RUGBY UNION

The Men Who Make the Game

RUGBY UNION

The Men Who Make the Game

Ian Smith

Book Guild Publishing
Sussex, England

First published in Great Britain in 2009 by
The Book Guild Ltd
Pavilion View
19 New Road
Brighton, BN1 1UF

Typesetting in Garamond by
Keyboard Services, Luton, Bedfordshire

Printed and bound in Great Britain by
CPI Antony Rowe

A catalogue record for this book is available from
The British Library

ISBN 978 1 84624 401 8

CONTENTS

FOREWORD

Sir John Hall had the vision to bring professional rugby to Newcastle and gave me the fantastic opportunity to build a team capable of taking its place in the top flight of English club rugby. Funds were made available to bring into the squad established, quality players and very quickly the team got the results that led to promotion from the Second Division in 1997 and winning the Premiership at our first attempt in 1998.

Whilst the focus at the top end of the club was to bring in established players we recognised that this was not sustainable in the long term and that structures needed to be put in place to attract and develop the young talent that would provide the nucleus of the Falcons squad in the years to follow. In developing our local network it became apparent that Ian Smith in his role as Director of Rugby at Northumbria University was an enthusiast for the professional game, an able coach and someone who was well respected by his players. It did not take a lot of persuading to get Ian on board to establish the Development Team set up at Newcastle Rugby Club in the summer of 1996.

Ian was joined in the November of 1996 by Paul MacKinnon who as a full-time member of staff assumed overall responsibility for the Development Team structure. Two different characters who complemented each other and developed and implemented a robust coaching and mentoring system that produced a seemingly endless line of talent that has gone on to play Premiership and international rugby. Ian and Paul's determination to get the best out of their players was commendable and the record of the Newcastle Falcons Academy is there for all to see.

In addition to his role at the Falcons, Ian guided Northumbria University into the position of being one of the strongest rugby universities in the UK, with four National Finals in his eight years as Director of Rugby.

When I heard of Ian's desire to write a book with the hope of encouraging youngsters into the game I was not in the least surprised and very willing to support. Helping people to reach their potential in all aspects of their lives is a trait I have observed at first hand over the last 13 years and the willingness of the players to take part in the project indicates the high regard in which Ian is held.

I believe that the individual journeys that the players have described in each of the chapters of this book will be of interest to fans and inspirational to the next generation of top-level performers.

Rob Andrew, MBE
England RFU, Elite Director of Rugby

INTRODUCTION

I am not sure what it was that unlocked my interest in Rugby Union, being from the soccer-mad North-East of England and to this day a Black and White through and through. Whatever it was I started playing Under–19 Colts rugby at Blaydon Rugby Club when I was 14 years of age and since then I have been hooked as a player, coach, commentator and fan.

My playing days were well before the professional era and, even if professionalism had arrived in the 1970s, there is simply no way that I was good enough to earn my living from rugby so to support the family I worked as a chartered quantity surveyor in the construction industry. In August 1993 I moved from industry to join the teaching staff at Northumbria University as a tutor in the School of the Built Environment and my work and rugby lives dramatically changed.

After class one day early in my first semester at the university one of my students told me that the lads knew that I was a coach working at Blaydon Rugby Club and they wanted to know if I would take First Team training for the university side. They had some good players that year he told me.

That conversation was the starting point of eight years as Director of Rugby at Northumbria University and they did indeed have some good players that year. Martin Corry was the club captain, lifting the Universities Athletic Union Championship at Twickenham in March 1994 after a 13–9 win over West London Institute who were captained by Richard Hill.

A very short time later in the middle of the 1995–96 Northern Hemisphere season the game of Rugby Union went professional and in the North-East of England Sir John Hall appointed Rob Andrew as Director of Rugby at Newcastle Rugby Club. Rob was given the funds to buy a team that would keep the club in the Second Division and then take them forward into the Premiership. Top-class players who had played under the amateur regime were brought into the club and formed the first cohort of professional players.

The professional era had arrived in Newcastle and I was asked to help establish the development structure at the professional club. As Director of Rugby at Northumbria University and coach at Newcastle Rugby Club I was in a very special place, a very privileged position.

Some 13 years later I have worked in different ways with lots of players, watched a lot of rugby and witnessed some fantastic occasions. I have watched players perform at the peak of their ability knowing all of the physical and mental effort that has been expended to enable that 80 minutes plus stoppage time to be the very best it could be.

I had been considering writing a rugby book but was very unsure about the format. My first university captain was Martin Corry MBE and after a chat with him in the spring of 2008 I became enthusiastic about the idea of taking each of the 15 positions in the team and producing a book that would be of general interest to fans and hopefully inspirational to the next generation of professional rugby players.

The 15 contributors are players that I have worked with in some way or simply been impressed with when watching them play. I have talked to all of them about growing up, their early involvement in rugby, standout moments from their careers to date, motivations, ambitions and their thoughts on the mental and physical demands of the game.

My motivation for writing this book comes from my respect for the players who play Rugby Union and a desire to share the experiences of elite performers in the hope of inspiring others to make the sacrifices needed to play at the top of the game.

Ian Smith

December 2008

ANDREW SHERIDAN

England; British and Irish Lions; Sale Sharks

The position of prop is very technical and demands a particular physical make-up that makes it unlikely that a person who plays at the elite level in a different position could also play at that level as a prop. I can't think of anyone apart from Andrew Sheridan who has played a particular position over a period of time and then moved into prop, both at the elite level of the game.

Andrew played professional rugby for Richmond and Bristol Shoguns and toured South Africa with England in 2000, playing in the second and back row but made the decision to move to the front row.

'At 21 I was playing for the First Team at Bristol Shoguns. I was on the bench quite a lot, played in the second row and a little bit in the back row but I didn't have a definite role. The line-out was becoming a more competitive area and I realised that, whilst I could win my own ball, it wasn't an area of the game that I was particularly good at.

'My aspirations were to play at the top level and I think you have to look at yourself as a player, you have to be self-critical. I felt that I had to decide – do I want to keep on bobbing along, or do I find a more definite role, a definite position? So it would be around that age, 21 or 22, that I made the move to prop.

'I found it a great help talking to Phil Keith-Roach, the England scrummaging coach, and he gave me a lot of advice. Peter Thorburn came in as Head Coach at Bristol and he was happy to give me as many chances as I wanted in the Second Team as a prop which was important for me.

'I could hit the scrum machine many times and look good but it's facing my opponents that's important. The first game I played at

1

prop for Bristol was against Newport and a prop called Rob Snow. After the first half I sat in the changing room and I couldn't get my chin off my neck.

'Peter gave me a very good run in the First Team at Bristol as a prop and I had some good days and others where I looked like I didn't know what I was doing; and probably didn't sometimes! I think it was very good of him to persevere as I was pretty inconsistent – things went well sometimes and other times I got myself into a mess.

'I was fortunate in the sense that most coaches wouldn't have had the same patience, and certainly that wouldn't happen now; I just don't think you would be given that number of chances at First Team level. I've worked very hard though, always trying to learn and trying to improve.'

The inner resolve and self-confidence needed to make the change that has seen Andrew establish himself as one of the top props in world rugby exists in bundles in his massive 1.93m 122kg frame. His combative and aggressive performances on the international stage have rightly brought the plaudits they deserve and you could be forgiven for attaching to Andrew the stereotypical image of a big prop who has tried plumbing at college and completed a Level 2 NVQ in Bricklaying.

The reality is somewhat different in that he is unassuming, quietly spoken, very thoughtful and intelligent – he has 13 GCSEs, 3 A levels with two at grade A and completed the first year of a History degree at Royal Holloway University before the pressure of rugby curtailed his studies.

'I managed to get 13 GCSEs with seven As and two A*s. England schools rugby did impact on my A levels and I remember I didn't really enjoy that time. I didn't enjoy exams and got agitated by nerves with the A levels. I remember being away with England a lot and having to do an awful lot of work in the 12 weeks before the exams because I just hadn't done enough before then.

'I was doing Latin, History and Religious Studies so there was a lot of information to remember and I didn't really understand Latin but I got a D and As in History and Religious Studies. It was tough. I put an awful lot of work into my Latin A level. I got my GCSE

OK but it was a big step up to A level and, despite trying my best to remember and cram in as much as I could, I just didn't have enough knowledge of the subject so I struggled.'

This propensity to work hard appears to be a consistent factor in 'Big Ted''s make up. Andrew was born in Bromley and at 11 years of age attended Dulwich College, which holds lots of good memories.

'It was just an enjoyable experience; it was a very good school. I think I'm very privileged to have gone to a school like that. Most of the kids wanted to learn. I've not got anything to compare it to but I've talked to lads who've not gone to such good schools and then perhaps got a scholarship to go to one like Dulwich College and it's just a big difference.

'It must be very different being at a school where it's the normal thing not to turn up to classes and then going to a school where there's actually a bit of a competition going on in terms of who can get the highest grades. I think History was probably my best subject and I enjoyed it as well, the Tudor period particularly and the Stuarts. I think we had some good History teachers, which helps as well to be honest. A teacher who's passionate about the subject helps. English was also enjoyable.

'I wasn't very good at Maths but did get a GCSE. They put us into different tiers for exams so I got the lowest grade. I wasn't good at Physics and Chemistry but I quite liked Biology. I guess I remember mostly the sport really.'

Dulwich College has a rich history since being founded by Edward Alleyn on 21 June 1619 during the reign of James I, and sport is an integral part of school life. The following extract from the independent schools website identifies a fantastic environment for aspiring sports stars:

Sport is an integral part of life at Dulwich College

Amongst the 60 acres of playing fields are two full-size and one practice Astroturf pitch, a synthetic athletics track, 12 rugby pitches, 10 football pitches, 10 cricket squares, 8 Astroturf nets and 9 all-weather tennis courts. There is also a large, fully equipped PE centre which houses a 25 metre 6-lane swimming pool, two fitness suites, a sports hall with room for 8 badminton courts and an air-conditioned exercise studio.

The Sheridan family have no great history in sport. Andrew's father, Dan, played football but not to any significant level, however within the family there is agreement that the standout sportsperson was his grandfather on his father's side of the family. Richard Sheridan sadly passed away when Andrew was only one year old, but family stories and photographs on the staircase wall of Siwan and Andrew's home in Timperley, south of Manchester, identify an army officer who was an all-round athlete into boxing, hockey and athletics.

Before his time at Dulwich College the young Sheridan used to kick a football about with his mates and with an imagination fired by American football on TV he started playing Under–9s rugby at his local club, the Old Elthamians.

'I used to play football with a couple of lads. When we were about nine years old we sort of had a casual group who on a Sunday would turn up with their dads and we'd play football. There were a couple of these lads that used to play rugby for a club in the morning and then come along in the afternoon and I think they suggested that I would enjoy it.

'I remember I used to watch American football; it was on television at the time on Channel 4 and I enjoyed watching it. I got into rugby through that; rugby had a certain similarity. I went along to Old Elthamians; they had a decent young team. I just enjoyed it and took to it like a duck to water.

'I played there from Under 9s onwards. I went to Dulwich when I was 11 and continued playing until I was 13 or 14. I'd play Saturday morning at school and then play on the Sunday for the club. You can't do that as you get older as GCSEs come along and at 15 years of age rugby was becoming more serious. I was playing for the First Team at school and concentrating on that.'

Whilst rugby was already a pastime for Andrew before he went to Dulwich College he was certainly not a one-sport youngster and tried his hand at lots of different things including athletics, swimming and football.

'I played a bit of football, mainly in defence, and did some ·

swimming. I enjoyed athletics and when I was growing up I did cross-country, 800m and 1500m, but as I put on some weight I didn't run so far so it was shot-put and discus. I did them to a reasonable standard – London Schools and England Schools – came fifth in the shot-put. I wasn't technically that good at it; I used to just lob it. I enjoy the sun and like watching athletics. Competitions would hopefully be on sunny days and I would sit back and watch all the sprinters!

'Other sports were enjoyable but I liked playing rugby, up to Christmas for the school and then the trials and representative stuff after Christmas.'

A crop of good rugby players entered school in the same year group as Andrew and they had a formidable team, remaining unbeaten from age 11 right through to age 18. The players were very competitive both in games and in training. Training sessions were very hard, three rugby sessions a week with players doing extra weights sessions and extra running.

All of the hard work was rewarded on the National Schools rugby scene when at Under-15 level the team won the *Daily Mail* Cup beating Bristol Grammar School in the final 37–0. The final was played at Twickenham and gave Andrew his first game in the magnificent stadium.

'We had a good school team the year I was in and we won the Under 15 *Daily Mail* Cup. It was the first time I had played at Twickenham and standing in the tunnel before the final, I was very excited. I suppose there weren't many people watching but it was just great to play there at such a young age. I was lucky enough to play there again the following year at Under 16 and also the following year so I had three years on the trot.

'I had represented England at 16 Group level and played again at Twickenham in one of the games I played for England 18 Group.

'They were good memories.'

Andrew's parents had invested a lot of money into the education of Andrew and his elder brother, Robert, at Dulwich College and it is typical of the man that even at young age he felt a responsibility to give it everything and work had to achieve his goals.

The end of sixth form was a difficult time owing to the pressure of work that had built up by being away with England but his parents were very supportive. Rather than pressurising Andrew to work for his exams they gave him the responsibility of choosing to do them if he wanted to. That personal responsibility is a consistent thing that comes out when considering the make-up of achievers in all fields.

'A levels were tough and I was pleased with my grades because I'd put in quite a bit of work in that last period of time. You can get quite a lot done in ten weeks. I was thinking that I'd gone to a good school and had been there quite a few years; it would be a shame to have left with poor grades and I wouldn't have made the most of my opportunity. I think that was what was playing on my mind when I was trying to cram in as much as I could for those exams. I don't want to have to do exams again!

'My parents let me get on with things. I don't remember any kind of pressure. My dad was always saying that you've got to have something to fall back on; but at the same time to go for it one hundred per cent.'

On leaving school Andrew joined the professional set-up at Richmond Rugby Club and pursued his interest in History when he started a degree at the Royal Holloway University but it proved to be a difficult year.

At the start of the year Andrew was a part of the Development Team set-up and juggling the time between training and studies was manageable. However, he was promoted to the First Team squad and played about seven matches. The First Team squad were all full-time players and very soon clashes with training and attendance at university crept in. There then came the added difficulties caused by the owner of the club deciding to pull out.

'I quite enjoyed university but was struggling with making it work. Professionalism was in the early stages and the owner of Richmond pulled out leaving little chance of the club surviving. We were all sacked.

'I took my first-year exams and passed them all, but I had to decide what I was going to do. The university said that as I'd passed the first year I could always come back to it and do the final two years. I'd had an offer from Bristol Shoguns, though not on a particularly significant salary, so I thought: Well, I could always go back to university, why not give rugby a whirl?'

Bristol at that time were under the management of Bob Dwyer and Dean Ryan, and Andrew started his time in the West Country in the Bristol Academy. By the end of that first season however he had ten games in the First Team, signed a new contract and was chosen as a second row for England's Summer 2000 tour to South Africa.

Although he did not get a full cap on the tour he played alongside Steve Borthwick in the midweek games. 'That year it all happened pretty quickly in that I started in the Academy then played for the First Team and then was selected for the England tour.

'I'd say the midweek tour games were more intense than Premiership games. It was quite tough out there. I remember the games being very physical, but then rugby every year seems to have stepped up in some way. I know physically it's harder but there always seems to be some element changing – I mean these days everyone has to compete for the ball. I remember my first years at Richmond and also some at Bristol when you'd be able to take the ball into contact and place it back. There was never this mad fight to try to nick the ball back off you. So things like that make it more intense. The breakdown is far more competitive; it's people fighting for the ball.

'It was really good; the whole thing was a really good experience. I took it seriously but everything happened very quickly and I just went along with it! I was pleased to be involved.'

The tour also gave Andrew an insight into how the senior professionals went about their business. 'I think I got more of an insight into how some of the senior players like Richard Hill and Martin Johnson worked, how they behaved in terms of training and their whole demeanour really.

'At the time I was still pretty young and, even though I took it seriously, looking back there were probably aspects of the game where I could have worked harder. I wouldn't go as far as to say I was just happy to be there because I wanted to play in a test match and I was obviously trying very hard to do that.'

A word or phrase to describe you at 21 years of age?

Decision Time...

At 21 I was playing for the First Team, I was on the bench quite a lot but I didn't have a definite role and I felt that I had to decide: did I want to keep on bobbing along or do I find a more definite role or position? I analysed my game and knew that if I kept on playing in the second or back row there would be clear weaknesses to my game. It would be at around that age, 21 or 22 that I made the move to prop.

In the two seasons following the Summer 2000 tour to South Africa Andrew had made the transition from second row and part-time back row to loose head prop. The transition was not an easy one but hard work and perseverance paid off as he started finding his feet in the front row. However, all was not well at the Bristol club and during the 2002–2003 season club owner Malcolm Peerce announced that he would quit at the end of the season and it became clear that the club's very existence was under threat. Rumours were rife in the town of possible moves to Oxford under the ownership of Firoz Kassam and a merger with bitter rivals, Bath. Bristol were relegated at the end of the season as the off-field difficulties raged on.

For the second time Andrew had to look around to other clubs to secure his rugby future. 'It was a difficult year but as a player you had to be a bit selfish. By being selfish it's not just about yourself but it's about trying to contribute in helping the team, when it gets like that at a club it's about survival. We knew what was happening. The owner said he wasn't going to keep it going so you knew you had to try to play as well as possible on Saturday in the hope that another club would be interested in offering you a contract.

'I enjoyed playing for Bristol and I enjoyed the professional rugby lark but I needed to play as well as possible, while it was all falling apart, to try to get an opportunity to move on.

'At 19 I was happy-go-lucky. I wouldn't say I was a free spirit but I was carefree, then you grow up. I was happy going on a trip to

South Africa and playing a bit of rugby and it was great to get paid for it! I'd had a taste of club problems with Richmond going bust, but I was paid £9,000 per year so I was never going to live it up every night and I was never going to lose a great deal either – I was a well-off student. But when I got to 21 or 22 and made the decision to move to prop, I was thinking I could play for another ten years. However, for me it was a case of getting things lined up in my head so that I knew what I was going to do if it all fell apart.'

Andrew secured a contract with Sale Sharks and he made his debut in the front row against Northampton Saints at the start of the 2003–2004 season.

The words of his dad from his time at Dulwich College must have been returning to the front of his mind – 'You've got to have something to fall back on; but at the same time to go for it one hundred per cent' – and he gave everything he had to Sale Sharks but completed his Level 2 Bricklaying NVQ at night school.

'For me, I made that move to prop and got the contract with Sale but it coincided with my decision to take the bricklaying course. I'd done bits and pieces including a plumbing course when I was at Bristol but I finished my bricklaying course while at Sale. It was nice to have the bricklaying two nights a week, something away from the rugby. A completely different set of people with no interest in rugby, just nice people.'

In December 2003 the now front-row forward played for an England XV against the Barbarians immediately following England's triumphant World Cup campaign in Australia and full international honours followed in November 2004 when he came off the bench to make his debut in the match against Canada. The transformation to prop may not have been complete but to gain full international honours was a fantastic achievement, and it was not even at loose head.

'I came on at tight head prop and I was a loose head. It was a hard enough transition to go from the second row to prop but to have to play both sides! I think there was only one prop on the bench and I said I'd come in and cover. We practised a bit, did a few scrums in the week and that was that; I came on as the tight head.

I was excited and nervous at the same time before I came on. It was nice to know you've finally been capped for England. I'd prefer to have been loose head but beggars can't be choosers.'

Since that first cap Andrew has established himself as the cornerstone of the England pack and his reputation continues to grow as he continues to learn. He demolished the Australia pack in his first international start in 2005 and was Man of the Match. He loved beating Australia, describing those days as 'good days'. The 2007 World Cup in France was also very special with the final being a vivid memory. 'Those are moments you remember...'

Technical deficiencies in the front row have been overcome with a combination of learning and pure strength and weight training has always been a big part of his preparation. 'I like strongman competitions. I just got into weights and trying to lift as heavy a weight as possible; it's always a competition. It is just something I've always done and enjoyed. I don't need to be motivated to train. I think that when I turn up and have a hard session, or it's raining, windy, whatever, it's still a pretty good job to have. In 15 years I'm probably going to struggle with my body being out of shape, hobbling along, but you could do a lot worse with jobs. So I don't think I need any more motivation. I just enjoy it.

'I get bored with some things in training like the line-outs and drills. I like laying bricks but when someone is laying their 300th line that would be boring as well. My job is like other jobs in that sense. Some days it's not as enjoyable as others... It's the same as any other job.

'Not long ago we had to go into an office. I've never had to work in an office; it was open-plan and everyone had their own cubicle. It was 8.30 a.m. and the people did not leave until 8 p.m., they were just stuck there in front of a computer. You see things like that. They might be highly paid but that's boring.

'I love what I am doing, playing in front of crowds, in big stadiums – playing a sport I've always enjoyed playing – but there has to be some element in you where you say you're going to maximise your earnings while you can, that's the nature of the sport. You pick up so many injuries that will take their toll on you in years to come when you're finished playing, but I just enjoy playing.'

Andrew is right. Sportsmen and women are retired a long time, as you have to give up playing the game at an early age, so making the most of your earnings potential while you can is very important to ease the transition back into the normal world that most of us inhabit.

Building up to games is a different process for different players. For Andrew it is having a routine. 'I'm quite relaxed about it but I like to follow a routine. I like to make sure I've done certain training things during the week, gym work, leg session, upper body, rowing, scrummages. I like my routine building up to a game.

'Come the day of the game, like everyone else I will be a little bit nervous but looking forward to playing. For me the warm-up is important, making sure that's where you're ready to play. If you build yourself up too early you just get tired.'

A word or phrase to describe you now?

Still ambitious but reflective...

I still want to get better but I'm 29 now so it's just the realisation that I'm not that young. Not very long in the future I'll have to call it a day, maybe at 33 or 34, or with the nature of the game it could be sooner. I guess it's what I am thinking about, what I am going to do then?

I guess I could get involved in personal training or work on the strength and conditioning side. I enjoy laying bricks; I am quite happy. I've had times where I've trained twice at the club on a day-off and then gone out and laid bricks for six hours. We'll have to see.

At 29 Andrew still exhibits all the signs of someone with a lot to give to the game and a desire to continue improving as a player. It goes without saying that silverware for Sale Sharks is an ambition as well as continued international recognition. The forthcoming British and Irish Lions tour to South Africa in 2009 is also on his radar. Already a Lion on the difficult 2005 tour to New Zealand, he still has the desire for more.

'It was a good experience but we just weren't successful playing-wise. It would be nice to be picked but I think before that my goals are just about improving and trying to be consistent. This can be difficult given the number of games you're playing and the length of the season.'

Outside of the game Andrew is a very private music man in that he plays the guitar and writes songs, although they do not get the benefit of an audience apart from a select few. When forced up to the front of the bus by club and International teammates to 'give us a song' the Bromley boy usually gets his tonsils around 'Country Roads'. Country music is his passion and provides a release from the pressure of elite-level sport when needed.

Andrew's wife, Siwan, enjoys rugby, watches the games and understands the demands and benefits that come with the job. In the same easy, unassuming manner that typifies everything Andrew does he articulates the couple's lot very well. 'I enjoy playing rugby and I'm happy enough to take the money so we put up with me being away. Siwan never complains about me being away seven or eight weeks on tour. We have a nice house, nice standard of living, she enjoys watching rugby herself. We can complain about things and moan but it's not a bad position to be in.'

Never believe in stereotypes. Big Ted is not your normal big, aggressive, bricklaying prop.

2008–2009 Season Update

The 2008 England summer tour to New Zealand did not go to plan for Andrew as he picked up a nasty eye injury which forced him out of the tour, but solid performances for Sale Sharks and England led to him being selected for the 2009 British and Irish Lions tour to South Africa.

Andrew Sheridan: Statistics	
Date of birth	1 November 1979
Birthplace	Bromley, Kent
Height	1.93m
Weight	122kg
Position	loose head prop
School / university	Dulwich College
Present club	Sale Sharks
Previous clubs	Richmond
	Bristol Shoguns
Nicknames	Sheri, Big Ted
Favourite TV show	anything – I don't watch much TV!
Favourite film	*Back to the Future*
Favourite music	country, acoustic
Favourite book	biographies and autobiographies
Favourite food	steak and mash
Most like to meet...	Ben Johnston; Mike Tyson; Eric Clapton
Least like to meet...	nobody
Best moment in rugby	2007 World Cup final
Favourite place to visit	Darwin, Australia; would love to go to the East Coast of Africa
I love...	boxing
I hate...	nothing

RORY BEST

Ireland; Ulster

A small village situated between Tandagree and Newry and straddling the boundaries of County Armagh and County Down in Northern Ireland, Poyntzpass contains the farm of the Best family and was the birthplace of Rory and his two brothers, Simon and Mark, who have all played rugby for their province and country at various levels. Mark has represented Ulster at Under 21s and Ireland at Under 19s but it is Simon and Rory who have played professionally for their beloved Ulster and also for the Irish national side.

In a place as small as Poyntzpass with a population of around 2,100 people the elevation to the world stage of two of its residents did not go unpublicised as support was given to the two front-row forwards before the 2007 World Cup in France. 'People in the village have been very supportive. There was even a banner up in the village when we were away in France saying "good luck to Simon and Rory Best for the World Cup". It's a small place – only a couple of thousand live there – but it's great.'

As it turned out Ireland had a difficult competition and never performed to their potential, but worse was to come for the Best family as Simon was rushed to hospital with a heart complaint during the actual competition. In the intervening time Simon's condition has been diagnosed and thankfully is now under control but he has had to retire from the sport.

Rory, however, has continued to play at the top of the game as captain of Ulster and an integral part of the Ireland national squad. Although the 2007–08 season has not been the best in terms of results for Ulster he has enjoyed the responsibility brought about by captaincy.

'It's a great honour captaining Ulster but it's strange taking over from Simon. The Ulster management asked me if I would take over as captain and told me that they'd have a conversation with Simon if I wanted to take it. Blood is thicker than water so I phoned Simon to discuss the situation as I knew he felt he still had stuff he wanted to do. We agreed to meet the coach together the next morning but at 9.15 a.m. Simon phoned me and said he thought it unfair to me if he didn't step down. He was not happy with the way it was done, but he was happy that if he wasn't going to be captain I was. It was a very bittersweet moment.'

I've known the two brothers over many years and it is typical that one would not stand in the way of the other when opportunities arise, irrespective of the circumstances. The captaincy has given Rory a deeper sense of responsibility and focus.

'It hasn't been a brilliant season for Ulster but I've enjoyed being captain with a wee bit of extra responsibility. There are times when the going gets tough in games and, instead of going off and saying I've had enough of this, you have to knuckle down – when you're captain there's no hiding place. If you feel yourself slipping into a "let's just get through this game" mindset you think: Now hold on, people are looking to you to keep them going.

'In training as well I know I have to give the lead to the young boys. It's good – it keeps you focused.'

Rory grew up around the farm and school was initially in the village school in Poyntzpass before moving on to junior school in the local town of Tandagree and then Portadown College when aged 14. 'Up to the age of 11 I went to a tiny school in the village. There were about 70 people there when I was going. After that I went to junior school in Tandagree, which is 4 or 5 miles away. You go to junior school between the ages of 11 and 14, then do transfer exams and go to either grammar school or high school. I went to Portadown College from 14 to 18 years of age.

'I really enjoyed school. I liked Maths and the sciences, Geography, anything practical; I hated English and French. I enjoyed French at junior school but it got a bit complicated! Sport at the school was great.'

Sport plays a big part in the Best family. Rory's mother was very good at lacrosse and claims honours at 400m hurdles though no evidence has been seen! His grandfather on his mother's side of the family was a good footballer, playing in goal, and Rory's father is equally well known in Ulster as a farmer and a rugby man with legendary status within Banbridge Rugby Club.

'Dad was always big into rugby. He played a bit for Portadown when he first played senior rugby then moved to Banbridge. Portadown was the more senior club in those days. With the farming, though, he couldn't be there in August and September for pre-season and the start of fixtures. They gave him a bit of grief so he went to Banbridge, the junior club. They were just happy for him to turn up on a Saturday. Now the tables have turned in the last couple of years and Banbridge are the more senior club.

'Dad played 20-odd years at Banbridge. When he was President he was still playing, normally on the bench, so he'd go into the club with the shirt and tie to do pre-match speeches. When the game was about to kick-off he'd sit on the bench in his shirt and tie, then he'd pull on his boots and stuff. He played prop.'

School provided the opportunity for Rory to get involved in many different sports. Like most kids growing up in Ulster the youngster was a big soccer fan, playing with his mates in school kick-abouts.

'I was always a big fan of soccer. I wasn't great at it but I'd play at school and I also played for the school First Team at cricket. I would throw things at sports day, mainly the javelin, but I wasn't that good at it! Probably at school it was the cricket and rugby that I liked best. With rugby we were training three times a week and playing Saturday. That then leads you into the cricket in the summer.

'I just really liked getting out, being outside. When the rugby season was over you would get home at four o'clock and you'd be looking for something else to do. That's why I enjoyed the cricket; it got me out and about and sometimes out of class!

'I didn't play much rugby out of school as the rules in Ulster are that if you play school rugby then you can't play club rugby, but at the end of the season in my last school year, once the school rugby season was over there were a couple of club senior games left so I played with my dad and my other brother, Mark. It will have been for Banbridge 4th or 5ths, something like that, probably up at Enniskillen in the middle of nowhere.

'Mark's a scrum half, a very big scrum half at that. He played Ulster Under 21s and Ireland Under 19s. He's very useful and is probably the most sporty of the lot of us. He's one of those that whatever he picks up he's pretty useful at it.'

Rory's rugby was starting to take up more of his time as he represented Ulster and then Ireland in his sixth-form years. During this time the balance of study and sport became difficult to manage as examination time came around.

'I studied Geography, Biology and Chemistry at A level but with Chemistry I bit off more than I could chew. In the first-year sixth form everything went well, then it got a lot harder in the second year. I was away a lot with Ireland Schools rugby and I'm the kind of person that if I'm not enjoying it then I struggle. The subject was getting harder, I was away a lot and getting behind, and there were subject timetable clashes. When these clashes happened then I'd always choose not to go to Chemistry.

'When the exams came nearer and I looked at it I thought "no!" Cramming wasn't an option. The first two of the four modules I did all right in, but the last two were awful and it completely destroyed me!

'I very nearly didn't end up at university in Newcastle. We were away with Ireland Schools on tour in Australia when the A level results came out. I needed two Cs and a D to do Agriculture but I got B, C and N. It was OK points-wise but I only got two A levels.

'Simon was already on the course and was at home at the time so he said he'd phone the university for me and speak to the tutors. Luckily enough for me they were quite light at the time and so they were happy enough to have me.'

Rory was following in the footsteps of his father and brother Simon by being a prop, but his ability to also play hooker was utilised by the school. 'I played Ulster Schools for two years. I was a prop who could hook; it was one of those things. I played a bit of hooker at 12 or 13 and moved to prop at 15. In that first year of sixth form the school had three good props and so me being the youngest of the three I was asked if I would mind moving across – so OK!

'I was put forward at the Ulster School trials as a prop so I ended up hooking for the school and propping for the trials. The next year

I played mostly hooker and propped a bit as well. My representative stuff in the last year was at hooker. That's why I came away from school playing a bit of both.'

School was a close-knit community and a lot of friendships were formed that are still important to Rory today. Good friendships and good memories. 'My first year in the sixth form we didn't end up doing very much in the Schools Cup, although we did beat both of the finalists in that year, in fact we beat one of them by 30 points.

'The Schools Cup is something I will never forget. I remember the week leading up to the first match; I just couldn't sleep with nerves. I've never known anything like it and I remember the night before I must have slept about two hours! Looking back it probably seems a bit silly but it was just anticipation, thinking that we'd had a tough draw and, if we got through this, then what would we do? We ended up getting beat in the last minute and it started snowing too. Everyone was trying to keep warm. It was freezing.

'I'm still very friendly with a lot of the boys from then; some of the boys would be a year older than me and I have quite a few memories from that year. We'd play the match, go home and eat, and then meet up in the pub and stuff in the evening. It was a very good social environment. We all got on very well.

'The next year was good too. I was captain and I enjoyed the extra responsibilities. I was also line kicking and goal kicking at that stage!'

It was in this year that Rory eventually got capped by Ireland in the 18 Age Group Schools side, with his first cap being gained against England Schools at Banbury. The nervousness felt before the Schools Cup game was a vivid memory for the boy from Portadown College but, whilst he was a bit nervous, he really felt the great honour of playing for his country.

There were two other boys from Ulster but he was the only one from his school and this only fuelled the pride he felt. 'I remember being excited and a wee bit nervous. Obviously you like your mates around but at the same time playing for Ireland is all the more special if you're only one of three from your province. There are still a few of that team kicking about – Dennis Leamy, Matt McCullough, Roger Wilson, Frank Murphy ... Gavin Duffy was the captain.'

So it was that in September 2000, with a year of International

19

Schools rugby under his belt and his A level results sufficient to gain him entry into Newcastle University to study Agriculture, the young Ulsterman arrived on Tyneside.

In the same way that Simon had studied at Newcastle University and played rugby at Newcastle Falcons, so Rory came into our academy. Some may see being able to play both hooker and prop as a benefit, but in the academy I think we struggled to find Rory's best position, which I at the time thought was as a prop!

When in the Newcastle Falcons academy Rory's international career progressed through the age groups, with him playing Ireland Under 19s in his first year at university and Under 21s in his second.

Simon returned to Ulster at the end of his studies but for Rory the call to come home came a little earlier as the Irish RFU exerted more control on the development of their players and took him back to Ulster at the end of his second year of studies. 'The RFU put a bit of pressure on me to go home to Ulster. They were conscious of the travelling back and forward and being at university. I enjoyed all aspects of student life and was a wee bit heavier than I should have been!

'In my first year in Newcastle I played Ireland Under 19s and then in the second year played Ireland Under 21s. That was a defining moment really for me going back, as I'd played Ireland Under 19s until I got injured. When I then went to Under 21s next year, the fella behind me was now starting and in the Five Nations I only got two games, both from the bench, literally five minutes and then fifteen minutes, and I said that's it.

'I thought it was because I was away that they were not picking me, so that was the defining moment where I said I've got to come home.

'I had another year at Under 21s and so I thought I had to be under their noses for them to see me. They were very supportive in getting me back. I came into their academy system. When you're a young elite player, you play for your Provincial Under 21s team and then you play for your club. For me that was Belfast Harlequins. I played for them for three years.'

Finishing his studies back in Ulster was important for Rory, but it was not an easy transition as Queen's University Belfast needed some persuasion to allow the farmer's boy from Poyntzpass on to their agriculture course. 'I tried to transfer to my last year at Queen's University Belfast but they weren't happy. At Newcastle my first year was mostly science – chemistry again! – and I failed one of the modules. However, they let me do my second year and drop one of the modules but I had to get an average 50 per cent in the second year to progress. As it turned out, I was getting 70 per cent.

'Queen's weren't buying any of that – all they could see was that I had failed a module. Basically I had to do another second year and then do the full third year. It all turned out well in the end.

'I didn't want to start another degree, as I see myself going into farming when I finish with rugby. Luckily enough for me, my dad is a well-respected farmer and in the International Farmers Union, and in the end they were more than happy. There were people on my course who hadn't even seen a farm before, so the university were happy with me with my farming background.'

Graduation from Queen's took place in July 2003 and that was also the time that Rory was offered a professional contract with Ulster. It all worked out perfectly for him as he felt he would have had difficulties balancing full-time studies with being a professional player.

'I see guys now doing one module a year and trying to balance studies with their rugby. That must be really hard. I was lucky enough to have the academy stuff, which was flexible; you had a couple of lectures in the morning and then training in the afternoon or vice-versa, and you'd train with your club on Monday, Tuesday and Thursday nights.'

The first season at Ulster saw the young hooker continuing his playing with Belfast Harlequins in the All-Ireland League. Three hookers in the Ulster squad led to the youngster starting out as third choice and, whilst training with Ulster three days a week, he trained with his club side on Thursdays and played Saturdays. If it hadn't been for the confidence of Andre Bester, the South African coach of the Harlequins, Rory's progress may have been slower.

'I was very lucky in that the club coach with Harlequins was Andre Bester and he worked with me a lot. When I first came back from Newcastle the Harlequins had Ritchie Weir who'd just left Ulster. Andre picked me ahead of Ritchie, even though at that stage he was a better player, more finished off. He picked me when he didn't need to, when other people wouldn't have.

'He was trying to build a team for the longer term. In that first year we finished fifth or sixth in the league and missed out on the play-offs, but in the next two years, under him, we made the play-offs.'

A word or phrase to describe you at 21 years of age?

Knuckling down...

I liked to party a bit and I was constantly getting myself into minor scrapes. I have a scar on my arm from when I was with Ulster 21s. After one of the games I ended up having an argument with a glass window and I thought: You know, it's got to stop, you either continue the way you are or you can try to play rugby professionally. I decided that I had to concentrate a bit more on my lifestyle and training.

When I was coming up through the school set-up we weren't a bad school team but we weren't brilliant, so you could, sort of, get away with it. I was always pretty good compared to everyone else and even at Harlequins I wasn't too bad. But then it got to the stage that, if I wanted to go to the next step, being quite good for your age wasn't going to cut it. I was going to have to concentrate and so it was about that age that I moved from sort of being a bit of a loose cannon to a bit more focused on what I wanted to do.

With Ulster, Rory has progressed from a self-confessed loose cannon into a very proficient player, where his all-round play and especially his proficiency as a line-out operator caught not only the Irish selectors' eyes but also the eyes of the Ulster public as he was named Personality of the Year at the May 2007 Ulster Rugby Awards. His leadership qualities were recognised by Ulster as he replaced brother Simon as Ulster captain for the 2007–08 season and he joined Simon as a full International player on 12 November 2005 when he came off the bench at Lansdowne Road to win his first cap against the New Zealand All Blacks.

As happens so many times in sport, someone's bad luck provides others with the opportunity to shine. 'Frankie Sheehan had hurt his neck and the selectors were going to announce another hooker after the second round of the European Cup games. Shane Byrne was number one so it was between Jerry Flannery of Munster and me as to who was going to come in.

'I had quite a good game against Biarritz and we had won about 17 out of 17 line-outs. We were sitting at the airport on the Sunday evening waiting to go back to Belfast when I got a call to say that they wanted me to come down to the Ireland camp that night. So I flew to Belfast, quickly got home and then straight down to Dublin to the Ireland camp. I felt great pride and was overjoyed to get the call but that was quickly followed by "Oh Jesus, this is new." Ulster weren't doing well so there wasn't a huge representation, only about four or five of us in a squad of 35. I was being thrown into a completely new environment with boys whom I had barely played against.'

As a lot of teams find, things don't always go well against the All Blacks, and so it was for Ireland that November afternoon as New Zealand stormed ahead. Big brother Simon was the first Best to enter the fray from the bench but it was not too long before Rory got the call to replace Shane Byrne. Ulster legend and colleague David Humphreys, also on the bench, got the call to action at the same time as the young debutant and offered some words of wisdom before taking to the field.

'I could see myself and David Humphreys being called down at the same time so we're just getting our last stretches and tops off ready to go on to the field. He said: "Look, just go out there and you've got nothing to lose; just go out and enjoy yourself. You know this is maybe the one time you get a run-out at Lansdowne Road, so just go out and relax, go and get the ball, make tackles, do whatever you can."

'Coming on with David Humphreys made a big difference for me. He was coming on for something like his 80th cap, so it was him saying 'go out and enjoy it' and then coming on to a scrum with Simon ... a wee bit of familiarity made a big difference. 'It was a massive day for Mum and Dad seeing both Simon and me playing in the same game for Ireland at Lansdowne Road.'

Having graced the international stage, Rory wanted more and grabbed his opportunity, establishing himself in the national team during the 2006–07 campaign where he played eight straight matches and became an integral part of the Ireland pack.

Getting to the top is one thing but working hard to keep developing your game is another significant challenge requiring dedication, hard work and sacrifice. It goes without saying that physical preparation is important in a very high-paced and physical game like rugby, but mental preparation and the ability to execute precision skills when emotions are running high is also a vital attribute for the modern-day hooker.

'For me one of the challenges of captaincy is that having to talk a bit more can get me a wee bit more wound up. This is a big issue for me. Especially when playing for Ireland, I wouldn't sing the anthems because it's immediately before kick-off and, once the game starts, it could be kick-off, catch and then kick-out. Suddenly you're having to throw the ball into a line-out.

'If you're wound up as tight as a drum and you're having to throw in it's difficult. All it takes is for you give an extra 5 per cent more and it's an overthrow so I try not to lose it. I stay as calm as I can. In training when you're calm everyone can throw in well, but it's in the games that the pressure comes on. I try to keep the same rhythm; staying as relaxed as possible when throwing in is what makes a difference. I do a lot of visualisation on my throwing.

'We play on a Friday night so I'll do a lot of stuff on that on Monday, Tuesday and Wednesday. I'll maybe do a little bit on Thursday but I think from Wednesday night I try to go "Right, that's it – I'm not going to think too much about it." It's like back at school when I was doing exams. You revise, revise, revise, and some people do it right to the night before the exam and then they come in for the exam they have so much going through their heads they can't focus... It's a bit of that really.

'The night before a game we do a light team run so focus in for half an hour, but apart from that I try to take it easy. The day of the game I don't really get up too early; I get something to eat and try to forget about the game. I think you can spend too much time worrying about these things. The way I look at it is that if I've prepared well enough during the week then 24 hours before isn't going to make a difference. I enjoy playing for Ulster and playing with the boys that I play with so it's fun.'

In the physical aspects of the game Rory has worked very hard on his general fitness, and specifically his speed, a weakness he recognised in his game. He has also had to work at securing the ball on the floor and turnovers, previous domains of the back row that are now a big part of all players' skills set. Fighting for the ball on the floor and the importance of turnovers is so much a part of the modern game.

'The speed of players generally and the stuff on the ground are major factors in the game. If you have the ability to make three or four turnovers in the game you're suddenly talking about another back rower. Players like Paul O'Connell have a massive impact on games. He does the second row donkey work tremendously well but is always involved around the field. In the Heineken Cup Final against Toulouse he forced two vital turnovers near the Munster line that changed the game.

'Obviously fitness is important, and I think my fitness has always been good but it used to tail off a bit towards the end of the season. At the end of my first season as a professional I realised that you can't just do your pre-season work and think that that's it. So I had to work a lot harder throughout the season.

'Around the time I started for Ireland for the first time I thought about my game and my fitness and went off the drink for a year. In that year I changed my whole body shape and I went down from 110kg to 102kg. I felt lighter, sharper. I was looking forward to training and that opened my eyes further again. As a 21-year-old I thought I'd cut back a wee bit. I'd still drink sometimes but that year I cut it out completely and I saw what I could achieve. This year, I rarely go out and it wouldn't be a slaughter-session, a few pints and home.

'I've worked very hard on my speed and have been very lucky in that one of the Ulster fitness coaches was a sprinter and played quite a high level of rugby too. On my days off I do a lot of work with him on the pitch or at the track. I'm conscious of the fact that I've never been that quick.

'With the new Experimental Laws this year and the general direction in which the game is moving you need to basically be a fourth back rower. As a hooker your core skills are still hooking and throwing but you also need to be good on the ground. You need to be able to make a minimum of two or three turnovers in a game and be an effective support player around the field.'

Playing for Ulster and Ireland has been a hugely enjoyable experience enhanced by the fact that up until the World Cup in France, Rory had done it with Simon at his side. Coming on to the Lansdowne Road turf from the bench to go into the front row with Simon on his debut was a fantastic memory surpassed only by the day they were both in the starting line-up for Ireland. The match was the Six Nations clash with Scotland at Murrayfield on 12 March 2007 and the 19–18 result in favour of Ireland won them the Triple Crown.

However, the defining memory from Rory's career to date was the unforgettable match in the 2007 Six Nations when Ireland took England to the home of Gaelic Games, Croke Park in Dublin, and demolished them. The history, the occasion and the raw emotion made it a very special day.

'The game against England at Croke Park, it's by far and away been my defining memory. The whole atmosphere, the day, the result, everything, I had never experienced anything like it. It was just one of the most perfect games for our boys. We never lost a line-out that day, everything we did came off.'

A difficult World Cup in France in 2007 and 2008 Six Nations campaign have seen changes in Ireland's management and, with Michael Bradley in charge, the players have been challenged with shorter but sharper, more intense training practices. The Summer 2008 tour to Australia and New Zealand saw Rory's rivalry with the Munster man Jerry Flannery continue as Jerry started the first match of the tour against New Zealand and Rory started the second test match against Australia.

At this point in his career Rory is focusing on the captaincy at Ulster and trying to be a regular starter for Ireland. Like everyone he has dreams and ambitions but he recognises it is important to live life 'in the here and now'.

'Obviously I'd like to be successful with Ulster and keep starting for Ireland but I just need to try to keep in this moment as much as I can. In the last couple of games for Ulster this season I realised that you can get too far ahead of yourself. I started worrying about the summer tours and I didn't do the amount of practice that I had been doing in terms of throwing. It cost us in a couple of games. We lost a couple of key line-outs that we hadn't lost in two years and I thought, hey you can't get ahead of yourself, so I went back to practising an extra couple of times a week, throwing a couple of dozen throws a day.

'You obviously have your ambitions and dreams but I see it that you keep yourself in the here and now and keep working hard if you are to realise them.

'I'd say a Lions tour would be a massive honour, a dream come true, but it's a long, long way off.'

A word or phrase to describe you now?

Enjoy the moment...

I'm trying to live in the here and now and enjoy the moment. I realise how lucky I am to be where I am. I am in the Ireland set-up and captain of Ulster but it's easy to get ahead of yourself and think that I'm going to do this and do that.

Especially with Simon retiring and David Humphreys retiring I've realised it's a short enough career. They did a montage of David's career over 15 years, and I remember being on the terraces when he scored that try or made that incredible kick. The reality is that it doesn't seem that long ago.

If I'm lucky I could have another six years or seven years in the game. I've been a professional now for four years so I want to live in the here and now and enjoy every moment. The end will come along quickly but sometimes enjoying the moment is easier said than done.

Enjoying the moment can be difficult when your profession is being in the public eye with individual and team performances open to all to comment upon. Rory has learnt some hard lessons, lessons that youngsters coming into the game sometimes struggle with as they start to believe their own press.

'The media are very fickle and can make it difficult. I've learnt in the last couple of years not to read the media. When you first come in to the game and you're fresh and green you get into the Ireland set-up and you're reading the papers. Through the Six Nations before the World Cup the media couldn't get enough of us. We were the best and then suddenly a year later those same players aren't fit to play club rugby.

'You have to be very thick-skinned.'

Outside of rugby Rory has recently got engaged to his long-term girlfriend, Jodie, whom he met at Portadown College when they were both 15. I sense anxious times ahead for Rory when he needs to buy wedding anniversary cards in the years to come. He's only been engaged two months but he couldn't remember if it happened at the beginning or the end of March!

The support offered by Jodie and also his mum and dad are important. Rory believes that his personal life doesn't impact on his rugby but that is not the case in the other direction. 'I don't think my personal life impacts on my sport but there's no doubt that my sporting life impacts on my personal life. I struggle to talk to anyone after a poor training session, or more importantly a bad game, and always end up taking it out on my mum and Jodie in particular. I know I do not make it easy for them but they are very supportive and I'm sure they understand.

'My rugby experiences have changed me as a person. Being captain this year I've realised you can't take everything home and I try not to take things as personally as I used to. I'm very hard on myself in terms of my own rugby but in terms of what other people think then, if I'm happy with what I'm doing, I don't take any notice of what they say.

'With Simon being a bit ahead of me with Ulster and Ireland, Mum and Dad know exactly what's involved in getting to this sort of level. The support of Jodie and my family is very important.'

Marriage in July 2009, building a house on the 11 acres he has bought near Poyntzpass, getting his golf handicap down and moving into farming at the end of his playing days are how Rory sees the future. As he thinks about his journey to where he is today, his advice to aspiring professional rugby players relates to being self-critical and refining core skills – these, he feels, are the platforms that enable you to reach your potential.

'Work hard and be your own biggest critic. Certainly growing up, there were people who told me that I'd not be good enough, but if you enjoy it and you believe in your own ability go for it. The big thing is to work hard, especially as a hooker. If you can get good on your core skills you'll find that everything else comes along.

'For me personally, I know the good games are when I throw well. When you throw well your head comes up and you get an extra couple of yards, your confidence is up. Throwing well doesn't just come from pitching up on a Saturday and having a good day; it comes from the preparation during the week.

'You must enjoy it as well – if you don't enjoy it, you won't put the work in. It can be difficult, mundane, for kickers, scrum halves and hookers, who have to practise the same skills constantly. If it's windy or rainy you know you've got to get out there, that's when you need to practise, especially in our climate!'

My wife and I have always had a soft spot for both Rory and his brother Simon from their time in Newcastle, and over the years we have got a lot of pleasure from watching the progress of the agrics from Poyntzpass, even if it is from a distance. For Simon, the path to the top looked as if it was laid ready for him to walk along. For Rory, he has had to be his own biggest critic for him to make the changes to his lifestyle and work ethic that have elevated him to the captaincy of Ulster and the position of one of the best hookers in the home unions.

Seeing kids reach their potential is the joy of teaching and coaching, and I have had a lot of joy from watching Rory achieve all he has in the game. As we talk at the Ireland team's Cheltenham hotel before their game against the Barbarians at Gloucester, from the glint in his eye and the determination in his voice I have no doubt there is even more to come.

2008–2009 Season Update

Rory captained Ulster though the 2008–9 season but it proved to be a disappointing year, with the province finishing a lowly 8th in the Magners League and not getting out of their Heineken cup group as Harlequins and Stade Français moved into the quarter finals from Pool 4.

On the international front, being a part of a Grand-Slam-winning team was a massive achievement but the season will have been frustrating as the rivalry with Jerry Flannery continued for the hooking spot. Although Rory featured in every game, it was the Munsterman who started, with the exception being when Scotland provided the opposition.

Rory Best: Statistics	
Date of birth	15 August 1982
Birthplace	Poyntzpass
Height	1.80m
Weight	106kg
Position	hooker
School / university	Portadown College; Queen's University, Belfast
Present club	Ulster
Previous clubs	Belfast Harlequins
Nicknames	Frog; Mocky
Favourite TV show	*Prison Break*
Favourite film	*Old School*
Favourite music	all sorts, very mixed taste
Favourite book	John Grisham books; *The Da Vinci Code*; Paul McGrath's autobiography
Favourite food	steak
Most like to meet...	Lance Armstrong
Least like to meet...	serial killers
Best moment in rugby	Ireland v England at Croke Park, 2007; starting for Ireland v Scotland with Simon (brother)
Favourite place to visit	Dubai; Hamilton Island, Australia
I love...	the sun
I hate...	early mornings

CARL HAYMAN

New Zealand; Newcastle Falcons

There can only be one person who could be the thousandth All Black and 117 years after the Otago forward James Allon became All Black No. 1 the honour fell to the man dubbed in many circles as the best tight head prop in world rugby when he made his debut against Samoa in 2001.

To many that would have been the meal ticket to open many doors but the unassuming Kiwi from Opunake, whilst recognising the historical significance, typically plays down the personal recognition.

'A lot was made of it in New Zealand and there was a lot of carry-on in the media. It was a great milestone and a big thing for New Zealand rugby but I was just happy to be one of many. That's the way the All Blacks have always been. Someone had to get it and I guess I was just lucky!'

Carl Hayman arrived in Newcastle after the ignominious end to the All Blacks 2007 World Cup campaign. An unexpected defeat to France in the quarter-final of the competition, played in the National Stadium in Cardiff, stole the cup way from the team whose name many had predicted would be engraved on the trophy, even before the kick-off in the opening match.

The big Kiwi caused a bit of a stir in the press on both sides of the world when news of his impending 'Geordieness' was made public. A commentator in the *Journal*, Newcastle's morning paper, wrote: 'I can't stress enough what a big coup this is for the Falcons. Carl Hayman is a genuine global star – a player who could have gone anywhere in the world but he chose Newcastle. This is a signing that underlies the club's ambition. It's a signing that will make people sit up and take notice. It's a signing that will put Newcastle on the map.

All over the world people will be talking about Newcastle Falcons. That must be a good thing.'

The New Zealand take on the event was to question the All Blacks long-held policy of not selecting overseas-based players. Chris Rattue of the *New Zealand Herald* wrote: 'In the case of Hayman, why not have a dispensation? Something subtle – such as allowing Opunake born tight head props with beards who played for the Highlanders to be excluded from the residency rule – would do.'

Despite his reluctance to be in the media limelight, Hayman was in fine form as he coped with the media hype that surrounded his Newcastle arrival. In response to a question about the media reaction back home to New Zealand's exit from the World Cup his laconic response was 'I don't have any need for newspapers because I do not have a fire in my house. No offence intended.' Asked how long he had wallowed in post-traumatic depression after the World Cup exit his even more concise answer was 'Not long really. Life goes on.' When he revealed that he had spent time after the tournament on the farm docking the tails off lambs with a red-hot iron, one of the assembled press corps with a weak constitution made the observation that it must have been unpleasant. His response was equally straightforward: 'It wasn't much fun for the sheep either.'

The no-nonsense demeanour of the man comes as no surprise from a man of Otago farming stock, who has represented New Zealand at every level from the 16 age group upwards. Hayman entered the world on 14 November 1979; his birthplace, Opunake, is a small town on the south-west coast of Taranaki on New Zealand's North Island. Rugby is a central pillar in New Zealand culture; it's what youngsters do, so it did not take long before a rugby ball found its way into Hayman's hands.

'I started when I was in nappies pretty much, throwing the ball around. I got chucked in there pretty early and played for the Opunake club ... I played for them right through to when I went to high school. Then in Dunedin I played for the local high school team.'

The Hayman family are from a farming background and, when Carl was 11, the family moved south to the Dunedin area on South Island to take advantage of the opportunities that existed there. The move south took him to King's High School where his rugby development was nurtured. Life on the farm was something that the young Hayman loved but when he was 15 the family moved into the town of Dunedin itself when his dad changed employment and started driving trucks for a living.

'I pretty much grew up on the farm and the good things about it were neat. I was sad to move on. I still miss the farm. Pretty much all of Mum's family are into farming; they have dairy farms in New Zealand. So it's in Mum's family, a sort of a family trait. I think I'll have a crack at it at some stage.'

A consistent thing about Carl's teenage years in Dunedin was King's High School, which has good memories for him: 'I enjoyed school, it was a good time and I had a lot of mates. The subjects I enjoyed were Graphic Design and tech drawing; I was quite into them and also woodwork, that sort of thing. I got by in Maths and ended up getting Grade C so I just about did enough to get by.'

For a young lad the Kiwi upbringing always has rugby at the front but encourages involvement in all sports and that was no different for the young Hayman who tried his hand at almost anything until the demands of rugby pressurised his time. 'I pretty much got into everything I could. I played some summer sports like cricket then went on to soft ball and when not playing them we'd get the clubs out and play a bit of golf.'

This rounded sporting background is, I feel, so important in youngsters' overall development. When I was growing up I tried every sport I could and I am sure this helped me grow up by enabling me to meet different sorts of people and build up the self-esteem that is so important in life as we get older. Kids should be encouraged to get out with their mates and throw, kick or hit a ball about.

With the establishment of academies to produce the next generation of elite sportspeople in all sorts of sports there is a danger of forcing kids into a one-sport dimension that builds up potentially unrealistic expectations. This may not be the correct environment to encourage social and academic development as well as their sporting development. This is something that Carl also thinks is important. 'I totally agree with you; it's pretty healthy at a young age to join different teams, play a bit of cricket or whatever sport you can. As you get older you tend to focus on what you are good at but it is good to be involved in other things even if its only for three or four weeks of the year before you're back into training for rugby.'

As rugby took a more prominent place in Carl's life it brought pressures in term of schoolwork. 'I just about scraped through my exams but then ended up being in the New Zealand Schoolboys and Under 19s teams. Playing for both of those meant that I ended up taking a lot of time out of school; I was away a lot. So in the seventh form year, instead of doing university entry, the school did a sports course covering nutrition and weight training, things like that, which was quite valuable as it gave me an insight into the different types of training and looking after your body. At that stage New Zealand professional rugby was pretty much just starting, no one had thought about it as a profession and the physical demands on your body.'

With the importance placed on rugby in the New Zealand psyche, inter-school rivalries were intense and school rugby games exposed schoolboys to a big stage at that early point in their development. These big games, enduring friendships and the possibilities offered by the professional game all generate good memories from the big tight head prop's time at King's High School.

'The schoolboy games, at that time in your life, were great. There were big inter-school rivalries in New Zealand and some of them at that point in time were the biggest rugby occasions in your life. To play in front of a couple of thousand people when you're 16 or 17 was quite a big deal. So, looking back it was a fun time, a pretty enjoyable time to experience and I was very lucky to be able to do that.

'I was at school with Tom Willis; he was an All Black and plays for the Waikato Chiefs at the moment... We went through school together. So we were playing footie together in the same teams from fifth form and were training partners right through until eventually we were both playing professional footie for the Otago Highlanders. We have some good memories from schooldays. Developing and building up a good friendship with him and also with a lot of other people from schooldays. It was good fun and my good friendship with Tom was pretty special.

'I guess looking back on those days we were looking at professional rugby just coming in. I had been able to make the New Zealand schoolboys team and I suppose that was the first real time I had thought that if I stuck at it and worked hard I could actually make a career out of it. That was the first real time I sort of got a feel for it.'

On leaving school Carl went into senior club rugby and along with Tom Willis he was drafted into both the Otago Highlanders Super 14 squad and Otago NPC squad. When still aged 19 he came from the bench at Carrisbrook, Dunedin to make his debut on 12 March 1999 in the 46–16 victory over the Stormers from Cape Town, South Africa. He made his NPC debut on 27 July 1999 in the 68–7 loss against Wellington. It's a hard school and there is a big smile on the Kiwi's face when he says: 'It was odd coming out of school and playing at that level rather than in age groups. Tom and me were both in the same boat and we had to learn quickly.'

A word or phrase to describe yourself at 21 years of age?

Looking forward...

At that stage I was thinking and looking forward. I was always thinking long-term. When I was 19 I was in the Otago squad and so when we were training for games, you know where you want to get to in terms of your goals, but sometimes you have to take the long-term view in terms of your training and lifestyle.

I had to sacrifice a lot when thinking long-term about my objectives in rugby. At times it was tough because I came straight from school to that environment and all my mates had gone straight to university and were living the university life! Running up their bills and what have you. Overdrawn on the odd occasion! There's no way you can enjoy the lifestyle that a lot of them did. I guess the trade-off is you get your rewards in others ways – rugby has given me a lot.

With strong performances in the Super 14s it was not long before the All Black selectors were taking a significant interest in the Otago prop and it was in the New Zealand winter of 2001 that Carl was brought into the squad. Having represented New Zealand at all age-group levels it should not have come as a great surprise that an international debut would one day happen but it arrived very quickly. 'I'd played a lot of Super 14 rugby for the Highlanders and had a pretty good season, to be honest, from memory, it all seemed to happen pretty quickly – it seemed to happen just like that.

'I was drafted into the squad for the Tri Nations and the tours to New Zealand, Argentina and France in 2001. You dream of being an All Black but when you talk about it with friends when you are growing up you don't really think it'll happen. Then you're actually playing pretty well and you get named in the squad – you're rapped. It's pretty surreal really; you have to give yourself a reality check.'

Ahead of the Tri Nations competition it was the tours of France and Argentina that were to provide international games in Wellington and Christchurch, but it was the preceding game against Samoa played in Albany Stadium, Auckland on the 16 June 2001 that generated a piece of All Black history. Carl took the field as All Black No. 1000 and played his part in the 50–6 defeat of Samoa. The Tri Nations followed and then there were tours to Ireland, Scotland and Argentina where the All Blacks remained undefeated except for a result that must have annoyed a very proud man as Australia beat the All Blacks in his home town of Dunedin.

The media attention around that first All Blacks game was immense and it must have been a fantastic moment but also a relief to finally take to the field. Emotions would have been running high, but again the mark of the man is to keep things in perspective. 'I slept OK the night before the game; I've never had a problem sleeping for some reason. However, immediately before a game I think I am a combination of both nervous and excited really. Before my first test it was probably a 70/30 split, 70 per cent nervousness to 30 per cent excitement. It's important to control emotions when you get to elite levels in sport. I guess the big thing is going into the unknown.

'As a youngster I suppose it's difficult to develop those sorts of skills because you haven't anything to relate them to. Just to be able to trust in your skills, trust in what you do. I mean for my first test I was pretty nervous for the whole week. I was just doing everything extra I could. I just didn't want to do anything to screw it up.'

Carl had embarked upon an illustrious career and strong performances for both the Highlanders and the All Blacks saw plaudits flooding in for the man who became widely regarded as the best tight head prop in the world.

Many great games have been played as the All Black reputation has been enhanced around the world but the period between 2004 and 2007 holds good memories for Carl. 'Being involved in the All Blacks team at that time was pretty special. The experiences of touring as a team were pretty neat; the experience of winning test matches and being really driven each week to give a match performance out in the field that you can be really proud of. At that time it was a big driving effect to be able to win tests.

'We won the Tri Nations in 2005, 2006 and 2007 and were involved in the Grand Slam over here in 2005 when we beat Scotland, England, Ireland and Wales. Apart from the 2007 World Cup, to be part of all of that and have all of those experiences was great.'

Dealing with the elation of victory is relatively easy but coping with disappointment is much more difficult. The scars of the World Cup exit are going to be with the individuals involved in different ways. However, it is typical of the man that he manages to draw a line under things and move on quickly as all sportspeople need to do. In many eyes New Zealand were widely touted as winners of the tournament and their exit must have hurt. 'The 2007 World Cup is probably my biggest disappointment. That is, not just me as a lot of people poured a lot of time into it but when you break it down there are a lot more important things in life. I mean, no one died – I've still got my health.

'I think sometimes people lose perspective in those sorts of things. Yes, it was disappointing but you can't do anything about it – what's done is done. You can't do anything different after the event; you can't bring that back and keep beating yourself up, or you will eat yourself away.

'If you look at the Premiership, each week you've got a game so even if you've had a defeat or a victory the next week someone's out there who wants to mow you down. After a victory you enjoy the success but come Monday or Tuesday you have to push everything aside; just park everything up and go about your next week's work.'

This very pragmatic approach is typical of the man, but playing at the level that he plays at does not come easy. Weighing in at 115kg and 1.93m tall he is a real physical presence on the field but players need to align their physicality to a mental state that enables them to perform at their best. Carl has referred to the nervousness and excitement he felt before his first All Blacks test but, as he has matured into a seasoned player his mental preparation for games is well grooved.

'I'm pretty quiet. I just run through moves and line-out calls in terms of where I have to be on the field with certain plays being called and stuff like that. I think about scrummaging, knowing how I want to set myself up, knowing where I want to aim, and all those sorts of things.

'It's different for all guys. Some players like to get themselves really pumped up and get out there; I tend to take it easy. It's a balance really: you need to be motivated to push yourself hard but you also have to be thinking about key things within your performance on the field; you have to break down what you are going to do so that it's fresh in your mind for when you get out there. I just like to be calm. To be able to soak in what's happening around me, to have an idea of things on the field that might help the team.

'Physically you need to be ready to go and play but in your head taking in things. I think mentally that's one of the keys. Thinking of some of the guys I've played with at that top level, they are able to be well prepared and ready to go but mentally calm and clear.'

In the 2008 Super 14 season experimental laws have been trialled with a view to their being introduced into the world game at the start of the 2008/09 Northern Hemisphere season. These laws have promoted significant changes in the way the game is played and also the physical demands made of the players. What is expected of props and their core skills may be changing.

'I think rugby is moving forward. I think in general people are expecting props to contribute more; they want a lot more out of them, instead of a few years ago when they were there to just scrum and ruck and that's about it. Now, it's more of an all-round sort of job. You need to be fit and you need to be strong. You need some sort of explosiveness for ball carrying.

'The new laws potentially make different physical demands of players. I guess it's having that balance right if you're far too big and strong and can't run around you lose out on the field but then too small and you don't have the strength for the scrummaging and other things you have to do.'

Carl had decided before the World Cup that it was the right time to take up the challenges offered by a move to the Northern Hemisphere and, even though he was inundated by offers from the big European clubs, thankfully for us in Newcastle the big man arrived. 'I'd call myself a homely sort of person and moving across to the other side of the world was quite a big deal. Coming over here, I just think it was time for me. I'd given a lot of good seasons to Otago Rugby and the All Blacks, and after the World Cup I couldn't really see myself staying; it would have been staying for the sake of staying. It was time to move on and to experience something different, a new challenge...'

Former Falcons Ross Nesdale and Craig Newby spoke to Carl about the club and the region. Current Falcons Brent Wilson and Joe McDonnell also had their part to play in the negotiations to get him to Newcastle. In Otago, Brent Wilson had shared a flat with him and information from former All Black and Highlander front rower Joe McDonnell helped him in making his decision. 'Everyone only had good things to say about the club, the people and the city. My French isn't too flash and I couldn't see myself living in London, so Newcastle just seemed like the ideal option.'

A word or phrase to describe yourself now?

Reflective, thinking about my sport and life in general...

I think it's probably the same as when you're younger but maybe more so for me now as I get older – your mind starts to think about life after rugby. You still pour everything that you can of course into the game but you have to give it some thought. That's not taking anything away from the playing the game or rugby though. I still have plenty to offer but I'd say I am more reflective at this stage of my life.

Whilst rugby still is the first priority, the lines between rugby life and outside rugby life become even more blurred as time runs its course. Playing rugby at the emotional and physical intensity that he has, Carl – along with other elite sportsmen – has to have the ability to block things out at times, but experiences in all aspects of your life make you the person you are. 'I've never thought about it in that sense. It's quite funny really because I guess the last sort of 10, 12, 13 years, my whole life, have been directed towards rugby. To a certain extent I guess how you succeed in what you do is sometimes dictated by how you get there.

'I think it's quite hard to separate your rugby life and life away from rugby, especially when you're playing sport and you have some sort of emotional connection to what you do. If you don't really care about your work, then your performances are going to be pretty poor.

'For me, over the years it's been pretty important to have some sort of connection and whether that's right or wrong I don't know, but that's how I am … emotion spills over.'

When Carl moved to Newcastle he was joined by his girlfriend, Natalie, a television presenter with TVNZ back in New Zealand. Life outside of rugby revolves around the Kiwi love of the outdoors, but on the windy, cold North-East coast you have to be keen to surf! 'I do a bit of surfing at Tynemouth. Pretty much just like to get outdoors really, getting on the water, walking or anything like that.

'When I was with the Highlanders I had an arrangement with a local farmer in Dunedin to spend a couple of days a week on the farm. So when I had spare time I'd go up there and help out. It was fantastic. Something I very much enjoyed doing and at home I now have about 20 acres with some sheep and I spend time fixing fences and spraying gorse bushes etc. when I am there. When I eventually finish playing and we head back to New Zealand I plan on getting into farming.'

Travelling the world doing something you love obviously has its attractions to youngsters but there are not many that will have the physical and mental abilities to play at the highest level. 'I think if you're going to take it up seriously you need a balance in your life. You've got to enjoy things outside of sport, whether it's study or other things you've got going on. Throughout my career I've seen people who have had lots of things going on and I think it helps their performances; mentally it stimulates them and helps their sport.

'When I look back I didn't really have the opportunity, through being chucked straight into rugby, to have a trade, a few qualifications, training or something, but to have something like that is key. It is important to do it in your younger years for something to fall back on.

'Just from memory, the PRA [Professional Rugby Players Association] in New Zealand would come around the clubs, would pull out some team photos from each team from about three years ago and say oh, these are the guys that are still playing and making their living from playing. Generally, there'd only be a third of the team left; such a high turnover of players through injuries or contracts or other different things and it makes you think. It's an incentive to give rugby your all but you need to do other things.'

Carl Hayman has been a massive presence at Newcastle Falcons since his arrival, but as we moved towards the end of 2008 rumours abounded that the big Kiwi was to terminate his contract and move back to New Zealand. He is the model professional, a modest man with a pragmatic calm approach to life, and if he left prematurely Newcastle would have lost an irreplaceable asset at a crucial time for the club as it fought for Premiership survival. Early in 2009 Carl confirmed that he 'would still be around'. He was an inspirational talisman for the team as they left the dark clouds of relegation far behind them with a run of seven Premiership wins in eight games by the end of March 2009.

If as a youngster you are going to model your development and lifestyle on a current top-flight player you could do a lot worse. However, the thought of him bashing out his favourite Johnny Cash songs in the players' band and curling his 1.93m 115kg bearded frame into his VW camper van wearing bad-taste shirt and shorts and the obligatory Kiwi flip-flops is more than a little worrying.

2008 – 2009 Season Update

Around Christmas time the rumour mill ground out that the big Kiwi was homeward bound and he did indeed go home to New Zealand in January – to get married! The start of 2009 saw him confirm his allegiance to Newcastle Falcons and in no small measure the impressive form of the 1,000th All Black was pivotal in the club's steady progress towards the end of the season and Premiership survival.

Everyone at the Falcons is delighted that the big man has agreed to captain the side in the 2009–10 season.

Carl Hayman: Statistics	
Date of birth	15 November 1979
Birthplace	Opunake, Taranaki, New Zealand
Height	1.93m
Weight	115kg
Position	tight head prop
School / university	King's High School, Dunedin
Present club	Newcastle Falcons
Previous club(s)	Otago Highlanders
Nicknames	Zarg
Favourite TV show	*Fair Go* (girlfriend presents it)
Favourite film	*Band of Brothers*
Favourite music	Johnny Cash
Favourite book	Jon Krakauer, *Into Thin Air*
Favourite food	roast anything
Most like to meet...	Arnold Schwarzenegger
Least like to meet...	Robert Mugabe
Best moment in rugby	making friendships
Favourite place to visit	Canada
I love...	being outdoors
I hate...	nothing

STEVE BORTHWICK

England; Saracens

One of the enduring memories for me of the 2007–08 season was the end of the European Challenge Cup Final played at Gloucester's Kingsholm ground. The two finalists were Worcester Warriors, who had beaten my own Newcastle Falcons in the semi-final, and Bath captained by Steve Borthwick, who was playing his last game for the club after ten distinguished years of service.

My memory is not so much about the game but more about the minute or so after the final whistle when the big Cumbrian was shielded from the cameras by his teammates as he shed the bitter-sweet tears of the victory that he so yearned to bring to Bath, yet at the same time realizing that he would never pull on those colours again. His next visit to the recreation ground at Bath would take him through the changing-room doors and left into the away dressing room after so many times turning right. The enormity of the moment had caught up with him and, whilst he is renowned for meticulous preparation prior to playing, nothing could prevent the outward expression of emotion for the supporters and a club with whom he had established a close bond since arriving as an 18-year-old.

'Bath is a great city and it's a fantastic rugby environment. I've had an amazing ten years and it's been special to be part of something that is such an institution; the club is right at the heart of the city and I also live in the city centre. It's been a fantastic experience and a fantastic time.'

It was BBC's *Rugby Special* that introduced me to grounds that I have only visited since my involvement with Newcastle Falcons. I have been to some magnificent stadiums but I love going back to Bath Rugby's spiritual home the recreation ground known to all as

'The Rec'. The old ground is in the centre of the beautiful Georgian city of Bath and is so close to the River Avon that the ground staff must have nightmares every time it rains. The ground may have seen better days, with the facilities being a relic of times past, but to be in the press box of the old timber stand, looking down on a pitch that has had so much history played out on its surface, staring with wonderment at people hanging from vantage points in the period townhouses above the clubhouse, and being lost in the splendour of the magnificent hill in the background beyond the temporary stand, is just so special.

Steve is very aware of the history of the club and the squad's responsibility to write the current pages of the club's story. 'There have been many great players at Bath over the years and some of those guys still come around occasionally. They bring a lot of great influences, fantastic players to learn from and be friends with, to listen to what they have to say and watch how they do things, how they handle themselves. There is a rich history and it's been fantastic to be a part of it. All of the players know how special it is to play for Bath. There is something unique about it.'

However, after ten great years at The Rec, Steve has decided to move on to face a new challenge with Saracens for the start of the 2008–09 season. 'The end of the season will be the culmination of my career at Bath. I've always given Bath my all and I am determined that the last time I wear the Bath shirt there will be nothing left to give to Bath at that point in time. I've spent a huge amount of time trying to learn from my experiences, talking to and listening to people. I read a lot, normally a book a week, to see how other people have acted in situations to help me learn about myself. I have decided that the time's right for me to challenge myself in other ways and decided to move and play at Saracens next year. I will give everything I possibly can up to my last day as a Bath player. Then that period in my life will have ended and the start of a new period will be beginning.'

Steve is originally from Carlisle in Cumbria. His father's work took the Borthwick family to Preston when Steve was nine years of age. It was in Preston that his rugby started to develop, both at Hutton Grammar School and also at Preston Grasshoppers Rugby Club, the former rugby home of another England second row, though from the amateur era, Wade Dooley. It was not, however, rugby that was the first love for the young man. Even though the family was involved in Carlisle Rugby Club and Cumbrian rugby, it was his father's love of football that captured his youthful imagination.

'My dad was a footballer and I was influenced by him. He played local league football in Carlisle, which is why I started playing football. I used to watch Carlisle United and then when we moved to Preston it was Preston North End. I was never very good but just enjoyed playing with my mates.

'I hadn't seen a rugby game, hadn't tossed a rugby ball until I went to secondary school at the age of 11. Hutton Grammar School actually played rugby and didn't really play football, so in my first year I played rugby on Saturday for the school and Sunday football for a local club. At the start of the year I leant towards football but as the year went on rugby took over and football sort of fell by the wayside.

'I enjoyed rugby at school. It was what me and my mates did. We had a successful team and it was great fun. It wasn't a conscious decision to concentrate on rugby; it was more to do with me being very big and not being very good at football. It was something that just evolved and I became a football watcher.

'I was also actively involved in other sports at school. Due to my height I enjoyed volleyball and basketball and that ultimately helped my rugby; athletics field events and cricket, where I was a good fielder, but did not offer much else.'

Hutton Grammar School holds a lot of good memories for the big Cumbrian, who had an early interest in mathematics that quickly turned to dislike and was soon to be replaced by a leaning towards geography and the social sciences. Sport became of growing importance as he became older and representative honours placed demands on his time that had to be balanced with the qualifications he would need to realise his desire to study at university. Sixth form, where Steve studied Geography, Economics and Chemistry, was a particularly challenging period, but he demonstrated an inner resolve to set challenging goals, to focus and to work towards achieving them. There are many young players in all sports that have difficulty balancing the demands of international sport and study.

These qualities have evidenced themselves many times over the subsequent years. 'At about 14 or 15 years of age I started going to representative trials as a back-row forward. In the first trial I wasn't going to get picked and one of the coaches decided to play me in the second row so I got to play my position by default. I played county rugby for Lancashire, managed to make the North of England side and got picked to play for England Under–16 Group making my debut at Twickenham against Wales.

'When I think back to that point in time, in the tunnel before the game it was just nerve-racking. I'd never dealt with anything like that before. Playing in this fantastic arena that you see on the television with probably between 15,000 and 20,000 spectators, which is small in terms of numbers inside Twickenham but for someone used to playing in front of couple of hundred at people at most, that was so very nerve-racking. We worked very hard as a team and we won. It was a phenomenal feeling to represent England, to actually represent your country at that age.

'It was a very busy time because, through England Under 16, we had weekends together training, which meant that I had to do all of my schoolwork during the week. The following year in 1997 I was chosen at 17 years of age to tour Australia with England 18 Group. Several of the squad, the likes of Mike Tindall, Iain Balshaw, Jonny Wilkinson, Anthony Rock, James Lofthouse, Lee Best, Lee Mears, were finishing school and were then joining professional clubs, not necessarily senior squads but they were going on to play rugby. I was actually going back to school for my upper sixth-form year and that was challenging in the sense that suddenly you've been away all summer – I think we were there six or seven weeks. Virtually all of our school summer holiday we were away on tour, very competitive and daily training, which was very demanding. Then suddenly I was back to school.

'When you're a kid you dream of playing professional football and you can go and watch footballers and think that's a fantastic thing to do as a job. With professional rugby starting in 1995 I suddenly had the idea that perhaps you can do that through rugby, perhaps be a professional sportsman. The idea got implanted then in 1997 after the Australia tour. Three of the squad, Iain Balshaw, Mike Tindall and Lee Mears, joined Bath and to see the boys do that makes you think that you could be a professional sportsman.

'I knew what I needed to do. I needed to do well and I needed to take focus. I was at a good school with good teachers who supported what I was doing. There was a lot going on and it was challenging to focus, but to be honest I was very fortunate to be playing rugby with my mates. When you are doing that all you're thinking about is winning the games you're involved in and that is relatively easy. It's when you're not involved in rugby and trying to focus academically that it is difficult.

'It did take some work to concentrate on my studies as well as my rugby but I knew I wanted to go to university so I knew I needed to get the qualifications to meet the entry requirements. Although I wanted to be a professional rugby player, another goal along the way was to finish my A levels and do well.'

Steve came to a three-day session that we held at Newcastle after the England 18 group tour to Australia in 1997. As a young lad of 17 years of age, he was intelligent, had a significant physical presence and simply spent the three days smashing people; he loved contact. We desperately wanted him to come to us, but our loss was Bath's gain. At the end of his A levels in June 1998 Steve joined Bath and moved to The Rec literally a week after finishing his exams. He moved straight into the First Team squad where he was suddenly rubbing shoulders with the idols that he had seen only on television. The team ethos at the club meant that he was integrated into the squad, looked after and helped by the senior players, but the shirt is never 'given' to anyone and has to be earned.

'Bath had a fantastic group of players at that time. The calibre of people involved was immense. I stood in a huddle on the pitch looking around at people I had only seen on television, players like Ollie Redman, Martin Haag, Mike Catt, Phil de Glanville, Ieuan Evans, Victor Ubugo... It was phenomenal the way things were and still are at Bath in that the guys look after you and will help you along the way, but they don't make it too easy, you are tested to see if you are up to it. Wearing the Bath shirt is special so it's always been made a big thing to earn it. It's never been given to anybody.'

Rapid progress carried on as he established himself in the powerhouse of the Bath pack as a 19-year-old in the 1998–99 season. It was the Saracens who provided the opposition at The Rec on the 18 December 1998 for his First Team debut. 'It was awesome. I was involved in the squad in the Anglo-Welsh games with Cardiff and Swansea but my debut was against Saracens and I managed to hold my place in the starting team all that year.'

International honours were also on the radar as North and Midlands Under 21s defeated the South African Under 21s at Leicester's Welford Road. Selection for England Under 21s followed with the South Africans again providing the opposition at Twickenham and again coming out on the wrong side of the score line. These games took place in the autumn of 1998 when Steve had just turned 19 years of age.

South Africa was becoming a favourite word for Steve when in 2000 at 20 years of age he was included in the full England squad for their summer tour. Whilst he did not get his first cap on that tour, he did manage it against France in the Six Nations championship on 7 April 2001 in a 48–19 victory.

Standing in the Twickenham tunnel before his 16 Group England debut against Wales had been 'nerve racking', but in that same tunnel on the afternoon of the 7 April 2001 those thoughts had been replaced by excitement. 'My overriding emotion was excitement. There had been a huge amount of work put in to get to this point, and as I walked out of the tunnel, saw the packed stadium and felt the atmosphere, I realised what this was. I was hugely excited but had to put that to one side and be focused because I had a job to do.' In a very short period a lot had been achieved by the big second row with many memories already locked away.

'Up to the age of 21 I had had some fantastic moments in the game. My Bath debut was awesome. My first England tour to South Africa in 2000 at the age of 20 was pretty awesome and my England debut against France when 21 years of age gave me fantastic memories and was pretty phenomenal. A lot happened at that time and I was also studying at university as well. That was also enjoyable in terms of getting involved in other things outside of rugby and meeting different people.'

A word or phrase to describe yourself at 21 years of age?

Ambitious ...

I was an ambitious young man trying to learn as much as I possibly could and trying to play competitively. I got more than I was expecting, playing for Bath, for England 21s, getting into the England Senior tour and getting England caps, were all things that made me even more determined to work harder and achieve more.

Success came at a very young age for Steve and in the intervening years he has established himself on both the club and international stage. He has been captain of Bath, captain of England A and, during the 2008 Six Nations campaign, captained England to victory against Italy in Rome when Phil Vickery fell ill on the day of the game. The latest accolade is being named Martin Johnson's first captain of England for both the Summer 2008 tour to New Zealand and the Autumn internationals.

Once again, however, balancing his rugby commitments with his studies as an Economics and Politics student at Bath University was challenging. 'Bath University was fantastic and some of the tutors were brilliant. They understood some of the pressure that was upon me and were great with it, but ultimately I had a responsibility to them, I had to give as well. First and foremost I had to deliver on the rugby field every week in training and in games. I then had to be effective in the student group. Sometimes after training it was into the car in dirty rugby kit straight up to the university to do presentations.

'There was certainly one presentation where my group met in the evenings to do the work and organise who's responsible for what but, as always, it comes down to deadlines. Unfortunately for one deadline the group was meeting a couple of hours before the final presentation to do the editing and see the final version of the work and of course I was training, so couldn't make it. So they left my part of the presentation outside the door of the room for me. I belted up after training still in my rugby kit and picked up my presentation from the floor, went into the university room and did the presentation with the group!

'That was a great experience – playing and studying; you know, to get up first thing in the morning and study before training. I was allowed to do examinations earlier or later than the rest of the group as they took place when we still had games. They were challenging times though really, really rewarding, and I learnt huge amounts about myself.' The image in my head is one where this big, sweating, dirty rugby player is at the front of the class reading his prompt cards.

Life in Bath has been a very positive thing for Steve in all sorts of ways and finishing his degree in 2003 was one of the standout moments that he will never forget. When he talks about the standout moments in rugby, it's clear the bond with Bath is very strong and there must have been a lot of thought when deciding to turn his back on the West Country and move to Saracens. Captaining Bath, in particular, has been a great honour. '[It's] a huge thing, to see your name on the club's honours board. I think the most important thing is that you have earned the respect of a group of people that you have a huge respect for. The team are your peers and their view counts. They are the people who work with you day in and day out. To have the opportunity to lead them out on to the pitch is pretty phenomenal and I am happy to be judged by those quality people.'

In amongst all of this success there have been disappointments but it is how these are dealt with that is important for professional sportspeople and there are lessons that carry over into more normal existences. 'I have great job, an amazing job, the best job in the world as far as I'm concerned, but it does have a downside. One of those is when you're dreaming of playing for England and they don't pick you, people are writing you off and saying all kinds of things. What I think you have to do is know yourself very well and understand the fact that when selection is made, that is one person's or a small group of people's view of you at that one moment in time and that doesn't define you.

'Because they don't pick you does not mean I'm suddenly not

worthy, not that good. As you get older, knocks come along the way, people are not patting you on the back all the time and you need to know yourself tremendously well, know what you are, what your strengths are, what your weaknesses are, what your areas to improve are. As long as you know these things, it doesn't matter what anybody else thinks at that point in time; as long as you have your own set of values, you carry yourself and hold yourself the way you want to, then that's it.

'Other disappointments can relate to injuries. It's quite a horrible thing when you're injured and can't play because as a rugby player you want to play and there's no point being sat in the stand. To reconcile myself with that, whenever I've been injured – and fortunately I've been very lucky – I think of it as an opportunity. It's an opportunity to develop your skills in other areas or an opportunity to rest. Ultimately when you play week in and week out you don't always get that opportunity, so being injured can be used positively. I've always tried to think of injury as an opportunity and fortunately for me that opportunity has been very rare.'

Steve is one of the most positive people I have ever met, though some may think that utilizing downtime due to injuries as an opportunity may be stretching positive thinking to the limits. However, one of the traits of top-level performers is the ability to draw a line under things that have happened, both positive and negative, reflect on the experience, learn the lessons and move forward. These mental abilities are much sought after in the business world. Steve concurs: 'The key aspect is that drawing of the line but also very important is the need to reflect. The challenge as a player is to find the right balance: don't spend too much time, deal with positive or otherwise situations quickly, take what lessons you can and move on.'

In the past it may be that the balance has been difficult to get right as Steve admits to having reflected too much on things that had happened in games and beat himself up about his own mistakes, but as maturity comes he is philosophical about the nature of a player's performance. 'We all make mistakes and I have learnt that it's possible to dwell on things too much. What is it they say? To be old and wise, you have to have been young and foolish.'

Getting the analytical and emotional balance right is vitally important and Steve's approach is certainly thoughtful. The onus for him is to get his personal preparation right and to this end he spends a lot of time studying the opposition as well as analysing his own team. 'The whistle goes and you're in; that's not me. I am more preparation and plans, but like anything there are times when something goes wrong either before or during the game. The bus gets lost on the way to the ground, kick-off gets delayed, or something happens in the game that you do not expect.

'All these different things happen and I suppose the answer is that you have to be flexible. Physical arousal but mental calmness is something that most players learn by experience.'

The weekly cycle of training is obviously an important part of the physical preparation needed to perform at the top level but also provides the opportunity to work on strategies that have evolved from analysing your own individual and team's strengths and weaknesses as well as your opponents'. In my years in the game I have observed both 'good' and 'bad' trainers, and not everyone enjoys training, especially if they see it as a means to an end. Some players need to be stimulated by their training. Simply turning up and putting in the work is not enough and I think Steve has this mindset where his striving for improvement is again very evident.

'I enjoy training in the sense that I enjoy making improvements. When you identify something you want to improve, be it certain skills, a lift in the gym, reaching a target on the treadmill, whatever it may be, you train, see the improvements and attain your goal – I really enjoy that.

'Lots of stuff in training is rehearsal, practising skills so that under pressure you can perform that skill. A lot of things are a matter of repetition but what I tend to do is ensure I'm focused on the next challenge. I look to identify what the next challenge is so that I'm not doing something for the sake of doing it. I'm doing it for something else, for the attainment of a goal.

'As a player I feel a great responsibility with the other players that are part of the team to perform at an optimum level to fulfil my role. Everything I do is for team success so whilst at training I'm doing things to get better personally, and I have individual goals, but they are to make me more effective within the team.'

A word or phrase to describe you now?

Focused and excited...

I am focused on achieving with Bath what this group of people deserve and I hope that is trophies at the end of the season. I am also excited and eager to see what's going to happen when I go to Saracens. I have a new place to live, a new group of people and lots of new challenges ahead of me.

Away from the rigours of training and playing, after completing his degree in 2003, Steve has spent time concentrating on and developing his rugby. Five years of juggling his rugby life with his academic life left him feeling the need to focus on rugby and his responsibilities as captain of Bath fully. However, active minds need stimulation and he has started learning French, and at some point in the future wants to study an MA in Management to which he feels he could bring his experiences from sport.

I feel that Steve is a man who knows himself very well. Like all of us he has his strengths and weaknesses but maybe, unlike the majority, he has the ability to maximise his strengths, recognise his weaknesses and take the positives from situations. The 2007 World Cup in France was a very frustrating tournament and one in which he did not feature as much as hoped. 'I wouldn't have been me had I not felt some anger. I'm fiercely committed to what I do and I'm very ambitious, so when things go badly I take it to heart. That's my personality and it's unlikely to change, but I dealt with that anger as I always deal with it by analysing my performance, identifying the things I should have done better and resetting my goals.'

The big Cumbrian's elevation to the England captaincy has been an extremely testing time as Martin Johnston's charges have struggled to compete with their Southern Hemisphere opposition on both the 2008 Summer tour to New Zealand and the Autumn internationals. I am not aware of any other England captain who has had the responsibility of leading his side against Australia, South Africa and the All Blacks on three occasions in his first six games in charge –

five of the greatest challenges in world rugby. The Pacific Islands provided England with a somewhat simpler challenge in the sixth game.

The 2009 Six Nations tournament brought with it its fair share of criticism but England showed that they can play an expansive game and wins against France and Scotland in the last two games of the tournament maybe gave an indication of better times ahead for England and its captain. I feel sure there has been a lot of analysis and feelings of anger over the last few months, but it is said that anger is simply hurt turned outwards and I think it is true to say that to get hurt you have to care. There is no doubting that Steve Borthwick cares deeply.

When Newcastle have played Bath over the years we always have a chat. It may only be two minutes on the stairs but that's normally because I can't stand the smirk on the big Cumbrian's face after another Bath win! I hope Sarries don't continue the tradition.

The lady who transcribed my interview with Steve put on the bottom of her notes: 'He sounds like a really nice man.' She is a fine judge.

2008–2009 Season Update

May 2008 to June 2009 has been a significant challenge for the big Cumbrian. His move to Saracens saw him immediately made club captain but, yet again, Saracens failed to satisfy their ambitions on the field and, as the season came towards its end, it was off-the-field matters and the aims of the new South African owners that created the headlines.

At international level, as England captain, Steve handled himself brilliantly in the face of mounting criticism of Martin Johnson's England set-up and the team's stuttering performances. He will also have been massively disappointed not to grab the attention of the British and Irish Lions selectors.

Steve Borthwick: Statistics	
Date of birth	12 October 1979
Birthplace	Carlisle
Height	1.98m
Weight	114kg
Position	second row
School / university	Hutton Grammar School, Preston; Bath University
Present club	Saracens
Previous clubs	Bath; Preston Grasshoppers
Nicknames	Borthers
Favourite TV show	*24*
Favourite film	any James Bond movie
Favourite music	U2
Favourite book	Gregory Roberts, *Shantaram*
Favourite food	Thai Massaman curry
Most like to meet...	Winston Churchill (if I had a time machine)
Least like to meet...	nobody
Best moment in rugby	captaining Bath and England; England debut against France
Favourite place to visit	Thailand; Australia
I love...	the ocean
I hate...	people who show no respect to others (and things generally)

HUGH VYVYAN

England; Saracens

The game of Rugby Union went professional in the middle of the 1994–95 season and in Newcastle Sir John Hall persuaded Rob Andrew to head up his push for rugby to take its place alongside ice hockey, basketball and the Geordie mad passion that is football in his vision of the Newcastle Sporting Club.

At the end of that season I was asked to jump on to the bus that nobody really knew the destination of. I was asked to set up and run a Development Team, and we did what we thought was right but the truth is that we did not really know where we were going or how we were going to get there!

As we found our feet we felt we were moving in the right direction with player recruitment and development, but in those first few months I did not have the comfort and good guidance of my very good friend Paul MacKinnon, who is now in charge of youth development for the New Zealand RFU. It is Paul that should rightly take the credit for developing the structures that have enabled so many players to come through the Newcastle Falcons system, but back in that formative time, particularly at the start of that first season, I got whoever turned up.

As Director of Rugby at Northumbria University I had a pretty good handle on students coming to our university but with Newcastle and Durham universities it was a little more difficult to get the information about students who were of a good enough standard to be involved with the Newcastle Club.

As the students arrived at the start of the academic year we attempted to make contact with prospective players and so it was that on a Tuesday night in mid-September 1995 I watched my flock of prospective

61

players jogging around the back pitch at Kingston Park and noticed this big skinny ginger kid who was way over six foot tall and had played most of his rugby at fly half.

I feel very privileged to have worked with Hugh Vyvyan in his early days with Newcastle and then watch him make his way in the game as a professional rugby player. Like lots of things in life you don't miss it until it's gone, and it was only when Hugh left Newcastle for pastures new at Saracens that I realised the significance of losing not only a very good player but more importantly a natural leader who embodied all the values that we had tried to drill into our young charges in the Academy. In professional sport as players develop, new opportunities arise. Movement between clubs is simply a fact of life but Hugh was the first of our home-grown professional players to move on and that was significant at lots of levels.

I hope that all of the youngsters that have come through the Falcons Academy system have received a good grounding in the game, but it was the arrival of Andrew Blades the World Cup-winning Wallaby as forwards coach in 2002 that made the biggest impression on the young second row. 'I was identified as a second row by Paul MacKinnon, whom I have a lot to thank for as the Academy Coach at Newcastle, and then Dean Ryan worked with me in the First Team set-up, who I think is an excellent coach; but after he left Andy Blades arrived from Australia and for me he was the best coach I have worked with. He got so much more from that group of players and transformed a pretty average Newcastle team into a cup-winning team.

'Pat Lam had left and Peter Walton had retired so there was no natural Number 8 and Andy moved me to the back row where I had played some rugby in the Development Team set-up. I had a couple of good years working with Andy and learnt such a lot from him. I was made captain in his second year at the club, which also turned out to be my last year.

'He got the best out of us as a squad and we played some really enjoyable rugby with the highlight being the Powergen Cup Final. It was my third cup final with Newcastle. I'd been on the bench against Wasps in 1999 and played most of the second half against Harlequins in 2001; however, in 2004 against Sale I managed to captain a winning team in one of my last games for Newcastle. It was a great day and a really fitting way to be leaving Newcastle.'

Whilst on the surface things looked like they were on the up for both Hugh and the club, that cup-final success masked some significant issues at the Falcons. The club captain was at a pivotal point in his career, as he was knocking on the door of his ultimate career ambition, an England cap, and he was also recognising the signs that his personal circumstances were changing.

'Although the cup-final occasion was fantastic I was pretty frustrated with the set-up at the club in all honesty. I think Newcastle totally lacked any ambition to go on and win the League. I was in the last year of my contract and I would have committed myself to another couple of years if the club had been willing to sign a couple of really good players to bolster the squad. We had some excellent young players, the nucleus of a very good squad, and I felt we only had to sign a few established players in key positions to have a realistic chance of pushing for the top of the League. I spoke to Rob (Andrew) at length and he felt his hands were tied financially.

'Playing for England was a big ambition for me. At that time I was getting into the England squads but always with the A Team and I felt a move away from Newcastle might help my international career. I'd captained England A at the Churchill Cup and worked well with the coach, Steve Diamond, who was newly appointed coach at Saracens. Saracens were interested in me joining them and what really caught my imagination was that they seemed to have a huge amount of ambition to take the club forward and were also talking to some great up-and-coming players like Alex Sanderson, Dan Scarbrough and Glen Jackson.

'A couple of years earlier I'd met Kate whom I was pretty keen on and, although her family are from the North-East, she was working in London. It all seemed to be pointing in one direction.'

When difficult decisions have to be made we turn to people whom we trust and it was to Andrew Blades that Hugh turned to for guidance. 'All of this was going on, so I rang Bladesy and arranged to have a drink with him in Gosforth. I let him know I was thinking of leaving and he told me that he'd been offered the forward coach's job with Australia and the likelihood was that he would be taking it. I suppose him taking the Wallabies job was the final nail in the coffin for me. I had great friends and teammates, but Bladesy moving on made up my mind for me – it was the right time.

'We were a tight-knit squad who always worked hard for each other and I loved my time at Newcastle – the players, the supporters and most of all the community – but I felt I would have always regretted it if I didn't move. I was 26 or 27 with a lot of ambition to further my career and it felt the right option for me at the time.'

In the same way as he had within the England A Team set-up, the Saracens coach wanted to utilise Hugh's leadership talents and made him club captain before he had even played a game. Vyv, by his own admission, has always been vocal and outspoken both on and off the field and the reason for this may be in his upbringing as the youngest of eight children.

The Vyvyan clan comprises Richard, Jonathan, Simon, Charles, Kate, Paul, James and Hugh with a 16-year gap between the eldest and youngest. With eight kids it is not going to be possible to be the only receiver of parental attention so Hugh spent a lot of his time in his brothers' company and in a sports-mad family the best way to get noticed was through sport.

'When you're the youngest of eight kids obviously you are not going to get constant attention 24/7. We were kicked out into the garden with a tennis racket, cricket bat or ball and told to play. I was looked after by my older brothers quite a lot and get on with them really well. I kind of wanted to show off to my brothers, I suppose, so that I would be noticed and the best way for me was through sport, particularly rugby.'

All of the brothers played rugby: Charlie played at the top level for Sale and James still plays for Richmond over 35s. One of the family's proudest claims to fame is the fact that the seven Vyvyan brothers made up their own team and reached the final of the Penryn Sevens on five occasions, winning it three times.

The love of sport comes from both their parents, Mary and Tony, with Richmond Rugby Club playing a big part in their lives. 'Dad met my mum at the Middlesex 7s so I suppose rugby's always been very much in our lives. Dad was originally from Cornwall but his work as an accountant took him to London. He played rugby for the Army, Coventry and Richmond, was 6 foot 4 and played inside centre. Back in those days he was one of the biggest on the pitch.

'I remember and have fond memories of going to Richmond Rugby Club on a weekend with my dad who was heavily involved with the club. All six of my brothers have actually played at the club for one of the teams; ironically, I'm the only one of the family not to play for Richmond at any level. My mum's from South-West London and she is also from a sporty family. She's 71 years of age now and still plays tennis; she's pretty fit. Sport's always been in the family.'

The Vyvyans were all born around the London area, with Hugh entering the world in Guildford, but when he was ten the family moved back to his dad's native Cornwall when Tony became the accountant for a mining company. Tony had been brought up in Africa where his father was a policeman, but had been schooled back in England at Downside School, a private Catholic school, and all of the Vyvyan brothers followed in their father's footsteps, attending the school between the ages of 13 and 18.

'I was very fortunate to go to Downside School, which was a private school, and I really enjoyed my time there. I made some excellent friends and sport was an important part of my education. I was really fortunate to play all different sports. I did OK at school academically and studied Theology, Classical Civilisation and Spanish at A level. I thought Spanish would be useful, though I only got an E so that probably wasn't a good decision.

'With rugby I was in the First Team right the way through school and I captained my age groups all the way up. Jon Callard (Bath and England) was at the school for my last three years as a Geography teacher and was also the First XV rugby coach. Even though the game was amateur in those days, he was very dedicated and trained hard. He gave me a good insight into how hard you have to train in order to be successful at your chosen sport.'

Jon Callard gave Hugh one of the highlights of his time at the school when he took on the current England fullback in a kicking competition. 'I played scrum half and fly half for most of my school career up to Upper Sixth and did the place-kicking. I used to practise my kicking with Jon and was always fairly erratic whereas he was the current England fullback. The only time I ever beat him at a kicking competition was the week before his international debut when England played the All Blacks. Anyway, England went on to beat them and Jon kicked the three or four penalties. He learnt it all from me!'

Kicking practice victories over England Internationals may have provided good memories but the skill may also have planted a seed of doubt into the heads of the selectors who have had a significant influence over Hugh's England ambitions. 'I played for Somerset Schools at Under 18 levels but I never progressed above that level. I played fly half and scrum half right through school and it was only in my last year when I grew about a foot and a half that I moved into the forwards. Ironically in one of the final South-West Schools trials I later learnt from one of the selectors that I bumped into ten or so years later that it was Andy Robinson who did not approve of me getting into the team. Apparently I kicked the ball into touch in my own 22, and he did not approve of that from a Number 8.'

At the end of his time at Downside it was in fact cricket that enabled the future professional rugby player to spread his wings as he took up an opportunity to spend a year in South Africa prior to taking up his offer from Newcastle University. A South African cricket coach worked with the First Team at Downside and the previous year had organised for a couple of the lads to go and coach in Cape Town. When the opportunity arose Vyv did not need any second invitation.

'I spoke to the cricket coach and he said there'd be no problem. I literally got on the plane on my own, rocked up in South Africa and was totally unprepared. I turned up and met this guy, but didn't know what I'd be doing; the only thing I knew was that I'd be working at a school. I remember boarding the plane and thinking what the hell am I doing?! I went to Edgemead Primary School in the northern suburbs of Cape Town and worked with kids up to 13 years of age. I was coaching cricket, taking PE classes and giving some tennis lessons. Basically, I was the general dogsbody! I also played cricket for a team called Bergvliet and had a great time. I met loads of local people through the cricket club.

'The first month in Cape Town I was in a car crash. I had put all my money into buying a car and smashed it up. I had no insurance and no money, so in the evenings to make ends meet I worked in a bar; I even made juggling balls with birdseed and balloons and sold them in the market in Cape Town to make some money. I was living in a dodgy part of Cape Town which was pretty rough and I didn't have a lot of money, just enough to make ends meet.

'When the rugby season started I went to the Villagers rugby club for pre-season training. I was the only English person there but I met a lot of South Africans and made a lot of friends. Once they accept you into their team, then it becomes easier on the social front; you almost have to gain acceptance and then everyone became much more warm and friendly.

'They had two or three teams and said that I would probably fit into one of the bottom teams, which made me more determined to do well. I suppose there is a different attitude in England in that if a South African or Kiwi turned up to a local rugby club in England they would probably be pencilled into the First Team.

'I played cricket but wasn't too fussed about how my cricket career went. At that time I wanted to do well with my rugby and took it quite seriously. I think that experience in South Africa was important for me. There were some brutal games played and that step up from school to Under 21s in South Africa was a huge step for me. It was a big step for my development and gave me lots of confidence returning to England and Newcastle University.

'In my last year at school rugby I went professional and applied to Newcastle University because Sir John Hall had bought Newcastle and employed Rob, Dean and Batesy. I decided to go to Newcastle to study Religious Studies after I got an A in Theology at A level.'

A year in South Africa under his belt, Hugh arrived in the Toon to take up his studies at Newcastle University. Embarking on Religious Studies at university may give the impression that a career in the priesthood was more on the ginger kid's mind than professional rugby, but in reality the course turned out to be a very enjoyable means to an end. 'I enjoyed my time there. I knew Religious Studies wasn't going to be particularly time-consuming to be honest. You didn't have to be a religious person to benefit from the course; it's more history of religion. I studied a bit about Buddhism, Hinduism, Islam, Christianity and I did my dissertation on Saudi Arabia, oil and Islam, highlighting the difficulties of massive oil revenues in an Islamic state.

It was a really interesting dissertation to do and I think it's pretty relevant today.'

Hugh came into a Newcastle University rugby set-up that boasted a lot of good players and, as coach of their city rivals, Northumbria, I remember with fondness the times we beat them and with not quite so much fondness those when they beat us. Players of the calibre of Simon Best, Johnny Spence, Jimmy Cartmell, Jimmy Rule, Paddy Seymour, Johnny Marsden and Richard Wilkes were all either involved at Newcastle (Falcons) or within professional set-ups at other clubs. The following season the likes of Tom May and Hall Charlton turned up to bolster the ranks even further.

University rugby in Newscastle was of a good standard and provided a good environment for the development of players, but Hugh's development was fast-tracked as he found himself not only a key figure in the university club but moving quickly through the ranks in the professional Newcastle set-up. 'University rugby was great and I lived university life to the full. I was also asked to join the Newcastle Falcons Academy, which was the break I needed. By the end of that first year of uni, I had managed to get on to the field with the Falcons First Team a handful of times.

'I remember being invited to train with the First Team and being so nervous because I was training and playing with some of the people I idolised: Nick Popplewell, Rob Andrew, Pat Lam, Inga Tuigamala, Alan Tait and Gary Armstrong. There were some unbelievable players in that team and it was such an honour to be invited to train. I remember being so nervous of my own teammates rather than the opposition in case I played badly and because I didn't want them to think I was a crap player! That was a huge driving force.

'I played for the university on a Wednesday and benched for the First Team on a weekend. Back in those days professional rugby was just finding its feet and I am sure it would not be allowed to happen today, but it was brilliant and in hindsight was a great way to start my professional rugby career. I was going out on a Monday and Wednesday with my friends at university and then at the weekend with the Falcons players on Saturday.'

Whilst progress was there for all to see, with the youngster regularly getting game time from the bench for Newcastle's First Team, international honours eluded him. In writing this a lot of memories came back to me about my fights with the RFU relating to lack of representative honours for Newcastle Falcons players who were also students at the two universities. I remember causing a bit of a stir when I raised this issue, which got printed up in one of the national papers the day of my last BUSA cup final as Director of Rugby at Northumbria University. Hugh, I always felt, was the first to suffer from the up-north, out-of-sight, out-of-mind syndrome.

In his final university year I was asked to coach the North of England students against the South at Bisham Abbey and made Hugh captain of the side, which also included Dave Walder, another of our Newcastle players but a student at Durham University. The North had a comfortable victory and Vyv's representative duck was broken later that year when he played for England Students against France. 'I played against France and Wales for England Students and I thoroughly enjoyed it. It was a great experience and a good opportunity to play with people from all over the country. We drew against France, which was good because they always had a pretty strong Students' team and we narrowly beat the Welsh. There were only two games but it was brilliant.'

After such a long wait to pull on the shirt with the red rose, the youngster was feeling fantastic before kick-off. 'I was very nervous and excited; it was fantastic. There were not many people there and we sang the National Anthem over this crackly old sound system but it was excellent... I loved it. Representing England had always been a dream so it was a very proud moment in my life.'

A word or phrase to describe you at 21 years of age

Ambitious and excitable...

I was probably still finding myself as a person, but the year I was 21 was my second year at university and I learnt a lot about myself during that year. I really wanted to make it as a player and could be quite excitable at times but in that year I had three operations and played virtually no rugby. It was very frustrating and I learnt such a lot about myself.

Hugh's rugby ambitions were being satisfied as he prepared himself for his second year of studies at Newcastle University. Newcastle Falcons had been promoted to the Allied Dunbar Premiership at the end of the previous season and prepared themselves for the challenges ahead with a pre-season tour to Agen in France. Newcastle only took a 30-man squad but Vyv was selected for the trip and the season of frustration started.

'I was pretty honoured to be involved. I was due to bench for the first game against Agen but I had been feeling pretty rough when I was in France.

'It was the new physio, Marten Brewer's, first week at the club. I was new to the First Team squad and had been ill for a couple of days. I was rooming with Peter Walton and I didn't want to say anything about being ill, so he was telling me to get up and I did a little bit of training but couldn't do much. I went to Marty because I was sweating and feeling awful and he took me to a doctor. They tested me and it turned out that I had peritonitis – a burst appendix. They called an ambulance and I was pretty much out of it, nearly unconscious. They rushed me to hospital and then I woke up the next morning without my appendix ... all very bizarre!

'The day before the game Marty pretty much missed everything, looking after me, and the likes of Alan Tait and John Bentley needed treatment but he wasn't around! They didn't know where he was and they gave him a hard time. I think it was a memorable introduction to the club for him as well as for me.'

Hugh got over his illness and his rugby season started but came to a grinding halt very quickly.

'I came back and played a couple of games but then dislocated my shoulder. I did my rehab, came back, played a couple more games and dislocated my shoulder again in a game at Welford Road against Leicester Seconds. That was the second time I'd dislocated it in six weeks and this led to me having a shoulder reconstruction.

'That was my season over. The great thing was that instead of moping around I had university to get on with and a lively set of flatmates to get up to no good with. I had a pretty vibrant university life to fall back on which I think was very important. I learnt a lot about myself coping with that disappointment.

'I can't believe people leave school and, if they have the academic ability, choose not to go to university – for me it's a given. It's a life experience thing more than anything and socially you learn so much, most people at that age need an outlet. I'm not advocating young rugby players going out on the lash all the time but sometimes it does help! I've seen a lot of young guys wanting to be professional players, but they don't have any social skills, they have no idea how to act in public. When you are at university and you're mixing with different types of people socially you soon pick up how to behave and you take that into your professional rugby life. You know what the protocols are and I think that is a big lesson in life.

'For any young player coming into the game I'd say you've got to take your rugby seriously but you have to have a release and relax at times. University can do that for you.'

As Hugh left university he was given a professional contract at Newcastle Falcons but in his last year as a student he was on a bursary of £3,000 and had actually started around 15 games for the First Team. He got match fees on top of this bursary but Newcastle certainly got good value. However, he always felt he was 'a student rugby player rather than a rugby player studying'.

As Hugh made his way in the game he had great players around him to pass on their experiences. 'I was very lucky because as a young player I had Doddie [Weir], who was quite a good mentor for me, and also Arch [Garath Archer]. They were both so different, like chalk and cheese in terms of character and how they played on the field. Doddie's line-out was fantastic whereas it was Garath's scrummaging, clearing of rucks and ball-carrying that were great.

'If I ever got the opportunity to play with Garath it was fantastic. I thought my strengths complemented his; I think he was one of the most underrated players in the country, a great player. I was very lucky to have those two players around and then Grimesy [Stuart Grimes] came to the club, again a very underrated player with whom I played a lot of rugby in the second row.'

The young second row was establishing himself as a quality Premiership player and the influence of Andrew Blades helped him progress to the point where he was certainly in the frame for international honours. It is Hugh's flirting with international rugby that has probably caused him the greatest disappointment, as his ambitions to represent his country were repeatedly frustrated. The 'nearly man' had his first England tour to Argentina in 2002 but the tour turned out to be a bitter-sweet experience, with elation at being on the tour and benching in a test match but despair at not getting on the field.

'My first trip was to Argentina with Clive Woodward and Andy Robinson as coaches. England always saw me as a second row but I was playing Number 8 at Newcastle so there's a little bit of an issue about my best position. I went on the bench against Argentina but didn't get on and I was gutted. England had a great win in Buenos Aires but I didn't play. I was really gutted after that game but it made me really, really determined to get the chance again.'

Putting the disappointment behind him, Vyv had a really good pre-season back on Tyneside and further developed his abilities as a top-level performer with a couple of good seasons at Newcastle. Eventually the international selectors came knocking at his door again but it was to lead the A Team into the Churchill Cup in Canada and the United States as a Number 8. It was a very proud captain that led his team in the tournament.

'It was awesome to be named captain for the tour. We played Canada, USA and Japan twice. It was a really good tour and meeting the other players made me realise that most people involved in the rugby community are easy enough to get on with. You always have a perception about other players, but you know a lot of them are different on and off the pitch. A player that you might think is a right pain in the backside on the pitch usually turns out to be a really nice bloke. It was good to meet the other players from other clubs and also to learn some new skills. You can develop as a player much quicker, I believe, by learning from other players, and tours are a good way of learning new techniques and skills.'

Leadership is something that coaches have seen in Hugh ever since his days at school when he captained the team every year. In the Falcons Academy the captaincy role is one that he embraced wholeheartedly, and a defining moment for Paul MacKinnon and me in the way we saw Hugh as a positive influence on the field was during an evening game in Scotland against Glasgow Hawks.

72

Back in those days Scottish professional rugby was struggling to find its feet and Newcastle's Development / Under 21 team regularly took on Scottish Division One opposition, which was a big ask of the players but a wonderful development opportunity for them to show us that they could step up to the plate.

During the game in question Newcastle conceded a try and were not playing very well. In the huddle under the posts the big ginger captain got hold of that team and talked to them in a really inspirational manner, but words are easy if not backed up by actions and Hugh set an example in the way he played that demanded a response from his teammates. The response came as the very young Newcastle team swept away their senior opponents and we were left thinking we had someone special in our ranks.

Some say leadership comes naturally; others say you have to work at it. Hugh sits on the fence when thinking about how he approaches the role, especially when called upon to do so for his country. 'I think that it's something you continually work on and you pick up but it's something that has come relatively naturally to me as I've always been vocal, probably as a result of wanting to be heard when you have seven elder siblings. For me, the key for a captain is to know different personalities and treat people differently; I have read some books on leadership and I find it an interesting topic. Communication on and off the pitch is a very important part of rugby. However, most of the time on the pitch you are reacting instinctively to how the situation unfolds, so what you say and do must come naturally.

'I was very nervous being captain of England A because there were some good players on that tour. In my first meeting as captain I was thinking about what people thought about me, and anyone who says they're not bothered about what people think is lying. I believe that everyone wants to be perceived well, so I was pretty nervous, but I hope I came across quite well. It was a successful tour in that we won all of our games so it definitely goes down as a positive experience.'

Hugh captained England A in the Churchill Cup tournaments in both 2003 and 2004 and his performances at the level just below the full national team were screaming out to be noticed. He eventually achieved that coveted first cap on 13 November 2004 and, whilst it is high on his list of standout moments, the shine was taken off to a certain extent by the nature of the opponents.

'It was bizarre really. My one cap came against Canada whom I'd played about five times in the two previous seasons in the Churchill Cup. I came off the bench for about 20 minutes, scored a try and it was a proud moment for me, but I felt a little bit flat because when you envisage playing for England you think of South Africa or New Zealand and I don't mean any disrespect to Canada but it was a bittersweet moment. However, that kind of drives you on. Great to get a cap, don't get me wrong, but I just always wanted to get more.

'That season was tough because I felt I was playing good rugby for Saracens but I just couldn't get into the squad. Coming into the Six Nations there were a few injuries in the back row so I felt I had a real chance of playing against Wales but it was never meant to be.

'Selection is all pretty subjective really because the coaches probably felt that the other players would do a better job than me, but I disagreed with them! I felt that year was my big chance to play a couple of games for England and it never happened. That's the saddest part of my career really. Your game's never perfect and you wish you could do things differently but of course you can't.

'The England coach at the time was Andy Robinson and I'm sure he's got a particular view about how rugby should be played. When I was 17 years of age he left me out of the South-West Schools team because he didn't like the way I played rugby. Perhaps later in my career he still didn't like the way I played rugby. Ultimately it is down to the individual and I should have taken all selection issues out of the coaches' hands by being the best player in that position. I was not, so I did not get to play any more for England – simple as that.

'I've almost played 200 Premiership games and I'm very proud of that, but ultimately I wanted to play more games for England and I have no one to blame but myself. There was a big thing in English rugby about being powerful and I've always been lightweight. It's the one thing I would have changed in my career, getting in the gym more and eating protein powder. I always did extra sessions but maybe not enough. That could have made a difference.'

The move after the 2003–2004 season to Saracens preceded that England cap and the ambition that was felt to be lacking at Newcastle Falcons is constantly evident at Sarries, as the great underachievers of the Premiership strive for consistency and the Holy Grail of success. 'My time at Sarries has been excellent, frustrating, but always exciting. The one thing Saracens don't lack is ambition. Every year they're desperate for success, desperate to get the best players in, and that was one of the key reasons why I came here.

'With all that ambition why hasn't there been more success? First, I think there has been too high a turnover of the coaching staff. Coaches need to be given time to implement change but with Eddie Jones I believe Saracens finally have the right man at the helm. Secondly, Saracens need to find more of an identity; they are called Saracens as they had no home ground or clubhouse and always played away fixtures, wandering from game to game. This identity crisis needs to be changed. I know over the last few years the players and staff have worked very hard to create an identity and this has gone a long way in helping us to become a successful team.

'The current set-up at Saracens under Eddie Jones is by far the most professional that I have ever been involved in. The coaching, strength and conditioning and medical staff are all first class. The players are looked after very well and only have to concentrate on their rugby. It is a huge step in the right direction and I am very confident that Saracens will be a force to be reckoned with over the next five years or so.'

A word or phrase that describes you now?

Relaxed...

Now I'm really relaxed about my rugby. I think when I was 21 I was pretty intense and focused and I sacrificed a lot more at 21 than I do at 32. Now I'm doing more stuff outside rugby and I have a fantastic family life with Kate, my wife, and our daughter, Grace.

I'm really enjoying my life in rugby now. I came to Saracens and was made captain before playing a game for the club. →

> That time was quite hard and very intense for a while, but in the last two years I haven't had any responsibility as captain and I've really been able to knuckle down with my rugby. I'm not sure if it's because of the lack of responsibility taking some of the pressure off or the fact I am getting more relaxed as I get older and have a steady family life, but I'm really happy and enjoying things.
>
> I've realised playing is not going to last for ever so I've sort of reinvented myself as a player, which I think you've got to do, and I have really enjoyed the last 18 months as I try and play each game as if it is my last.

At Saracens, Hugh's contract ends at the end of the 2008–2009 season and he was hopeful that he would stay with Saracens for another year or two before the inevitable comes around and he hangs up his boots. However, nothing stays the same in sport as well as in life and since our interview changes at the top of the club have seen Eddie Jones leaving and the futures of several of the Saracens squad brought into question. It may be that Hugh is one of the casualties of the new regime and may have to look elsewhere to finish his playing days at the top level.

Looking back over his career his one cap and try for England is a proud moment, but there is no hiding the disappointment of not being capped more than the once against Canada. However, there are many other high points to cherish as the years role by. The brothers Vyvyan winning the Penryn Sevens will always have a special place in the memory. 'For us, a bunch of slow people to win a Sevens competition once was great but to win it three times was remarkable. I think we're all telepathically linked.'

His last game for Newcastle Falcons, the Powergen Cup Final against Sale, where he captained his team to victory and lifted the trophy at the home of rugby, Twickenham, is remembered with fondness. 'The last game for Newcastle with all my mates, with some really close friends in the team, was so special. It was just an awesome occasion. Everyone says it was an entertaining game and Sale were a really good team including the likes of Jason Robinson, Mark Cueto and Charlie Hodgson. We played probably the best rugby we'd played all season and deserved to win.'

Whilst not at the top level of the sport, the aura of playing Barbarians rugby also holds a special place in the memory for Vyv as he took his place on the summer 2007 tour. He was a member of the squad managed by the great All Black Zinzan Brooke and captained the side in both of their games against Tunisia and Spain. 'A fantastic experience and so much fun. Probably one of the best weeks I have spent as a rugby player.'

Outside of rugby, as the Sarries second row moves towards the end of his playing days, it's the City and world of finance that is his focus. An interest that maybe he gets from his accountant father. 'About two years ago I was having an off season, struggling with injury, and to be honest struggling with enjoyment. It made me think about what I would do when I finished. I started looking into life after rugby and sourced an opportunity to do some work experience at Merrill Lynch in one of their Global Wealth Management teams. I took them up on the offer and 18 months later they can't get rid of me!

'I actually think that it is helping with my rugby; having another focus away from rugby can be a positive thing. I commit to a day a week and have been very fortunate to find a mentor who gives me as much flexibility as I need. I think that I am naturally very competitive and I really want to be successful at my next career. I will always feel as if I should have done better in rugby and that will drive me on in my next career.'

Whilst the City is Hugh's ultimate destination he is passionate about making the most of his time left in the game and still has ambitions. 'I want to keep on enjoying it. A dream come true would be to play for England again but I'm realistic and at 32 years of age it's not going to happen. I'd love to win silverware with Saracens; the Premiership would be very special. I'm coming up to 200 caps in the Premiership and I'd love to become the most capped Premiership player by the time I pack it in.'

The intense, excitable youngster has come a long way as a rugby player and a person since his adventure to the frozen North of the country. Emotion is a massively important attribute of successful people as it resides within the hearts of people who care about what they do. When things are not going as we hope, which happens to all of us at some point, emotion can get the better of us and turn into a negative force. Vyv's wife, Kate, is an important influence in helping him keep things in perspective. 'My wife is a great stabilising force for me and gives me the best advice. She tells me to stop being miserable and get on with it, but when I tell her to stop being miserable and get on with it, now that's quite a different matter!'

We had chatted over a coffee at St Pancras Station and as Hugh left for an afternoon of work at Merrill Lynch and I wandered off in the direction of Kings Cross for my train back to Newcastle there were a lot of memories running around my head. They all reinforced my view that Hugh Donnithorne Vyvyan is one of life's good guys!

2008–2009 Season Update

Saracens' off-the-field re-organisation, with new owners taking the club in a new direction, would have been a very unsettling time for all involved at the club as press rumours abounded about comings and goings. Hugh was out of contract at the end of the 2008–9 season, but in May any uncertainty as to his rugby future was removed as he signed a two-year deal that will almost certainly see him finish his playing career with the club.

Hugh Vyvyan: Statistics	
Date of birth	8 September 1976
Birthplace	Guildford
Height	1.98m
Weight	102kg
Position	second row; No. 8; blind-side wing forward
School / university	Downside School; Newcastle University
Present club	Saracens
Previous clubs	Penryn RFC; Newcastle Falcons
Nicknames	Vyv, Big Red
Favourite TV show	*24*
Favourite film	*Lord of the Rings* trilogy
Favourite music	very mixed – Al Green to whatever
Favourite book	*The Kite Runner*
Favourite food	traditional Sunday roast
Most like to meet...	Winston Churchill
Least like to meet...	Pol Pot; Hitler
Best moment in rugby	the Vyvyan brothers winning the Penryn Sevens; Newcastle's 2004 Powergen Cup final win; captaining a Baa-Baas tour; England cap
Favourite place to visit	Amalfi coastline, Italy
I love...	my family
I hate...	negative people

MARTIN CORRY, MBE

England; British and Irish Lions; Leicester Tigers

As a teacher and a coach, I think the greatest pleasure comes from being around and enabling (in some small way) individuals to realise their potential, to be the best they can be in whatever activity they are engaging in. Not being the very best when judged against others but being the very best they can be.

For me this pleasure is heightened when you come into contact with special individuals who never reach a point at which they feel comfortable that their potential has been reached because they keep pushing themselves harder and further in pursuit of higher achievement. They grasp opportunities that present themselves along the way and succeed through hard work and determination At the top of their chosen field, their journey can often be full of challenges and disappointments and the retention of the personal traits and enthusiasm that originally endeared them to you can so easily be lost as life experiences harden them.

There will be no doubt that Martin Corry will be more worldly-wise than he was when we first met in 1993 but when chatting to him in the bar of the Three Swans in Market Harborough I was delighted to be talking to the same person, now in his final year of professional rugby as captain of Leicester Tigers. His determination and enthusiasm to drive Leicester Tigers forward, to support the new management team and fight for his place, even though he is the captain, says an enormous amount about the man who has been at the top of his sport for over ten years.

We first met in the changing room at Northern Rugby Club before my first training session as coach to Northumbria University. One of my students asked me to help with the university team and I think that, when I turned up at the training ground on a dark Monday evening, the most pleased man to see me was John Elder, the former England coach. John is a truly lovely man who had helped with the university boys, but in his advancing years the thought of pulling on the tracksuit on cold dark Monday evenings maybe did not fill him with joy!

Martin was a second-year Sports Studies student at Northumbria University and captain of the university rugby team. It was an important year in education as polytechnics were given university status and Newcastle Poly became Northumbria University. In that first year as a university the team competed in the Universities Athletic Union (UAU) Cup previously the preserve of 'proper' universities. After defeating Tim Stimpson's Durham University team in the semi-final the 'poly' headed to Twickenham to face Richard Hill's West London Institute.

'It was special. It was the first time that the new universities were allowed in the competition. You were playing rugby with guys you were socialising with all the time, so there was always special camaraderie. We didn't know how good we were and that was the best thing. We knew we had a good side because a lot of the guys were playing for Gosforth, but we didn't realise how good until we beat Durham University in the semi-final. That was probably our best game.

'I look back and remember going down to Twickenham to play West London Institute, Richard Hill's side. Richard Hill was already a big name in the game and they also had Darren O'Leary and Andy Lee who played at Saracens but we were being told that we were going into the final as favourites. As a team we needed to be told that people thought we were the better side. We were a poly in the far north and we didn't expect to be taken seriously.

'I'm rubbish at remembering games and there's only a few that have stayed with me and that's one of them, it was special and we won 13–9.'

In the following years I coached Northumbria University to three more Twickenham finals in the rebranded BUSA competition but the first one was very special and gave me the opportunity of seeing first hand the future England captain lubricate his tonsils and hit the high notes on the karaoke stages of Richmond High Street!

The Corrys were living in Stourbridge near Birmingham when Martin was born on 12 October 1973, the youngest of three children having two older sisters, Jo and Rachel. When he was seven years of age the family moved to Tunbridge Wells in Kent, as his dad's job with a bank took the family south. 'Both of my sisters have the brains of the family. We're very close but when we were growing up there were times we were miles apart. In every aspect you'd have all extremes. One of us at one extreme, one at the other extreme and one in the middle! Jo was into sport and got her blue for netball at Oxford, though Rachel was not so much into sport.'

Like most kids growing up in England, Martin's first sport was football but it was in Tunbridge that he got his first involvement in rugby when he was taken along to Tunbridge Wells Rugby Club mini rugby on a Sunday morning to be coached by Dad, David. Mini rugby as an introduction to the game is a very positive, enjoyable experience and with his dad coaching it was just great fun. 'When we moved to Tunbridge I still played football, I was a goalie, but my dad played rugby and he would take me down to the minis on a Sunday morning. It was brilliant, just going along with your old man – he'd be coaching me or whoever and then there'd be drinks in the bar afterwards. You'd have a lot of mates there and it was just a great atmosphere.

'There was no conscious decision to concentrate on rugby. I played all the sports at school – rugby, football, cricket, basketball – and I played cricket and football for local clubs. As I grew up it was football on Saturday morning and rugby Sunday. I wasn't a good footballer, so footie died off and rugby became my passion. I don't know whether a sense of belonging is the best way of describing it but the rugby club was just a great place to be.'

Tunbridge Wells Rugby Club to this day holds a special place in Martin's heart and he played through all of the age groups, eventually ending up in the First Team playing senior rugby when 16 years of age. This provided some rich learning experiences for the gangly youth.

Some of the bar room tales of rugby are rooted in fairy tale rather than based on fact, but Bill Cuthbertson, the fearsome-looking, bearded London Scottish lock who had played in the international arena for

Scotland made a lasting impression on the young lad jumping at two in the line-out. Jumping against the 'old man' should have presented no problems for the youngster and the team were looking forward to a plentiful supply of possession. 'I was playing senior rugby at Tunbridge Wells, alternating between back row and second row. When I look back it was a great experience playing against men when I was still a kid.

'I remember playing against Bill Cuthbertson, the former Scottish International second row who played for London Scottish. I was only a skinny little thing at the front of the line-out playing against him. He was a big lump and I thought I'm going to have a field day. I went to jump for the first ball. Those were the days when we had pockets in shorts and he had his thumb in mine and said: "Today, son, you and me are staying on the floor and letting the others jump." It's little things like that that you remember. You take those experiences and you're streets ahead of those who've only played schools rugby.'

Tunbridge Wells Grammar School was a very enjoyable time in Martin's life. Whilst not a renowned rugby school, it did play matches in the second half of the winter term after Christmas. For Martin, representative rugby came when 16 years of age with County and Divisional honours and selection for the England 18 Group in his final school year.

Academically it was the sciences that interested him the most, but when things started getting more serious at exam time the realisation kicked in that Science was not the way forward. 'I wasn't the greatest academic. I did Maths all the way through to A level and enjoyed that, but when subjects got serious I realised it wasn't going to be science. A lot of enjoying subjects depends on the teachers and we had some great teachers. The Maths and Geography teachers were great and we had an Economics guy who was just completely eccentric. I loved that you know! I studied Maths, Economics and Geography at A level.

'I had a really good childhood and really enjoyed school. At senior school you go through everything – you discover beer, you discover girls and you think you're the first to do so! I wasn't a massive rebel. There were times I went off the rails a bit, but doesn't everyone? Once I started playing senior rugby I just thought that's it – I loved every aspect of it, the game, the socialising, everything.

'A vivid memory for me was when I was 16 or 17 and playing

for Tunbridge. My old man would come along to watch and after the game would give me £5 pocket money and tell me to go out with the lads for a little while and have a good time. One time I came home after being out and I remember falling back into the house. Mum and Dad were waiting up; I slumped on to the couch and Dad asked me if he had any change. I put my hand in my pocket and gave him some money!

'The lads I was playing with at Tunbridge, they had good jobs in the City, and they'd say, "OK come on, we'll look after you." Looking back you would think a spotty lanky 16-year-old, what a pain in the bum, but they really looked after me. They put me in a corner with a drink and I never had to buy anything.'

In his final school year the 'spotty youth' went through the schools trials process to gain selection for England 18 Group, with his debut coming against Scotland in Glasgow. The final trial at Nottingham was a nerve-racking experience, but the build-up to his actual debut had emotions running at high levels and he had to fight back the tears when arriving at the ground on the team coach.

The pre-match anxiety was heightened by the fact that most of his rugby that year had been in the back row, but he was selected in the second row alongside Garath Archer, who would end up being a teammate of Martin's at both Gosforth and Bristol. Before kick-off the future England captain confesses to being very nervous. 'I was wetting myself. With the match you know what you're doing; you switch into autopilot and just go out and play, but with the build-up at that time I didn't know what to expect.

'We had a really good year in terms of the guys who were with us. There was a lot from the London area and Garath Archer was in the team. Even though I was very nervous I felt comfortable with the guys. I remember that there was not going to be any national anthems before the game and that really hacked us off so we all sang it in the changing room before we ran out.

'One of the players' dads had video-recorded the match and me and Arch watched the game afterwards. We hadn't done that before, we'd never seen games on video. That was all pretty remarkable.'

That first international appearance was the start of a very successful campaign as England won the Triple Crown and Grand Slam.

The England schoolboy completed his A levels and his rugby connections were a big influence in choosing which university to study at. Rugby was going to be the focus of Martin's life and he wanted to find a way that allowed him the best opportunity to develop his game. Coaches that staffed the RFU summer training camps at Nottingham Trent University were not only from the RFU but also drafted in from leading clubs, and these coaches were not slow in identifying talent and trying to get that talent to their clubs. Gosforth were no different and Mick Mahoney, the club's coach, tempted the young Corry to Geordieland.

'I really didn't have a clue what I was going to do at university, just no idea. Although it was still an amateur game, my only focus was playing rugby, so it was a case of what was going to allow me to progress furthest in my rugby. Mick Mahoney explained to me that Gosforth were working in partnership with Northumbria University to enable you to play for both the university and Gosforth. He said: "Drop us a letter and hopefully I'll get your acceptance dropped a couple of points as an elite athlete." At that time doing my A levels I thought I'd take all the help I could get! So it was just a really good fit – a good university with strong links to the club.

'At that time I didn't know how far away Newcastle was from Tunbridge! To be fair, it worked brilliantly for me. I'd served a year's apprenticeship in the Under 21s and then got a lucky break, well lucky for me, but it was courtesy of Brian Chick splitting his head open and I was in the First Team.

'The game then was very amateurish. I was training at the club Tuesday and Thursday, training with the university on Monday, and playing Wednesday. I look back now and try to make comparisons but you can't because training was nowhere near the intensity that it is now. It was easy to manage. Mick used to ring me up and say: "I know you've had a UAU game and a few pints but it's Thursday morning get out and have a run and make sure you're nice and loose and ready for training tonight." That was the norm. It's changed completely now.

'I just wanted to play rugby.'

From being around Martin from his second year at university, I can vouch for the fact that rugby was his focus. Looking back, he feels his life was rugby first with studies and socialising a joint second. However, as my eyebrows raise, with a big smile on his face he says: 'That's a lie; it was rugby, socialising and then studies.

'There were times when it looked iffy that I'd get a degree because the last month and a half of my Sports Studies degree course I was selected for the England A tour to Australia and Fiji. I'm not one of these people who can plan ahead and organise myself to do all of the work. I did just enough to get by.'

Everything was falling in to place: a completed degree achieved by hook and by crook, a growing reputation at club level, selection for England Students, England Under 21s and then the England A tour to Australia and Fiji aged 21 gave him the confidence he needed to fuel his ambition to take his rugby to another level.

'At first when you go into senior rugby you're thinking, "Can I do it? Can I make it?", and I had all of these uncertainties, but after my time in Newcastle I knew I wanted to pursue my rugby even more.'

A word or phrase that describes you at 21 years of age?

Enjoying the time...

When playing for Newcastle I wasn't stressing. I was taking it seriously but I think about how it's been over the last few years and how much thought and preparation goes into the game. I remember how different it was back then.

I'm really meticulous about my diet now but back then the Saturday morning before we played for Newcastle I'd go round the corner and buy two full breakfast stotties! I used to take them to Matt Long's house [Northumbria University, Gosforth and Moseley prop forward] and eat them there. We were so laid-back.

When we were playing we were giving it our all, but the little things, the whole life, it wasn't just all rugby – there were a lot of other things in my life apart from rugby.

Gosforth Rugby Club had been going through a bit of a hard time and were a mid-table team in the Second Division after being relegated from the First Division at the time that Martin finished his degree in the summer of 1995. It was a pivotal time when big decisions were made to enable him to achieve his ambitions in the game. The breakfast stotties stopped and his lifestyle changed to enable him to feel the full benefits of structured training.

Leicester were interested in the young back row and discussions took place with Tony Russ in charge of rugby at that time at Leicester, but Martin felt he needed to be playing regular First Division rugby and, with the likes of Dean Richards and John Wells in the Leicester squad, the thought of playing second fiddle was not an attractive one. 'Me and Arch sat down and said, "What do we want to do?" We wanted to play First Division, we wanted to be in a club that was up and coming, part of a young squad and we wanted to make sure we'd get into the side. We looked around and saw Bristol, and so we talked to them and they showed us around. The England Under 21s coach was at Bristol, which really helped. It was a fit for both Arch and me.

'It seemed the place to be so we went from one corner of the country to another!'

The two ex-Gosforth players made an immediate impact and Martin was made club captain in his second year. The game was still amateur, but the club helped find bits and pieces of work that enabled them to train three times a day. England Under 21s had fitness consultants who gave the two players fitness programmes to follow, but sometimes too much enthusiasm and a certain lack of knowledge caused problems.

'I remember doing a plyometrics session. We wanted to give it all our energy so we looked at the programme, which indicated bands of 10, but we thought they must mean 10 sets of 10! We did 2.5 hours of plyometrics. We couldn't walk for two days afterwards. We literally couldn't walk up the stairs. We were trashed! It was a learning thing.

'Bristol was brilliant for us. It established us as First XV players and we were able to really concentrate on our training. That's when I started changing as a person and as a player. I started putting a bit of bulk on, because I was always a lightweight back row player. The people at Bristol were good. We had all the right training and nutrition advice so I filled out a little bit. I had a good two years there.'

After two good years at Bristol the two players were on the move again. During their time at Bristol the game had gone professional and they had one full season as professional rugby players when Rob Andrew took Garath Archer back to the new Newcastle Gosforth Club and Martin was courted by Bob Dwyer the World Cup-winning Aussie coach who was in charge at Leicester Tigers. Martin's dream was to play for England and the Leicester selling point played to this.

'Bob Dwyer came to have a chat with me again and I thought, well, now's the time. He sold it by stressing that if you succeed at Leicester and play well then you'll play for England. The England goal was always a dream but I didn't really have it as a goal because I didn't think I could achieve it. If someone had come up to me and said, "Do you think you'll ever play for England?" I would have said no. Playing for England was almost like the Holy Grail. I wanted it but had built it up to be such a huge thing that I never really thought I'd ever get it.'

However, it was before pulling on his Leicester Tigers shirt that the dream of a full cap was achieved. Martin was selected for the 1997 summer tour to Argentina and was still actually a Bristol player. However, the achievement of his first cap did not necessarily bring the satisfaction that might have been expected. It was a capped tour, but the British and Irish Lions were on tour in South Africa at the same time and a rather heated discussion with England coach Jack Rowell took the shine off the moment.

'We had a massive barney because he wouldn't give me an opportunity to play. It was still the time when a tour's a tour and you have two, three or four warm-up matches and I just wasn't given an opportunity. I remember I said, "Look, Jack, I need to have a chat with you." He said, "OK, yeah," and I asked if we could go somewhere private, but he said, "No, we'll sit here in the hotel lobby." All of the players were coming in off the team coach and I thought, well, OK if it has to be here, it has to be here and so I said, "What the ****'s going on? You brought me here. Give me an opportunity to show you what I can do." He said that there were a lot of good players in the squad, and I agreed with him but that I believed in my ability and wanted the opportunity to show him what I could do.

'Thankfully he did on the Tuesday before the test. It went well and so I got in from there. For me it was such a battle that actually getting the cap meant everything then.' When Jack Rowell announced the side he couldn't remember it, and Martin's natural pessimism surfaced. 'I'm naturally a pessimistic person and felt that Jack had made a mistake even after he announced the team. When the side got announced Jack was reading through the team: "Number 1 Kevin Yates; Number 2 Richard Cockerill; Number 3 ... Who have we got for 3 and 4?" He couldn't remember it and I'm sitting there waiting for my name to be called out.

'He read it out and I'm sitting there thinking, well, I'm not sure if I'm playing because it could have been a mess-up somewhere. We went out to train after he read it out and I went out with the rest of the players, but in the back of my mind I was thinking he's going to tell me he's cocked up and read out the wrong team and I'm not playing. That kind of took the shine off the moment really.'

The actual test was played in a very hostile environment, as no love is lost between the Argentine crowds and all things English. As the team walked up the steps from the underground changing rooms they were pelted with oranges and roundly booed and jeered, but running on to the field into the noise and atmosphere is a memory that stays with the back rower. 'All you want is an atmosphere. If the crowd love you or hate you all you want is atmosphere. It was a brilliant place – a brilliant place to go and to get two caps. We won the first test but lost the second.

'My folks were out there, they followed me everywhere and it was great. I gave my dad my cap as a way of saying I wouldn't have been there without you.'

The tour took place at the end of the first full year of professional rugby in the summer of 1997 and rugby has changed beyond recognition since then. At that time all things that were involved in the game were understated. Nothing demonstrates this more vividly than the awarding of caps. 'Don Rutherford just walked around and handed out the caps in the dressing room after the match. You look at how it's done now. You go up to receive your cap after the post-match dinner and it's a big thing but back then it was "Congratulations, you've got your first cap," and a shake of the hand.'

Now a full England international, Corry's natural pessimism made him reflect upon his achievements and gave him added resolve to get more. 'Getting my first cap was everything because that's all I wanted – a cap, but afterwards I thought, OK, I've got a cap but it's without the likes of Rodber, Dallaglio, Hill, Backy – those types of players who were away with the Lions. It made me greedy for more when everyone was available.'

The intervening years have seen Martin play at the top of the sport for Leicester Tigers, England and the British and Irish Lions, with his greed for more international caps being satisfied with a total of 64 appearances for England and 6 Lions appearances before his retirement from international rugby before the 2008 Six Nations campaign. A difficult decision but one based upon the fact that at the age of 34 his body could not keep up with the intensity of both top-flight club and international rugby.

I have seen at first hand his enthusiasm, which is infectious, and coupled with his uncompromising approach and ability to influence those around him, his effectiveness as a captain has been recognised by the management of all of the teams with which he has played. His achievements in the game can be matched by few others:

1997	England debut versus Argentina
1998–99	Leicester Tigers Zurich Premiership winners
1999	England Squad Rugby World Cup South Africa
1999–2000	Leicester Tigers Zurich Premiership winners
	Leicester members' 'Player of the Season'
2000–2001	Leicester Tigers Zurich Premiership winners
	Leicester Tigers Heineken Cup winners
2001	British and Irish Lions tour to Australia
2001–2002	Leicester Tigers Zurich Premiership winners
	Leicester Tigers Heineken Cup Winners →

2002–2003	Leicester Tigers Zurich Premiership winners
2003	England Squad Rugby World Cup Australia
2004	Awarded MBE in New Years Honours List
2004–2005	Zurich Premiership 'Player of the Season'
2004–2005	PRA 'Player of the Season'
2005	Appointed England captain
2005	Appointed Leicester Tigers captain
2005	British and Irish Lions tour to New Zealand
2005–2006	Leicester Tigers Guinness Premiership winners
	Leicester Tigers EDF Energy Cup winners
	Leicester Tigers Heineken Cup finalists
2006–2007	Leicester Tigers Guinness Premiership winners
	Leicester Tigers EDF Anglo-Welsh Cup winners
2007	England Squad Rugby World Cup France

With so many achievements to reflect upon as his career comes towards its end, high points are plentiful but certain things hold special memories. 'When I went out for the 2001 British Lions tour was very special for me. I'd been selected for the England tour to Canada and just got out there on the Tuesday and was straight on a plane to Australia to join up with the Lions. Backy [Neil Back] got injured in the first test. I didn't have time to think, was jet-lagged and didn't know what day it was when I arrived in Oz. When I landed one of the journos told me that I was playing in the next game.

'You get in a comfort zone playing with England. I was comfortable in that set-up but you get to the Lions set-up and you see Scot Quinnell, Keith Woods. I thought of those kinds of players as Lions legends and I'm in a huddle with them! Willie John McBride gave out the test match shirts and I was thinking this is so special. When

I think back the whole build-up to that occasion in Brisbane was just unbelievable.

'In 2001 just before the Lions tour, winning the European Cup with Leicester was special. At Northumbria University we won the UAU with the group of lads whom you view as your close mates, your friends, and that's what the European Cup was like. We went to Parc des Princes, which is pretty much the home ground of Stade Français and nobody gave us a chance. There was a 44,000 crowd with a lot of Tigers supporters in the ground and we went on to win 34–30, and then going out on the town for a big night with a great bunch of lads who are your closest mates – it was a really special day. When I look back 2001 was a real highlight.'

In amongst all of the highlights there have inevitably been frustrations and disappointments to cope with. Although he has won a remarkable 64 caps for England, the thinking of England's management has, more than any other factor, led Martin to reflect upon his ability to influence events and to develop the mental strength to cope with situations that have the potential to dent the confidence of weaker individuals. A selection policy that was rooted in the coach having a 'dream' was a banana skin that could not have been foreseen but one that needed to be coped with.

'I was always in and out of Clive's [Woodward] thinking. I used to wake up 2 a.m. and think, "Is he going to pick me?" I developed a sort of mantra, "All I can do is all I can do", and I'd use that as a test. When you're awake at that time, when everything seems huge I'd think, "Well, if I've done everything that I can possibly do it's just one man's opinion if he picks me or not." If I could lie there and say to myself that I'd done everything I could do, then I could sleep easy after that. I personalised it. This is about me and all I can control.

'Ed Moses was a big hero of mine growing up and he coined the phrase "control the controllable" and so I just went with that.

'In the 1999 World Cup qualifiers I played the first two games and Clive dropped me. He told me that his thought process was "I had a dream and I thought I'd go with this side." As a young lad to be told you're not playing because someone's "had a dream" was a bit difficult, but I just said, "Right, all it's got to be about is that

I don't lose sleep over wondering what his dreams are; this is all just about me," and that's when I went really into myself. I decided that I'd do everything that I could do and after that things went well. I still struggled to get into the England side but in the next couple of years I played the best rugby of my life.'

A word or phrase that describes you now?

Frustrated at getting old.

Everyone's saying that this is your last year but I'm not thinking about whether or not it's my last year. I want to really enjoy fighting for my position at Leicester, getting Leicester to finals and hopefully getting trophies.

My contract says it's over at the end of the year but I don't want to be one of these players who are winding down mentally. If my performance is suffering and if they think they'd rather have another player brought in, then they'll have to be playing bloody well to get in ahead of me!

We've started this pre-season with a new coach and I'm learning from him and I'm excited about it. I'm excited about what I can do this year because I'm older and there are a lot of youngsters coming into the squad. It will be a big fight for a position but that's brilliant. Throughout my career I've always had challenges and I like a challenge. I'm one of these people where nothing comes easily, but I think that as a result of that it means so much more to me because I've had to fight for everything.

Last year was a tough year. I gave up international rugby because I wanted to focus on Leicester and to get us to where we needed to be and that didn't happen. It was tough at the club, but I am excited about the new season and helping the club move forward.

It says a lot about the standards set by Leicester Tigers that a season that saw them once again take their place in a Heineken Cup Final is classed as poor and tough.

The Leicester Tigers captain has worked hard to get to the top and then harder still to stay there. He has constantly stretched the boundaries of his potential with a complete dedication and focus on his sport. Life outside of rugby has really been organised to support his rugby and he has benefited hugely from the support of his family and particularly his wife, Tara.

He talks with the obvious warmth of a proud father about his young family. His daughter, Eve, was born during the 2003 World Cup, necessitating a quick return trip from Australia to be at the birth. His son, Edward, was born in 2006. Both will be the beneficiaries of the time that will be generated as the rugby player chapter of his life closes and new opportunities arise. When thinking about the future, he has nothing planned to any degree of detail but many opportunities exist both inside and outside the sport.

'I do have a few things mapped out. I've got options and most of them as my major source of income are away from rugby. I'll stay involved in the game and that might start with taking my son to mini rugby and coaching them, and if that's what it is then I'll be delighted with that. I can't see myself at a club other than Leicester, but I also think the lifestyle of a coach is too volatile for me. It's quite an insecure life. My family's gone along with me buggering off all over the place so... I look at people like Dean [Richards]. He was my rugby hero. I played with him and was coached by him, but he ended up getting sacked by the club where he'd been for 23 years. As a result he had to take his family to Grenoble in France and now he's back in London at Harlequins.

'I want to feel in 20 years' time the same way that I do now about Leicester, and if you're going to be a coach you're going to be sacked somewhere along the line, regardless of whether or not you're great at it. I don't want to be a serial coach. If Leicester offers me some way to contribute that would be great but, if not ... well, I've got plenty of other options which I'll take.'

For youngsters who aspire to sporting careers Martin recommends taking part in as many sports as possible, as the crossover of skills from sport to sport is significant in developing the abilities to excel at the highest level in your chosen sport. Perhaps it is stating the obvious but you must enjoy your sport to give it your best.

'There's a time when you can take your sport really seriously but there's a time when you should go out and simply enjoy your sport for what it is. Yes, always try to win and always try to be the best you can, but when you look at some of the Under 8s, and you get a lot of pushy parents, I sometimes think, is there enjoyment there?

'I think it's important to teach winning and losing because it's going away from kids nowadays. You need the competitive edge to be successful in whatever you do and it's important to understand that the pain of losing is more than made up when you win.'

Age catches up with us all and it is an inevitable truth that at some point Martin Corry MBE will no longer pull on the shirt of Leicester Tigers and at that point the game will lose a significant presence. He has certainly come a long way from Tunbridge Wells Rugby Club where as a spotty lanky youth he stood at the front of a line-out with Bill Cuthbertson's thumb in his pocket!

2008–2009 Season Update

The body finally gave up and dodgy knees have put an end to a fantastic career.

Although not on the pitch, the Leicester club captain was at pitch side supporting the players and Richard Cockerill, the club's new coach appointed in mid-season. Nobody will have been more delighted at the clinching of the Premiership title at Twickenham with a 10–9 victory over London Irish or more disappointed at losing the Heineken Cup Final to Leinster 19–16 at Murrayfield.

His playing swansong was to captain the Barbarians at the end of the season with games against England at Twickenham and Australia in Sydney.

Before the England game Martin Johnson's comments were very much tongue in cheek when he said, 'Martin Corry is a fantastic player, a good bloke and a great example to any player about taking the highs and lows, and we are looking to make sure he finishes on a low'. But the last laugh was with the Baa Baas' captain as England were beaten 26-33.

Martin Corry: Statistics	
Date of birth	12 October 1973
Birthplace	Birmingham
Height	1.95m
Weight	115kg
Position	No. 8; blind-side flanker; lock
School / university	Tunbridge Wells Grammar School; Northumbria University
Present club	Leicester Tigers
Previous clubs	Bristol; Newcastle Gosforth
Nicknames	Cozza
Favourite TV show	*QI*
Favourite film	*Goodfellas*
Favourite Music	stuck in the eighties
Favourite book	Harlan Coben, *Tell No One*
Favourite food	any Indian curry
Most like to meet...	Ed Moses / Lance Armstrong
Least like to meet...	nobody
Best moment in rugby	2001 British Lions tour; 2001 Heineken Cup win
Favourite place to visit	would love to go to the heart of Africa
I love...	my family
I hate...	time-wasting

MARTYN WILLIAMS

Wales; British and Irish Lions; Cardiff Blues

Martyn Williams is an extremely likeable and humble man and his face shows embarrassment about the title of his autobiography published after the World Cup of 2007. However, I think the person who thought of using the title of the 1960s epic Hollywood film starring Yul Bryner, Steve McQueen and James Coburn amongst others deserves massive praise – *The Magnificent Seven* is the perfect description of the man from the Rhonda who has stamped his mark on Northern Hemisphere rugby as the most natural open-side flanker of his generation.

The year 2007 was a barren one in Welsh rugby with a poor Six Nations campaign, a troubled pre-World Cup tour to Australia and, by all accounts, a dismal showing in the World Cup with a quarter-final exit at the hands of Fiji. Although the decision had been made after the Six Nations championship, it was after the World Cup exit that on 1 October 2007 the Welsh open side announced his intention to retire from international rugby. The loss of the inspirational Cardiff Blues player who had been the Six Nations' 'Player of the Tournament' during Wales' Grand Slam season in 2005 was significant.

The Welsh post-World Cup autopsy led to the appointment of a new coaching team of Kiwi Warren Gatland, London Wasps coach, and Rugby League legend Shaun Edwards and former Wales scrum half Rob Howley. A very wise man once wrote that 'retirement takes all the meaning away from weekends' and there was no hard sell needed by Gatland to get Martyn out of his premature retirement with the 'Return of the Magnificent Seven' being announced in January 2008.

'It was after the last Six Nations I thought: I'll be 32, it's time to give someone else the chance to come in and after the World Cup I said, "That's it," but then Warren got in touch. He left me a message, asking to meet for a coffee. This was the first time I'd ever spoken to him and the first impression was so good. Warren's very laid-back and he speaks totally honestly. He didn't put any shine on it. He said, "You're going to work harder than you've ever worked before but I can guarantee you're going to enjoy it and that we'll have success." It was a 20-minute conversation and even though I said I'd need to think about it, I knew in my heart I wanted to come back.

'If somebody of the stature of Warren Gatland insists that you can still contribute, and that you still have something to offer, it tips the balance. My retirement lasted exactly one game, the friendly against South Africa, which I had gone along to watch, and felt very strange sitting in the stands. It's renewed my enthusiasm. I know I only missed one game but after speaking to other people I think it made me realise that you're retired a long time, so as long as you enjoy playing and you're playing as well as you can be then just keep going as long as you can.

'The boys have ribbed me from the moment I said I was coming back and it's not over yet. I'm still getting it! Massively. Unbelievably.'

Martyn may be struggling with the ribbing of his teammates in the national side, but his return has coincided with a revival of Welsh rugby fortunes, with their being crowned Grand Slam winners for the tenth time in the 2008 Six Nations Championship. Martyn was named 'Man of the Match' against the Scots and scored a try in the 29–12 victory over France in the National Stadium, the victory that clinched that tenth Grand Slam title.

The new coaching team has made a big difference and brought together a Welsh squad previously rumoured to be fractious and divided. They have an immense knowledge of the game and have harnessed that knowledge within an approach that is supportive whilst at the same time demanding. Training is very intense and has gone up a notch from previous regimes. The expectation of precision in delivering high-level individual performances has added a level of personal responsibility, as no one's place is guaranteed, but there is a lot of support.

'They give us great balance on and off the field because they know you need to relax as well. Warren's big on keeping the boys mentally fresh. So yeah, I think Shaun saw the bottom of a champagne bottle on the Saturday night we won the grand slam. It's good to see him in that light because there is a separation between players and coaches but you feel comfortable speaking to them. Sometimes a coach can be too familiar with players, or too distant. But they're spot on. You know who's boss but you're not afraid to approach them. It's a very difficult balance and I don't know how they do it, whether it's just natural or if it's something they work at.

'I just want to enjoy my next couple of years. I've got two more years on my contract but Gats has come out and said he wants me to play until 2011. I'm 32 now and I'm not sure the body can hold up until then.'

The Magnificent Seven has had a huge part to play not only in Wales 2008 successes but also for the Cardiff Blues as they fought their way to second place in the Magners League behind champions Leinster and the quarter final of the Heineken Cup losing to Toulouse in France.

It all started on 1 September 1975 when Martyn Elwyn Williams became a child of the Rhondda, in the small village of Maerdy which lies at the head of the Rhondda Fach Valley. The Williams family lived there until the family moved nearer to Pontypridd when Martyn was about seven years of age.

To this day he loves all sport but surprisingly in the Rhondda when he was growing up it was not rugby but soccer that the kids played. In the intervening years things have changed and the Welsh RFU now have coaching schemes and structures in place to engage the youngsters of the Rhondda, but they did not exist in the late 70s. 'It was moving to Ponty, that's when I first got into rugby. The Rhondda, well it's changed now in that it's more into its rugby and there's a good rugby structure in place but then it was more soccer. I didn't even pick up a rugby ball until I moved to Ponty.

'I was about nine years old and it was through school. I was at Coed-y-Lan Junior School and I can remember the headmaster coming in to the classroom and asking if anyone was interested in rugby. I love sport so fortunately, even though I was nine and in Standard Two, I was in the team with guys who were in the year above. That year we went on to win the Schools Cup – it was the first time our school had ever done it – and I was hooked from there really. I played all sports and loved them, but I set my heart on rugby.'

Martyn immediately took to the game and by the age of 11 he was representing East Wales in the second row or at Number 8. This representative rugby cemented his allegiance to the game and edged out football as his first love. He did, however, continue to play football and represented the Welsh YMCA as a centre half at Under 16 level. 'I was fortunate and picked rugby up really quickly. When I was nine I was quite tall for my age, but then things happened and I didn't grow like the others. I'm glad really because I started off in the second row and then moved back to Number 8. I didn't want to play second row but didn't play open side until I was 15.

'I loved football, that was my first love and I still love watching it. I'm a mad Liverpool fan! But where I'm from, Pontypridd, it's all rugby. There is soccer but being in South Wales, particularly Pontypridd, rugby's huge. As I was growing up, Pontypridd were fairly successful with Neil Jenkins there. When I was picked for Wales at U15, you're stuck then. That's what everyone wanted to do... No one pushed me to rugby but I naturally gravitated towards it.'

There is a recurring thread running through Martyn's youth in that he always seemed to play sport with mates who were older than him. 'When I was 14 I used to play soccer with the older guys; I played with the 16-year-olds so I could play with my mates. With the youth rugby I was really friendly with the 18- and 19-year-olds when I was 16 and, although people would say that I shouldn't be playing youth rugby at that age, I'd just go and play with them. They were my mates and I think it got me to develop quickly... It really did help.'

The young Coed-y-Lan schoolboy has many memories from his early years. His involvement in rugby had led to representative honours from the age of 11 when he played for East Wales against West Wales but a standout moment was being chosen for the Under 15 Welsh National Team, which was a big thing for a comprehensive school that did not have a big reputation for its rugby.

Mental strength and the competitive side of his character were also very evident in those early years. He moved from Number 8 to open side but his first experience of the position made him determined to work harder. 'I moved from Number 8 to open side at Ponty. We played a match against Cardiff and my opposite guy had an absolute stormer. He skinned me and was supposedly the next big thing. Then my coach said, "you know, you could be better than him if you want to," and I think from that day I concentrated and dedicated myself to getting better and by the end of the season he'd moved to 6 and I moved into 7 for the Welsh team.'

Coed-y-Lan Junior and then comprehensive school gave Martyn his education and he loved it. History, Geography and PE were the subjects that captured his imagination and he kept up his studies into sixth form where he studied History and PE at A level. 'I absolutely loved school. I was pretty good academically at school right the way through to early comprehensive. I enjoyed it, for the sports but also for all the interaction with other kids, and I look back on my school years as really good years... They were good times.'

He continued his education by starting a Sports Science degree at Glamorgan University but at the end of the first year professional rugby curtailed his studies. 'That year was my last year at Youth level and the year when rugby went professional. I was offered a full-time professional contract with Pontypridd and given a job with the company who sponsored Pontypridd.'

So with his university education on hold Martyn concentrated on his full-time contract at Pontypridd and a part-time job with the club's main sponsor. Professional rugby became reality very quickly and was a very new thing that clubs and players were trying to understand, find their way around and make work. In the rugby-mad area of South Wales there was a lot of money being thrown about, as clubs tried to establish themselves in this new professional era, but each player's circumstances were different and not all could afford to give up their main employment.

'Yes, it was a strange time because no one knew where it was going to go and there was no structure in place. When I came out of that last year of Youth rugby playing for Ponty Youth I was offered a full-time contract and a part-time job with the main club sponsor. It was mostly Development Officer stuff: PR and marketing, going out to presentation events at local schools and things like that. I was working at the same firm as Neil Jenkins and Dale McIntosh. I think because I was a youngster they thought they'd keep me on board, as the likes of Cardiff and Swansea were throwing money around at that time too.

'I just concentrated on training and I was fortunate to be able to do that, because a lot of boys were still working. They were getting paid by the club but they weren't paid enough to be able to give up their jobs. We were still training Tuesday and Thursday nights, but then some of the boys on full-time contracts with the club could train during the day.

'We just weren't sure where it was going.'

The Pontypridd open side was very much in the national selector's eyes in terms of age group rugby, but he made an unexpected jump to the full international stage very quickly after good performances in the Student World Cup in South Africa in the summer of 1996. 'I came from the Welsh Students tour in South Africa. I played really well out there and got a lot of good feedback from it. I wasn't really playing for Pontypridd at the time, I was more a backup to Ritchie Collins and then within two months I was suddenly put in the national side at 20 years of age.

'It all happened quickly but looking back I think I hadn't really earned my place; there wasn't any real strength in depth and we didn't really have that many options. It was a case of "Let's give the youngster a chance." We played the Babas on the Saturday and then France on the Wednesday, so they were my first two caps. It was funny, really, to play for Wales when you haven't really established yourself at club level.'

The elevation to the full national team happened so quickly that the whole experience was just a blur with no real memories to hang on to. Standing in the tunnel before going on to the field for the national anthems, into a stadium where the crowd generates an atmosphere to make the knees go weak and the hairs on the back of your neck bristle, Martyn describes his overriding feeling as one of shock!

The match ended in a 31–10 victory for Wales and Martyn kept his place for the non-Championship match a month later against France. This time Wales were on the wrong side of the scoreline going down 40–33 in the National Stadium and an appearance from the bench in the 31–22 victory over Italy in Rome's Olympic Stadium on 5 October 1996 completed his international year.

The following year, when Martyn was 21, he was dropped back

into the Under 21s squad, which he captained. It was an experience he describes as being 'hard to take at the time'. However, he continued to show good form for Pontypridd as the team enjoyed successful times at Sardis Road. 'Pontypridd is a very small club and you're always the kind of underdogs and you have like a chip on your shoulder constantly. I'm stubborn, really determined – that's the kind of person I am – and if I set my mind at something, that's what I will do. The players around me were from the Ponty area and if you're from that area I think that's the sort of upbringing and attitude you have.

'We were really successful, won the championship in 1997 and did well in Europe. I think that was a great start for me and I couldn't have asked for a better environment. I was there for four years until 1999 and then I went to Cardiff which was a huge move for me.'

A word or phrase that describes you at 21 years of age?

You think you are better than you are...

I'd say that I knew where I was going – I was playing for Pontypridd and it was really successful, and being in a small town it was quite a big thing but I think looking back I'd say I was naive. At 21 you think you know it all but you know absolutely nothing! I was capped at 20 against the Babas. At 21 I'd already kind of realised my dream to play for Wales and I thought, I'm invincible... I was thinking, yes, I've done it!

It all happened quickly then when I was 21 I was dropped back in to the Under 21s, which was hard to take at the time. I remember getting a letter from the Welsh Under 15s. At that level there were about four or five of us from Pontypridd and my old coach, my first coach at U15 said, 'You all think you've all done it but the hard work starts now. Now you're there, stay there.'

That's stuck with me from day one. A lot of the boys once they get their first cap, that's it, they sit back, but that's when you've got to work hard.'

In the time between those first stuttering international steps and the return of the Magnificent Seven, Welsh rugby initially struggled to put a structure in place that would provide a competitive environment for the very best of the wealth of youth talent to come through and find its way into the national team. The early days of professional rugby in Wales were difficult times as administrators fiercely debated the merits of a regionalised structure. Strongly held traditions and allegiances, based around the famous clubs that provided the sporting focus for their communities, were strained to the limits. Lack of both direction and progress did not help the performance of the national team as they struggled to be competitive and the national side were subjected to carping criticism as comparisons were made with the great Welsh teams of the 1970s. The performances like those that allowed crushing England victories were hard to take:

1998	England 60–26 Wales	(Twickenham)
2000	England 46–12 Wales	(Twickenham)
2001	Wales 15–44 England	(Cardiff)
2002	England 50–10 Wales	(Twickenham)
2003	Wales 9–43 England	(Cardiff)

'In Wales it's like being in a goldfish bowl. You're constantly under the microscope when you play for the national side. It's either feast or famine. You're either the best in the world or the worst – there's no in-between. It's really difficult. I remember my first cap was in 1996 but I then played my first Six Nations game up in England in 1998. We were just so depressed because you're losing to the likes of England, but especially by that margin, by 60 points, with what happened in the 70s, the history... It had never happened before.'

It wasn't only the performances against England that were difficult to take for the Welsh nation. For Martyn, the journey home from Dublin after the 54–10 hammering by the Irish at Lansdowne Road in February 2002 was a particular low point. Thousands of Welsh supporters in Dublin airport singing 'We have the worst team in the land' really hurt but professional sportspeople have to look forward and try to take on board the lessons.

'It was very difficult going to Ireland and losing by 50 points and then coming home through the airport. Wales is such a rugby-mad nation; the game in Dublin, it's like a Welsh international weekend in Cardiff – there's thousands of Welsh supporters there. As a team you have to walk through the airport and it's honestly so difficult, but you find out about yourself. It's easy when you're winning but you find out a lot more about yourself when you're not winning and when you're going through tough times.

'If you keep looking behind you all the time it'll drive you back, but you have to learn from your mistakes. I don't think you can totally forget them because you've got to learn from them. That's why the Grand Slams in 2005 and 2008 were so special because a lot of us had been through a Six Nations when we lost all of the games in 2003. We've come through the other end now though.'

Whilst nothing can ever be taken for granted in professional sport in general and Welsh rugby in particular, the regional structure comprising Llanelli Scarlets, Neath and Swansea Ospreys, Newport Gwent Dragons and Martyn's Cardiff Blues has eventually brought stability to the club game in the Principality and good performances in the Magners League, EDF Cup and Heineken Cup have to some degree healed the wounds of the early years of professionalism.

The national team have also had their moments of success. Whilst 2003 was not a good year for the team, some important building blocks were put in place that started the turn-around in Welsh fortunes. For Martyn personally it was the time that he grew into his role as the Welsh open side.

'We were fortunate there at that time in 2003 having people like Andrew Hoare, Scott Johnson and Andy Hansen come on board. Those people were huge influences. When you're younger you're quite naive, you think you know everything and there's not a need for a coach, but as you get older you realise how important they are. For me particularly, I was, up to 2003, kind of in and out of the side. I'd have good years and bad years, but I really found it hard at first when the new management team came in because they'd tell me home truths.

'I'd been an international for best part of six or seven years and I thought that these guys can't tell me what to do. I suppose it's a maturity process but after about a year or so I realised that these guys know what they're talking about and if I don't do what they say I could fall by the wayside. They told me that if I didn't do what they said that I'd not be able to play international rugby past the age of 27 ... and I'm still playing now at 33. I feel that if I hadn't done what they said I wouldn't still be playing now.

'In 2003 we lost to Italy 30–22 in Rome. We'd lost something like ten games in a row but we had that management team in place who were putting in the building blocks. There was myself, Gethyn Jenkins, Stephen Jones, Dwayne Peel and Tom Shanklin. All these boys are still going and it's probably because of those people... It's all because of unseen work. People don't see them so don't realise their importance to us.'

As Martyn has cemented his stature in the world game with top-level performances for both club and country, he has seen the game dramatically change. As an avid sports fan, satellite TV gives him the opportunity to watch games from times past and they make him cringe because they are so slow. When the game went professional there were no real structures in place and building those structures has at times been a painful process, but the science and training methods are now producing athletes who can cope with the strength, speed and power demands of the sport at a much younger age.

'What I find quite scary now is that when I was in the Youth we would go out and train with the First Team. If you saw us together you could tell who was the Youth and who was the First Team. When our Academy come with us now, the 18-and 19-year-olds' size is exactly the same as us, you can't tell the difference. They're still boys at 18 and 19 but they're just so physical.'

Martyn recognises that his mental approach to the game, harnessing that self-confessed stubbornness and competitive nature, is the key to unlocking his physical attributes. Despite that confession to feeling shock in the tunnel before his first international match, the passage of time and accumulation of experience have led to a relaxed individual who loves the build-up to big games. 'I'm quite relaxed really. The week before I'm fine – I think that's the best part really, the build-up, I love it. You can really feel the build-up to a big tournament.

'Saturday mornings are tough when you're waiting to go out there and play. You get pretty nervous then, but I love the build-up, I love the expectation. There are one or two boys who like to shout and stuff, but in the changing room, as captain, you have to say a bit but really I'm just sitting there with my iPod and just keep myself to myself until we have to go out. The younger ones in the squad sometimes ask questions and I try to help them, but I wouldn't go out of my way to impose myself because I know some people like to be left alone. If people ask then I'll help.'

A word or phrase that describes you now?

Content but driven…

Content, if you'd told me I'd achieve what I have when I was 18 I'd have bitten your hand off, but I still want to chase.

Coming out of retirement, it's renewed my enthusiasm – I know I only missed one game but it made me realise that you're retired a long time so as long as you enjoy playing and you're playing as well as you can be then just keep going as long as you can.

Content but driven, that's how I'd describe myself.

The game has changed massively in the professional era and maybe the most fundamental change is to come in the 2008–2009 season with the introduction of the experimental laws into the Northern Hemisphere's game.

The physical demands of the game could be very different for a lot of positions, but an open side who plays the game in the way Martyn does will be absolutely crucial as the time the ball is in play goes up along with the games pace. An understanding of the game, anticipation of what is going to happen next, and then having the skills to be effective when physically stressed, are the cornerstones of the way the Welsh flanker plays the game now.

'I'd say I'm an out and out 7 and couldn't play anywhere else. I haven't got the size to play anywhere else! The way I play I rely on anticipation and just reading the game and I'm fortunate that coaches haven't really tried to change me. With certain positions you have to work within a structure and you've got to do this and do that, but I've got freedom. I've got to get on the park and be into everything, that's why I love playing 7.

'I watch to see how the game is played but just playing is the most important thing. You can watch and you can analyse teams as much as you want but until you go out there and make the mistakes yourself and then realise you've made those mistakes you'll not improve.

'I'm not being arrogant but you do need an all-round game as a 7. You've got to be one of the main defenders in the team, you've got to carry the ball. Some of the time you have to link-play so you need to have scrum-half skills; you've got to be strong on the ground but putting all those other skills under pressure, possibly more pressure than other players because you are expected to be one of the first players into the contact area. You have to have a high work rate so aerobic fitness is hugely important at 7. If you've got a big engine then everything else will just fall into place.'

It's interesting that he does not include the drop-kicking skills he used when scoring a drop goal against Tonga in the 2003 World Cup, an event he describes as not the prettiest but good for his CV!

Outside of rugby, Sam, Martyn's wife, has accepted his return to the game after his premature retirement, but probably really knew he could not give it up at the time he did. Such a successful Six Nations campaign has, however, given her and their five-year-old daughter, Mia, a lot of pride as Dad has captured the public attention with fantastic performances. Their son, Cory, is too young to appreciate the way the nation has taken his dad to their hearts but that will come with time.

Away from the rugby field, time with the family is precious but Martyn just loves sport, no matter what it is. 'My wife will tell you that I'm just a mad massive sports fan. I'm a huge American football fan and watch it and read about it constantly, also football and golf. I will be watching the Euro football tonight, Sweden and Greece.'

When thinking about the future both inside and outside of rugby, ambitions in rugby take a short-term perspective, but outside of rugby the goals are longer-term. 'The Lions tour, that's completely off the radar at the moment... It's 12 months away, a long time in rugby. You've got your club to play for before the international games. I suppose you'd be lying if you said it wasn't in the back of your mind and it's something you want to do but I just want to enjoy my next couple of years. I've got two more years left on my contract. I'd love to win something with Cardiff because we haven't won anything since 1999–2000.

'Outside of rugby my financial advisors have worked with a few players over the last ten years. The company does corporate tax planning and have offered me a position in the office one day a week. They have a chartered tax advisor and a financial advisor in the company and I'm just going to start my exams, literally, in the next couple of months and hopefully I can go with them. I am fortunate in some ways. I've two years left on my contract at Cardiff but hope to get qualified and work there.

'I've always been daft really because I always just wanted to concentrate on my rugby, but it's been in the last three years that I realised that doing things outside of rugby was important. HSBC asked me to do a bit with them and at the same time I found I played much better.

'Some of the single boys will train in the morning and then be home by 2 p.m. and there's so much dead time. There's so much I wish I had done when I was younger. I'm lucky now because my profile's quite high and people come and ask me to do things but I know I should have been actively doing more when I was younger.

'There's a young boy, Jamie Roberts, just got his first cap for Wales and he's going to be a doctor. I know that Cardiff have been on to him for the last couple of years to go full-time but he's insistent that no, he wants to finish his studies to be a doctor first. I'd definitely recommend that way of doing it. Get the studying done.

'Looking back, I know I was determined that nothing was going to detract me from getting on with the rugby but, you know, it's all about getting the balance right.

'I can honestly see why a younger player gets caught up in it all. You get so involved and put everything in to get to the top that you don't want anything else to take your mind away from it. But as you get older, more mature, you realise it's all about getting the balance right. That's been a huge thing for me.'

As Martyn looks around the game today and sees youngsters take their first steps in realising their dream of playing the game at the very top levels, his advice is very simple and no different from any walk of life. 'You've got to enjoy it but also be willing to make some sacrifices. In Wales you know most rugby players will be from working-class backgrounds and at 16 or 17 years of age there are other things that can tear you away from it.

'I remember a coach saying to me that all the best rugby players in Wales are stood by the bar. I'd play with boys at Under 18 level and they had so much talent, I'd say much more than perhaps some of the boys I play with now, but because they didn't have the drive, they just didn't make the sacrifices and so they fell by the wayside. Just be willing to make some sacrifices.'

Martyn retired from the game but thankfully was persuaded to come back and enable us to witness his sublime skills as a natural open side for at least another two years. Seeing him score a try in the National Stadium to help defeat the French in the 2008 Six Nations championship and guarantee Wales their tenth Grand Slam was a great sporting moment and meant a lot to him.

'The biggest moment in my career is probably the France game this year for the Grand Slam. I made the decision to come back out of retirement and that for me was quite a decision because it could have backfired. To win the Grand Slam and score when I might not have even been playing is something I'll always remember.'

Strong performances in the 2008 autumn internationals and the 2009 Six Nations tournament, where he again captained Wales in the match against Scotland in the absence of the injured Ryan Jones, have reinforced the benefits to the Welsh team of having the Ponty boy on the open side. The 21–18 win over Australia in the Millennium Stadium will be up there with his other great memories.

Let's hope that the body holds out and Warren Gatland's desire to have Martyn playing until 2011 happens. Everyone except opposition fly halves have enjoyed 'The Return of the Magnificent Seven.'

2008–2009 Season Update

In my eyes, the Welshman is simply playing the best rugby of his life and selection for the British and Irish Lions was well deserved. The pain he must have gone through at missing that kick in the Heineken Cup semi-final shootout, after the drawn game against Leicester, must have been deep and long lasting. I hope that ridiculous system of deciding such a monumental occasion is consigned to the dustbin.

Martyn Williams: Statistics	
Date of birth	1 September 1975
Birthplace	Maerdy, Rhondda Cynon Taff
Height	1.85m
Weight	100kg
Position	open-side flanker
School / university	Coed-y-Lan Comprehensive
Present club	Cardiff Blues
Previous clubs	Cardiff; Pontypridd
Nicknames	Nugget
Favourite TV show	*Gavin and Stacey*
Favourite film	*Walk the Line*
Favourite music	country
Favourite book	Conn Iggulden, *Emperor* series of novels
Favourite food	seafood
Most like to meet...	Brett Favre (American football quarterback)
Least like to meet...	the grim reaper
Best moment in rugby	winning two Grand Slams with Wales
Favourite place to visit	the States
I love...	Christmas
I hate...	training and playing rugby at Christmas

NICK EASTER

England; Harlequins

As academy systems further develop in all sports, talent is being identified earlier. On the downside, however, youngsters' opportunities to try different sports become more limited as one governing body or another attempts to nurture their talent to the exclusion of other sports. It is very difficult for kids, too, not to have their expectations raised when their effort is put into maximising their potential within one particular sport.

It is unlikely, then, that the path Nick has followed will be repeated by many. The Number 8 did not find top-level rugby until he signed for Harlequins in August 2004 when he was 26 years of age. However, he did not take long to find his feet as he was named the 'NEC Player of the Year' for the 2004–2005 and 2005–2006 campaigns, scoring 19 tries in the latter.

Nick had played no representative rugby at any level until he played for England Saxons. He made his debut from the bench in February 2007 against Italy A, and only one week later he started his first full international against Italy in the Six Nations match at Twickenham. Subsequently he has become the first Number 8 to score four tries for England in a test match, a feat achieved in the World Cup warm-up Investec Challenge against Wales in August 2007. He was a cornerstone of the England pack during the World Cup in France and was named man of the match for his performance against the French in the Six Nations championship match in Paris in February 2008.

Prior to his contract at Harlequins he had graduated from Nottingham Trent University with a degree in Mathematics and Science in 1999, taught mathematics in Cape Town, South Africa, worked with a firm of investment bankers in the City and played National Division One rugby for Orrell before his move to Harlequins. To use the old adage 'He's seen a bit of life' and this has given him a mindset that not only gives him the steely determination to succeed but also the need to soak up and enjoy the fruits of that success.

A special moment for all players is to represent their country and it would be easy to think that someone coming late into the elite level of the game with no representative history behind them would have their international debut as their standout memory in the sport, but it is the later stages of the 2007 World Cup in France that bring back the most vivid memories. 'I'd say the quarter-final win over Australia and the semi-final win over France were pretty big moments... They stand out as highlights.

'We had gotten a bit of stick, as England do when they aren't winning everything, but we knuckled down as a team and put in some good, resilient performances. We put in an excellent defensive and disciplined effort in both games. We had done well on the pitch and I will never forget the nights out after those games as well.

'When we played Australia we were in Marseilles and luckily played in the afternoon. After the game we went down to the harbour and were hosted on an O2 boat to watch the New Zealand v France game. They had a big screen up in the harbour and when the French scored nine points in the second half we went to the end of the boat and watched the guys cheering. It was an amazing atmosphere ... the whole day was amazing.

'I think that's what rugby's about. Some people forget sometimes. Sometimes players are so engrossed in what they do, but when you're in your twenties or early thirties you have to remember to still enjoy where you are. There are plenty of times when it's right to lock yourself up in your team room, drink your lemon juice and eat your cayenne pepper or whatever it is! You know you've got to enjoy days like that because you never know when it's going to end. We're here for a good time, not a long time.'

Sport is at the core of Nick's family. His maternal great-grandfather Pieter Le Roux was a Springbok, capped by South Africa as a flanker on their first tour to Europe in 1906. Nick's father, John, was a professional squash player in the early 1970s and met Glynis, his

South African wife, whilst playing on the professional circuit in South Africa.

John may have been a professional squash player but is also a good all-round sportsman. Bob Hiller, the England fullback in the mid-1960s who ultimately gained 19 caps, six as captain, may have played a part in shaping the squash career of Nick's father. 'Dad was a very good sportsman at school. He was good at rugby but he went to Oxford University at the same time as Bob Hiller who was England fullback at the time. Fullback was also Dad's position and he thought he would not get into the side, so in the winter he played squash and in the summer cricket getting his blue in both. He took his squash from there and played for England and professionally in the late 60s and early 70s.

'That's when he played with Jonah Barrington, who's my godfather. In the UK Jonah was always Number 1 and Dad Number 2. Jonah probably had a better work ethic than my dad, though I'm not saying he didn't work hard, but Jonah was known to be a fierce trainer, ahead of his time really – a very fit man.' (Jonah Barrington is arguably the best-known squash player of all time due to the way he took training and match preparation to another level to fight off the challenge of the Khans of Pakistan and Geoff Hunt of Australia and keep himself at the top of the world game in the 1970s.)

As Nick and his brother, Mark, also a professional rugby player with Northampton Saints, grew up in Dulwich, sport was all around them both in terms of their everyday life and family history. Nick attended Dulwich College, the same school as Andrew Sheridan the Sale Sharks and England prop, but Nick was two years ahead of Andrew at school. Dulwich College is a fantastic environment for developing sporting talent but, although he was a talented sportsman, it was not rugby that did it for him in his early school years.

'When I was younger I was a good hockey player and I played cricket but I always enjoyed rugby. I really enjoyed cricket at school but the cricket season was in the summer and it was also exam time so we didn't look forward to that term as much. Rugby was at the start of the new school year and everyone who was involved in rugby looked forward to the rugby season.

'I loved my other sports but, with rugby, when it came to the rugby season I always had a bit more passion. We only played one term of rugby at Dulwich and I only played two years' rugby due to being ruled out through injury. I did play in my last year and enjoyed it. You always enjoy your sport at school when you are playing with your peers.' Injuries were a problem for the young sportsman in his early teens, with shin splints from cricket and a broken arm when in the lower sixth putting a stop on his rugby.

Peter Allen, Dulwich's rugby coach when Nick was in his last year, remembers the then tall second-row forward who started the year in the Fifth Team but was moved up to the First Team to take his place alongside the back-row player playing two years young, Andrew Sheridan. 'Nick was a very talented ball-player back then, superb hands, but wasn't so keen on training. Too be fair though he knuckled down when I told him I wouldn't pick him if he didn't. But he was always a bit more ambivalent about his rugby than the Sheridans of this world, partly because he was a very good cricketer and hockey player as well.'

I know the 3 to 1 female/male ratio was a factor in my eldest boy, Andrew, deciding to study in Nottingham and this may also have been one of the factors considered by Nick as he weighed up his higher education options. Whilst it was really Sports Studies he wanted to do at university, his loathing of essays led him into a Mathematics degree where he had comfort in numbers. So it was that the Dulwich schoolboy moved to Nottingham Trent University to fully enjoy all aspects of the university experience. 'I wanted to do Sports Science because it's very good at Nottingham Trent but I had to go through clearing and all of the places were taken. I was only really good at Maths so decided to carry on with that. They let me in luckily and it's where I wanted to go.

'With maths you didn't have to write essays! You knew when you were working out the problems that you were going along the right lines! People would say oh, you're doing maths, what are you doing that for? And I'd say well you don't have to write essays for start. There's no deliberating; you're either right or wrong.

At university, rugby provided the typical social life of a student as he kept his studies going whilst turning out for the university side, the local club side, Ilkeston, and a sevens team sponsored by a

Nottingham city-centre pub that benefitted from the thirsty student population. 'When I moved to university it was similar to school in that you always enjoy your sport when playing in age groups with your peers. Through that I got into the social side of university a lot more, which was good.

'I was playing for the university and a little club rugby. In the first year the university only managed about eight games in two terms … it was ridiculous. They had a league so you got a game week in and week out during the first term but then it was the knockout stages for the second term. Because of that a few of us decided after the first year that we'd got to join a rugby club because weren't getting enough rugby. So in our second year we played a little bit for Ilkeston on a Saturday as well as playing for the university on a Wednesday.'

Nick enjoyed his time in Nottingham and graduated in the summer of 1999 with a degree in Mathematics and Science and now had the daunting prospect of facing the big wide world. He went back home to Dulwich and managed to get temporary jobs while he pondered what to do with his life. Along with two friends the idea of travelling was floated, but the others had travelled prior to university and needed a year of work to get their finances in order before another expedition. Knowing his mates as he did led to a change of plan and Nick ended up teaching Maths and PE in Cape Town, South Africa in January 2000. 'I thought about a gap year and that it could be a bit more constructive than simply travelling. I'd seen others teaching in Australia and South Africa, and I quite liked the idea and thought, why not teach in South Africa? I'm half South African, I've got family out there still and it's not as far as Australia if things didn't work out. South Africa is a great country that loves its sport and I felt it was more constructive to go and teach; there's a purpose to you being there.

'I wrote off to various schools in Cape Town and Rondebosch Boys High School got back to me pretty quickly and that was that. Their schools run on the calendar year, from January to December and it was a great time teaching Maths and PE to 14- and 15-year-olds. I taught in three out of the six lessons per day so I had three lessons free where I'd go to the gym or into Newlands. It was great.

'The guys who'd gone out there before university, they filled in as substitute teachers, but I was given a much bigger role since I had my degree, more responsibility. I took the Under 15 A and B rugby. It was excellent and I had a really fulfilling time there.'

Nick used his free time effectively as he trained more regularly and played for the Villagers Club, a famous old club in Cape Town. Owing to the timing of his arrival in Cape Town he missed pre-season training and started playing in their Fourth Team but very quickly rose up the ranks with a couple of Third and Second Team games before gaining a place in the First Team in a championship-winning year.

It was at this point that Nick decided to utilise his undoubted sporting talent to good use and focus on his rugby. 'We won the league that year. It was between us and Stellenbosch, who are always very strong, and that's when I started taking the rugby seriously. At university and when I played for my Old Boys, if the chance occurred to go out the night before a game I'd go out. But when you're playing with Super 12 and Springbok players sometimes, depending on what time of year it was, you were playing at a high standard. It was a fast-paced game as well; there was only a little bit of kicking and there were tries galore. You're playing with very talented individuals at a high standard. It was at that point, that's when I started taking my rugby seriously and actually played my only representative rugby before England Saxons when I played a couple of times for the Western Province A Side.'

A word or phrase to describe yourself at 21 years of age?

Maturing as a person...

Nick was at an important point in his life in terms of his rugby. When he was at Villagers, Gary Gold was the coach, who has since coached at London Irish in the Premiership and is currently assistant coach to Cape Town's Super 14 franchise, the Stormers. Through his network of contacts he found out about interest in Nick from clubs in Ireland and France, but this was all happening in September and he was committed to his teaching post until December.

Nick was naive about rugby contracts and agents, so on returning to England in December 2000 he tried to resurrect the interest of clubs but it could not be made to work with the season half over and unattractive contracts the only thing on offer. After a month of soul searching, a job in the City was secured, with Nick prepared to 'give it a go'.

He did give it a go for six months but the lure of rugby was growing stronger. 'I managed to get a job in the City for about six months, so I thought, right, we'll see how that goes. That was in 2001 and the City had taken a bit of a hit on the investment and fund markets. It wasn't the greatest time to be there or the greatest job; I was a bit of a dogsbody if truth be told. In that year you also had the British Lions tour to Australia, which was a cracking series and drummed up a lot of interest in the City (where there is a big rugby following), and being frustrated behind a desk wasn't where I wanted to be so I decided to give this professional rugby a crack.

I phoned or emailed my old coach in South Africa and he put me on to an agent. There were a couple of professional rugby clubs interested; I had trials but nothing on the table and in came Orrell with a contract. I was thinking, they're not a Premiership club, they're in the division below, but he persuaded me it was the right thing to do. Dave Whelan had just taken over and it was going full time.

'I was playing for Rosslyn Park at the time, amateur stuff, and we played them in the Cup and I liked what I saw. They'd brought in some Rugby League guys from Wigan, were playing some exciting rugby, and I could see that there was a bit of a future there but in the end it wasn't to be.'

Dave Whelan, the former professional footballer for Blackburn Rovers and Crewe Alexandra, had stepped in to take Orrell back to the top flight of English rugby. At the time Whelan was owner of JJB Sports, the sports clothing retailer, Wigan Athletic Football Club and Wigan Warriors Rugby League Club. His dream was to see top-flight football, Rugby League and Rugby Union played at the JJB Stadium.

Maurice Lindsay, the Chairman of Wigan Warriors, was also part of the management team and Orrell was a professionally run club. However, Rugby Union just did not pull in the paying public. Orrell were second in the League and scoring tries for fun but could only attract small crowds, not enough to make a viable Premiership business. 'Virtually a week after being offered a contract I was up there training. They looked after me really well – it was professionally run but it was a pity that in a marketing sense it didn't really take off.

'The ground was nice but there was just no atmosphere because you were only getting in "one man and his dog", so to speak. We were getting between 600 and 700 people to a National One game when we were second in the league and scoring tries all the time. There were clubs below us averaging crowds over a thousand people. It was always going to be difficult in Rugby League land in Wigan and with the football doing so well it was difficult for it to take off, but I really do regret them not marketing it enough.

It was full-time rugby with full-time training. There was a group of us all in our early twenties and it was like being at university but with good salaries. We had a great time up there; it's a good night out in Wigan and there's always Manchester and Liverpool. I don't regret any of it. I learnt things and made some really good friends as well.'

After Nick had spent three years at Orrell the Australian coach Ross Reynolds became disillusioned. Despite finishing second to Worcester in Division One, Whelan was scaling down his interest in the club and cutting budgets. Reynolds described the end-of-season presentation night as a wake not even lightened by a video showing some of the 135 tries scored by his team during the season.

Reynolds moved to take charge of Rotherham, who had been relegated from the Premiership at the end of the 2003–2004 season. At the same time several of the Orrell players were coming out of contract and Reynolds wanted to take them with him to Rotherham. Although Nick's sights were set on Premiership rugby, he followed his coach to Yorkshire.

However, all was not well in his new home on the eastern side of the Pennines. After six weeks of pre-season the Rotherham players had not been paid. 'We were there for a month and the guy in charge, Mike Yarlett pulled his money. We hadn't got paid for a month or a month and a half in pre-season at Rotherham and we were thinking, what's going on here. It was getting silly, we all stopped training. We were thinking it must be that Ross Reynolds – he's a jinx! But it could have been any of us who'd come over from Orrell!

I was in limbo for a month trying to find a club and then Harlequins came along.

'Luckily Alex Bennett, a good friend of mine who played at Orrell, had also played at Saracens and he knew Mark Evans. He told him that he should take a look at me, so I met Mark Evans, he gave me a three-month trial contract, and it went well from there.'

The move to Harlequins enabled Nick to realise his dream of Premiership rugby and he was conservative in his targets for that first season when he set himself the goal of starting six to eight games. However, after coming into the First Team for his debut against Gloucester on 9 October 2004, he was a regular for the remainder of the season.

For the Harlequins, however, the season did not go to plan. 'We got relegated at the end of the season, which was obviously not good. I'd played a lot of National One rugby, gone up to the Premiership and really enjoyed it. Everything was a great challenge, a new environment, a new club, and then it was so disappointing to be relegated. It was already a good club and I think it was good for the club to have Deano [Dean Richards] come in. People were saying at the time: "Oh, it's just a year but you know a lot can happen."'

The predictions of an immediate return to the Premiership turned out to be well founded as Harlequins ran away with the First Division title and regained their place amongst the elite for the start of the 2006–2007 season. The club was much stronger and with hindsight the drop into National Division One proved to be a beneficial journey.

Nick continued with his good form for Harlequins and it was not long before the international selectors took an interest in the impressive back rower. However, it nearly did not go according to plan. 'I was quite fortunate. We played Bath on the Saturday the week before the Saxons were to play against Italy A. The squad were due meet up on the Sunday after the Bath game but I got sent off – I had two yellow cards, the second one for verbal abuse of the referee. I joined up with the Saxons, and Dorian West [England Saxons coach] said that they wanted me to start but couldn't name me in the team as I had to go back to London on Tuesday for the hearing. I'd had a good disciplinary record beforehand so they let me off.

'It was a misunderstanding and wasn't aimed at the ref – it was at one of my players – but I had heard that some referees felt that for verbal abuse it warranted a ban of six to eight weeks. Luckily I got off, was able to play the Saxons game off the bench and suddenly I was named in the starting line-up for England the next week. It all might never have happened because of that one misunderstanding.

'I obviously learnt my lesson from that – you have to watch what you're saying and watch who's there just in case there's a misunderstanding! You've got to learn from your experiences, that's what life's all about. People always say that I wish I was 21 again but only knowing what I know now, and that's absolutely right. It's funny how things work out and how different it could have been.'

So seven days after coming off the bench to take his place in the back row of the England Saxons pack, the journey from social rugby player at Old Alleynian's and Nottingham Trent University to international player was completed as he took to the field on 10 February 2007 to represent England at Twickenham against the Azzurri, in what turned out to be an uninspiring 20–7 win for the home side.

Standing in the tunnel waiting to walk out on to the Twickenham pitch, Nick felt that the game could not start soon enough. Players had talked to him about the pre-match events, the national anthems, the smoke, the noise from the 80,000 crowd, the fact that you can't hear the whistle blowing, but it was Martin Corry who gave a steer to the debutant.

'Oh I couldn't wait for it to start. Martin Corry actually gave me an excellent piece of advice. He said, "Do what you've been doing for the club, don't wait 20 minutes and think, oh, I can handle the pace of this." I thought that was an excellent piece of advice: just do what you've been doing for the club, get a touch of the ball and luckily I got a few touches in the first 20 minutes.

'It wasn't the greatest of games but it was a win and I was pleased with my performance and thoroughly enjoyed the whole day.'

Since that first cap Nick has been an integral part of both the Harlequins team, which has cemented its place at the top end of the Premiership, and also the England team, which has at times stuttered but which against the odds made the 2007 World Cup final.

In his schoolboy days he may not have been the most enthusiastic trainer but he has coped well with the physical demands of the game at the top level. His experiences outside of the game and the fact that he came to top-flight rugby later than most have influenced his mental approach and build-up to matches. 'I think mental preparation is down to the individual. People who have got into the game in similar way to me – you can call them late developers if you like – you know that they're out there to enjoy themselves. I think you can appreciate the moment a little bit more.

'If you're 16 or 17 and you're in your club academy and then progress to the National Academy, your sole goal is that you've got to play for your country. I'm not saying you won't enjoy yourself, but if things don't go well you can really beat yourself up. It's absolutely right to analyse and look for mistakes but you have to draw a line under it if you can. Compared to some people, I'm a bit more relaxed before a game.

'In preparing for a game I'm thinking about my role. For all players, you make sure you're physically ready; you feel strong, you feel quick. You've got to make sure you're right. Sometimes it's a fact that you wake up and you're in the right mood … you're just in that mood all day no matter what you have for breakfast, what you eat for lunch, when you get to the ground or how much stretching you do. Sometimes you've got to get yourself to that level.

'As soon as the game kicks off it's got to be right; your first role in the game, whether it be capture the kick-off, chasing, the first scrum you do, first line-out, you have to feel switched on. Being in my position you've got to get your hands on the ball early, you've got to get a feel of the contact early as well, try to make an impact, and you've always got to try to be involved in the game. There's no point waiting.

'At the end of the day you've trained all week but for me it's all about Saturday. If you train and it's crap all week but you win on the Saturday, then it's been a good week. If you train well all week and you lose on the Saturday, then it's not been a good week.

'As a late developer I think you just appreciate the whole thing a little bit more and can take it all in.'

A word or phrase to describe you now?

Enjoy the moment...

The way I look at it is that you have to have ambitions, goals and dreams but you have to be happy with what you're doing and get life in balance.

Whilst enjoying the moment, Nick's ambitions are focused on being successful for club and country. 'I am enjoying what I do and want to stay there as long as I can. Martin Johnson has just come in as England coach and I want to be in the EPS squad. Then there's the Lions next summer. It would be fantastic to go back to South Africa with the Lions.

'There's a young, excellent, talented squad coming up at Harlequins and the ambition is to win things with club and country, still be playing and stay reasonably fit... I just want to be successful.'

His performances since coming into the England side have been special and it is a great surprise that he was not been selected to be in the 2008 EPS squad announced at the end of June. He will have been hugely disappointed by his omission, but it says a lot about the man in that he got his head down, worked hard and produced strong performances for Harlequins. When injury created the need to bring players into Martin Johnson's autumn international squad it was the Dulwich boy who was called upon to fill the gap and actually started in all four games. The England management team recognised the error of their Summer 2008 selection decision, as the big Number 8 continued his international career with a starting berth in all of England's 2009 Six Nations games.

Outside of rugby, golf is Nick's summer sport of choice and, for a man who is well known for receiving dietary advice and sometimes even following it, cooking also provides an occasional distraction. However, like a lot of the England boys it is playing guitar that provides him with his main relaxation. 'I play a bit of guitar. The Newcastle lads have a go; Jonny's [Wilkinson] quite good and Floody's taken it up ... it's a social instrument. If it's there, somebody will pick it up. I'm not very good but it's a great way to fill your social time.'

Nick is determined to soak up all of the enjoyment from his life in the game but recognises that at some point the curtain comes down on playing. However, what he will do when he eventually has to make that decision is something that has not exercised his mind an awful lot. 'I don't really know! People always ask that. It's said that only 2 per cent of the population are in a job that they like but at some point you have to make ends meet. You will have to still fend for your family by the time your career is ending; you're having to put bread on the table and you're in a job you don't like.

'When I think about what I would actually like to do I'd like to be a singer-songwriter, but I know I can't sing so that's out of the window, but I'd love to be an actor – the Vinnie Jones of rugby or something like that! A Hollywood actor, now I could get into that! There's many more people qualified through the hard school of acting and I'm not sure if I have the ability, but it would be great to do.'

Nick is a larger-than-life character who hasn't come into the elite level of the game by the normal channels. His life experiences have identified him as a very talented individual who has the abilities to succeed at everything he does when he wants to do it and you can guarantee that he will enjoy it at the same time.

A very personable man, I am sure that life after rugby will provide no problems for him but a lot of opportunities. Being a singer-songwriter may be off the former Dulwich schoolboy's radar but the Vinnie Jones of rugby? Well, if he puts his mind to it, you just never know!

2008–2009 Season Update

Originally left out of Martin Johnson's first England squad, the big No 8 has worked hard to re-establish himself as an integral part of the England team. His club, Harlequins, have made steady progress and are now a force to be reckoned with in the Premiership. They came so close to something special this year, but a hard-fought Heineken Cup quarter final with Leinster and a Premiership semi-final against London Irish, both played at their home ground of the Stoop, saw them on the wrong side of the scoreboard.

Nick Easter: Statistics	
Date of birth	15 August 1978
Birthplace	Epsom, Surrey
Height	1.93m
Weight	113kg
Position	No. 8; blind side
School / university	Dulwich College; Nottingham Trent University
Present club	Harlequins
Previous clubs	Orrell; Villagers, Cape Town, South Africa; Old Alleynians
Nicknames	Minty
Favourite TV show	*Curb Your Enthusiasm*; *Entourage*
Favourite film	*Kodak* (I can't believe I wrote it down!); *The Godfather* trilogy
Favourite music	Dire Straits; The Killers
Favourite book	*Bravo Two Zero*
Favourite food	Thai green curry
Most like to meet...	Jack Nicholson
Least like to meet...	Robert Mugabe
Best moment in rugby	2007 World Cup quarter- and semi-finals
Favourite place to visit	Miami South Beach
I love...	all-you-can-eat buffets
I hate...	bad manners

MIKE BLAIR

Scotland; British and Irish Lions; Edinburgh

I do not think there could have been a prouder man than the captain of Scotland as he stood in the tunnel of the Vélez Sársfield stadium in Buenos Aires on 14 June 2008 before the test with the Pumas of Argentina. The match was to be his 50th cap for his beloved Scotland, an international career that started on the North American tour in 2002 with a try-scoring debut against Canada in Vancouver.

Scotland's 108th captain took over the leadership from the injured Jason White in the middle of a troubled 2008 Six Nations' campaign for the match against Ireland at Croke Park, Dublin. The performance against Ireland was an improvement on the preceding games against France and Wales but, despite a lot of possession and territory, they came out losers yet again. So it was on the back of three defeats and an increasingly negative press that Mike Blair led out Scotland at Murrayfield to play the old enemy, England.

Under a heavy Edinburgh sky, England were put to the sword and Calcutta Cup victory went to the Scots, with Mike putting in a captain's performance and being named 'Man of the Match'. The joy of victory was, however, not fully savoured. 'After beating England, when I went up to receive the Calcutta Cup in front of everyone, that is my favourite moment in rugby, but the Six Nations was a really stressful time. There was just a lot of negativity from the media and we felt a lot of pressure because we weren't playing well.

'Before we went out to play against England I was nervous because of the amount of abuse that we'd had. We were trying to play the best we could and were doing as much as we could to beat these teams. It hurts a lot when people say you're not putting the effort in. We try our best week in and week out and sometimes it doesn't click.

'As captain, I felt additional responsibility due to the pressure Frank [Haddon] was under. As captain, you have your own separate press conference where you get grilled for half an hour. I generally don't mind that but the media was very negative.

'When we beat England it was a fantastic achievement, given we are the smallest country, beating the World Cup finalists. The emotion should have been great joy, being happy with the incredible win we'd had, but when the whistle went it was just massive relief. We knew for a week that they'd be off our backs. Unfortunately we didn't beat Italy so they were right back on!

'It was a really stressful time. I felt more pressure going into those games than I had for a long time, but I still love running out at Murrayfield or wherever the international venue is.'

Rugby may be the sport that Mike has taken on to top international honours, but he is a gifted all-round sportsman who was able to develop his abilities in the Edinburgh Academy, an independent school where sport plays an important part in pupils' education. 'I attended Edinburgh Academy and was there from age of 5 until I left to go to Durham University at the age of 18. My dad was also at the school, as were my three brothers.

'Rugby was the sport I grew up playing the most. I played at school from Primary Four, which is seven years of age. I liked the team aspect of it; it was a more sociable thing to do. It's one of the big things with rugby. You don't get it as much with tennis and squash, which I played to District level. With cricket, I played Scottish Schools at 18s but I was basically better at rugby than cricket. I found I enjoyed the rugby a bit more and pressed on with the age-group stuff. I enjoyed it.'

Sport is a big part of the Blairs' family life, with two of Mike's three brothers involved in rugby – Dave is in the same Edinburgh squad as his older brother, while Alex, who is an extremely talented fly half, will almost certainly follow Mike and Dave into the professional game after finishing his education at Edinburgh Academy.

'My dad played at Edinburgh Academicals and was captain there in the mid-70s. My uncle played Scottish Schools rugby and also played at Edinburgh Accies. My mum's pretty coordinated and handles herself pretty well around the table-tennis table when all of us are at home. My dad's father was a very good golfer. There's a fair sporting background and I think there's always been some level of sporting achievement in my family.'

School was a good time for the Edinburgh lad and holds good memories. Edinburgh inter-school rivalries have a significant place in the minds of all involved in the schools – kids and parents as well as school staff. In rugby terms it is the rivalry between Edinburgh Academy and Merchiston Castle School that really gets the blood racing. There is a great tradition – the annual fixture, which has now been played continuously for over a hundred years, is the longest established inter-club match in existence anywhere. It is these big occasions that have stood out for Mike.

'When we got to the final of the Schools Cup for rugby in the 1997–98 season we played against Merchiston. It's the oldest club fixture in the world so there's a big rivalry there. We lost in the final; it was a huge occasion and a truly memorable day. There was a really pressured environment. Playing this fixture as a national final in front of your mates was huge. Every time we play against Merchiston it's like Scotland v England; there's a big hype about it with the players and the supporters.

'It's quite funny – Frank Haddon was teaching at Merchiston and coaching rugby when I was at Edinburgh Academy. When we have been together for Scotland I continually taunt him by telling him to count up how many international players have come through Merchiston as opposed to the Edinburgh Academy in the last five to eight years. A lot have come through the Academy recently – Ross Rennie, Dave Callum, Don McFadyen, Barrie Stuart and myself.

'I have been taunting him this year by saying Ross Rennie got his first cap this year and he was an Academy boy and that he couldn't claim Phil Godman because he was an Academy boy before he went to Merchiston.'

Whilst Mike is the first to admit the fact he didn't study maybe as much as he could, he did focus on the books when he had to achieve what he wanted to achieve. The private schools in Scotland do GCSEs and Mike passed nine GCSEs before moving into the sixth form and studying his Scottish Highers. 'I took four Highers in the sixth form – English, Geography, French and Biology. I was never really that much into the education side of things. I didn't study a huge amount; I did what I had to and tried to get away with doing as little as possible, but when the exams came I had to work. At that time I was really keen to go to Durham University and I knew that I needed good grades for that.

'The thing with Durham was that I had a strong sporting CV and they were interested in me because of that. I wanted to do the Sport in the Community course. I knew Dave Walder through the course, though he was in his third year when I started. There's not much interaction between the years. I did enough to get into Durham but the reason they took me was the sporting stuff. I played national age cricket, District tennis and squash too. I'm not an amazingly studious guy, though I'm not stupid – I managed to get a good balance.'

Whilst sport generally and rugby in particular played a large part in Mike's Edinburgh Academy life, it was a good experience in lots of other ways. 'I met my wife at school. She came to the school for the last two years – it's completely co-ed now but they came in at the sixth form then. A lot of guys I went to school with came all the way up from junior school so it was great, day in and day out, being with them. I don't keep in touch with them as much as I should; I'm not good at that kind of thing! It sort of fades away.

'Sport was a major part of it; it was just a great place to grow up. We lived close to the school and close to the sports ground. In our last year we'd have a bit of a training session in the morning then four or five of the guys would have lunch at my house. We would then go back out after lunch for the game. I remember that well, good memories.'

Whilst in the lower sixth the young scrum half made his debut for Scotland Schools 18 age group, a year young when he lined up against Ireland at Thomond Park, Limerick, the home of the 2008 Heineken Cup winners, Munster. Those early international games were difficult, with Scotland inevitably ending up on the wrong side of the scoreline, a fact that Mike thinks was primarily due to the physicality and size of the opposition, a situation that now seems to have been corrected. 'All the games I played at age group we seemed to be pretty well beaten and it always seemed to be a slog because physically we were smaller and we hadn't played at the kind of level the other countries had played at. I think it's turned around a bit now.

'When I played at that level I wasn't doing weights. There wasn't any conditioning in place, but now my youngest brother Alex, who played for Scotland Under 18s this year, he's been doing weights for two or three years now and you can definitely see a difference in his physique. That's something that's improved to such an extent that we're now playing off an even playing field.

'I think the age group eligibility dates changed as well. We used to be six months younger than England but it's more an even age group now. Scotland Under 18 this year only lost one game against England. They beat Ireland comfortably and France and Wales too. It's a lot more of an even field now.'

Selection for the game against Ireland came as a surprise, but the young scrum half did what he always tries to do and that is go out and enjoy it, have fun. He has the ability to not let things get on top of him, to block things out or deal with them – what is going to happen will happen so just do your best and get on with it.

'It was a kind of a shock selection really because Callum Cusiter, Chris Cusiter's older brother, had been playing. I hadn't been expecting to play and was told the Wednesday before that I was starting the match. I suppose it took a while to sink in. The kind of honour it was at the time. I tend not to let situations get on top of me too much. I'm not really a massive one for having that sort of mindset. A fatalist. You just get on with it. I play rugby because I enjoy doing it, and when you go on the pitch, in my head it's still essentially fun. It's something I'm wanting to do.

'I wasn't nervous, but it was lashing down with rain and I was worrying about how my pass was going to be and all these kinds of things. Again, I didn't let it get on top of me. We lost by about 50 points but it was good. I think Paul O'Connell played in that game. There are a few names I recognise from then who are still playing. I do that with all the age groups I've played against – look for who is still playing now.

'I was on the bench against England Under 18. When you look at the programme it's incredible the amount of guys who've gone through and played not just professional but international rugby –

David Flatman, Steve Borthwick, Andy Sheridan, Alex Sanderson, Adam Balding, Hall Charlton, Andy Goode, Joe Shaw – it's amazing the number of guys who went through that year. Only a couple of the Scotland guys, though, went on to play professionally. I don't know what happened. I think with Scotland at that time it was quite easy fall out of the sport, so if you didn't get picked up at that point for one reason or another, you could have faded into the distance.

'With the academy systems in England you're already picked up by a club when you're 17 or 18 years of age and you know exactly where you're going. They're changing that bit now and they are trying to put academies into place in Scotland with area institutes.'

At that time some people say that as soon as the game went professional they wanted to be a part of it, but this was not the case for Mike who was not particularly stressed about planning a future. He had decided upon continuing his studies in the North-East of England at Durham University and did well enough in his A levels to take up his offer of a place. Knowing the people at Durham University, I am sure they were rubbing their hands with joy at the thought of an age group international player wearing their purple shirt on the lovely racecourse ground pitch next to the river in Durham City. However, it did not work out quite as expected.

'I was led to believe that Durham was a good rugby university but I didn't get into it. I got the impression that it was who you knew not how good you were that mattered so I didn't really give it a shot. I travelled home to Edinburgh each weekend and played for Edinburgh Academicals and then Boroughmuir.

'I played for the National Sevens team at the end of my last year at school and even as an unconditioned 18-year-old I felt I had something to offer in the professional game, I felt I certainly had it in me. I don't want to say it was a matter of time but I think it was something I was progressing towards without thinking about it too much.'

Mike left Durham at the end of his first year and completed a Sports Science degree in Edinburgh. In his final year of studies he started getting involved with the Edinburgh professional team, although not as a contracted player. This increasing involvement at the same time he was finishing his degree created the opportunity for the move into rugby as a professional player. 'In my last year of university I was involved in the Edinburgh professional team. I wasn't contracted but there was only two scrum halves on their books and one was injured, so I was involved a fair bit. At the end of the year they said they wanted to sign me full-time. I'd got away with my Sports Science degree and managed to pass so I felt at the time it was something I couldn't turn down.

'It was quite strange how it all worked out. In my last university year I'd been involved in bits and bobs with the Edinburgh squad but I had been involved with the National Sevens team. I had played a couple of tournaments in Cardiff and at Twickenham and was actually the top try scorer at Twickenham, so I was pushed into the Scotland A Team in my Scotland Under 21 season. I played a couple of games for Scotland Under 21. I thought I hadn't played that well but they still pushed me through to the A Team.

'I actually got my first full cap against Canada before I had a professional contract. My contract started August 2002 and I was capped on 14 June. I hadn't actually played a game for Edinburgh as a professional player. It was a strange way to go about it and you don't see it now as guys are going into professional teams at a younger age.'

With his first cap under his belt and a contract with Edinburgh secured, Mike was on his way but felt that Scotland were trying to look after his development and were easing him into the international environment. 'I wasn't too bothered about it being a step-up in level because I was confident in my skills set and being able to cope. It didn't help that we lost, but again it was fun because I got my first full cap.

'We were in Canada with just five or six thousand people watching; it was like playing in a park so I still felt I was being eased into it. After the tour I wasn't involved in the autumn internationals but played for the A Team. I thought I hadn't missed my chance but certainly felt I was third choice.'

The mindset underpinning the way he plays the game is having faith in your ability to perform your core skills, whatever the situation. Whilst it may not work for everyone his performances are based on spontaneity and not thinking too deeply about his mental preparation.

The notion of having fun and enjoying the rugby experience is part of the Scottish captain's approach to this day. 'I am of the opinion that a scrum half does not have a different mindset when you go into games at a higher level. If you do your skills well then it doesn't matter what level you're playing at – Edinburgh Accies or the British Lions ... it doesn't matter. If you do your skills well, it doesn't matter what the opposition do; it doesn't affect your game so much.

'It's about constantly getting your pass away and, although there's not a huge amount of opportunities for clean breaks for scrum halves these days, if a gap opens up you take it. I like there being a flow to my game and when I'm playing well I'm playing naturally and relaxed. When I start thinking about things too much that's when I'm not so good.

'Whatever game it is, I try to go into it with that same kind of mentality. It's a game you go out to enjoy and if you're enjoying yourself you're going to play better. I think that's the kind of mentality that I've got but on occasions it's been almost impossible to do that... This year's Six Nations was a really stressful time.

'In the build-up to a game I know guys who plan out their day before the match, writing out what time they brush their teeth, shave etc., and mental cues for the skills they need to perform. But if I did that, I just can't imagine, it's the last thing I want to be doing.

'A psychologist worked with England in the 2003 World Cup and talked about "TCUP" – Thinking Clearly Under Pressure... Clive Woodward always went on about it. I can't remember the guy's name but he came in to do stuff with Scotland, and I don't know if I'm old fashioned or too simplistic but it just didn't do it for me. I just want to enjoy what I'm doing and if I start thinking about it more as a game I just won't enjoy it.'

It is refreshingly honest to hear someone in Mike's position talking about sports psychology in this way. In my experience of developing players and also working with executives in business the common trend is that people who are successful know themselves and are confident in their own abilities to do what they have to do whatever the situation. They trust themselves and find their own way to get the best out of themselves. I have seen sports psychology interventions with teams becoming almost a self-defeating prophecy as the idea is introduced, bought into by some of the players, but then take on a life of its own. Rather than being a support to performance it becomes another variable that can influence performance negatively.

A word or phrase to describe you at 21 years of age?

Trust your own ability...

I didn't let too much stress me out. If I didn't get chosen, then it was my mindset that it would happen in time... Trust your own ability.

On returning from the North American tour Mike got into pre-season training with Edinburgh and played in all of the pre-season games, but Frank Haddon, then the coach of Edinburgh, decided to start the season with the experienced Graham Burns at scrum half. Such is the nature of rugby, however, that Graham was injured in the first ten minutes of the opening game, an injury that was to sideline him for six weeks. 'Graham was out for six weeks with an injury so I played the next five games and played quite well. Graham didn't get a chance to get back in and I sometimes look back at that time. Little things like that build your career – if Graham's injury hadn't happened I would have progressed more slowly, but that's the nature of sport.'

The feeling that Mike had that he was being eased into international rugby and his position as third-choice scrum half were confirmed when he was not included in the Scotland squad for the 2002 autumn internationals, but the cotton wool came off with the 2003 Six Nations competition. 'Just before the Six Nations, I got a call to say that I was involved in the squad and I felt it was one of the happiest phone calls I'd ever had. I really didn't think I would be involved because of what had happened in the autumn. That was a really good moment for me. The good times I'd had previously I'd sort of expected because of the way I'd play or because of certain situations, but that was a one that came from left field.'

The great Scottish scrum half Brian Redpath was the Scotland captain in the 2002–2003 season and Mike knew his role was as understudy, getting bits and pieces of the action when called upon. However, Brian retired at the end of that season and the coaching set-up changed, as Matt Williams took charge of the national team. Whilst not taking anything for granted, Mike felt that now was the time for him to get his chance. A difficult period followed on the international scene as Chris Cusiter became the first choice.

'I was playing for Edinburgh and they'd done quite well getting to the Heineken Cup quarter-final for the first time. I certainly wasn't counting my chickens or anything and hadn't thought about it too much but I presumed my time was coming. Matt Williams came in as coach to the national team and he arranged a meeting about six weeks before his first selection for the game against Wales.

'He told me he was going to start Chris Cusiter and at the time I couldn't believe it. I remember at the time being gutted and couldn't believe that he could make that decision with limited information at that time, and I remember being really upset. We had two massive Heineken Cup games to play, we had about six weeks to go before the game and the need to name the team, yet he'd put all his eggs in one basket and said he wanted Chris.

'Matt was in charge of 17 games and Chris started 16 in a row and was then injured in the Six Nations game before we were to play England. In the week leading up to the game he couldn't walk at all, was on crutches and hobbling around the hotel. Matt said he'd give Chris until the Friday to see if he would be fit and I'm looking at Chris and he couldn't walk.

'I guess the point I'm making is that it was a very hard time then, but I really felt that whatever I did I couldn't influence Matt and his decision. From then I realised that you have to accept what people do. You can do your best, play as well as you can and do as much as you can, but if you don't get selected then don't get upset about it because you can't do anything about it. That's the main lesson that I took from that situation. I think that spreads into everyday of life. There's going to be times that no matter what you do, something's not going to work for you and I think that you just have to accept the situation.

'With the scrum halves that Scotland have now – Chris Cusiter, Rory Lawson and me – you know there's real competition. I think that with these guys if you're not selected you have to put your hand up, think that a really good player has taken the position, accept it and support the team.'

Matt Williams left the Scotland set-up after the Six Nations campaign in 2005 and Frank Haddon moved from Edinburgh to take interim charge of the national team for the summer games against the Barbarians and Romania and was appointed National Coach in September 2005. Under the current management regime Mike has found himself in the thick of international action.

Magners League and Heineken Cup rugby have provided Mike with the opportunity to show his talents on the club scene with Edinburgh but the Scottish Rugby Football Union have struggled with the structure of the game in Scotland and these problems were sharply brought into focus in the summer of 2007. A dispute between the franchise owners of the Edinburgh club and the Scottish RFU led to Scotland players including Mike being taken out of World Cup training as the problems escalated and the lawyers got involved. 'There was some trouble at Edinburgh in the summer of 2007 with the owners leaving us. The players didn't know the exact detail of the situation but it was a pretty depressing time for the club. Some guys in particular had a really hard time. I guess I was concerned about the situation but, with the focus on the World Cup, I was of the opinion that it would blow over by the time we got back.

'I had opportunities to leave at the end of last season and once I got back from the World Cup. It was something I thought about as some very good clubs were interested in me but I felt loyalty towards Edinburgh. Andy Robinson had come in and after a few training sessions I felt that he was a positive addition to the team. He's hands-on coaching every day, which he wasn't with England, and I think he's enjoying it ... it's his real passion. At the end of his involvement with England he got a really rough time. I think he's enjoying being away from it all.

'I do enjoy training and have done particularly this season. I think when you get a new coach in you get a buzz – a new voice, new training ideas – and that's continued throughout the whole season.'

Andy Robinson has had a big influence in Edinburgh and the players have responded to his coaching style and the ideas he brings.

As the Scottish National team management was reviewed after the 2008 Six Nations championship Andy Robinson has taken on responsibilities with the national team in the hope that the good form shown by both Edinburgh Rugby and Glasgow Warriors will be brought into international team performances.

Mike has two years left on his contract at Edinburgh but is unsure as to his long-term future. 'I don't know where I see myself going. I now have another two years at Edinburgh but I do see rugby as an opportunity, an avenue to explore something else. I always think it would be good to play in France for a couple of years. I do think rugby gives you great opportunities. You could go to Toulouse or Paris for a couple of years and they'll get you a job organised, look after you. When you have finished playing rugby you could decide to go to Paris for a couple of years, but it would be much more difficult to do, finding a flat and a job. I don't know if I'll end up doing that or not but I feel that it's something that, if I didn't do it, it might be something I'd live to regret. Some people say that even if you don't enjoy it, you've given it a go.

'Chris [Cusiter] is at Perpignan and he's having a great time, really enjoying it. He said it's really quite different but it's made me think about doing it but I am here for two years... After that I'm not too sure. We'll have to see where we're at because that'll be just before the World Cup year so that comes into play.'

Since taking on the Scotland captaincy the precious times away from rugby have been reduced even more and non-rugby activity has taken a back seat. Coffee with friends is taken around the demands of interviews, photo shoots and various club and Scotland visits.

Life after rugby is some thing that Viv, Mike's wife, tries to talk to him about but in the same way that he feels more comfortable in his rugby by going with the flow and not thinking too much about situations he doesn't like to think or worry about it. 'It's something my wife constantly talks about, how we have this lifestyle now, but what will happen in five years' time? I am just turned 27 and I haven't done a huge amount outside of rugby. I don't like to think about it or I'll worry about it.

'One of the guys on the board of Edinburgh Rugby is looking at helping guys out with some work experience. His point is that it's good for you to know what your potential routes out of rugby are. He talked to us about the ways in which we could start going about it. He's not talking about finding your perfect job now; he's talking about doing something for a day, trying it out, just when you can. Don't worry about it, no pressure.

'That seemed really good; it's not something I've thought too much about before now but his main point is that rugby is your number-one focus and if anything encroaches on that then you shouldn't be doing it.

'Duncan Hodge is the Scotland kicking coach but he has a full-time job as well. I think something like that would suit me – working on a particular skill with a group of elite professionals and having another job as well.

'You never know how things will work out. Sometimes things find you. I feel that, for me, after rugby will be affected by how well I do with rugby. If I play well and get x amount of caps with Scotland, then it may put me in a better place for after rugby.'

A word or phrase to describe you now?

Loyal...

That's a difficult question but I certainly feel that I'm a very loyal kind of guy; I think that what happened with Edinburgh in the summer is proof of that. Four or five top Scotland and Edinburgh players left. I had the opportunity, too, but I didn't want to be seen as 'the straw that broke the camel's back' and possibly throw the whole thing into freefall.

I feel that there's a degree of loyalty in my personality. I met my wife at school when we were 15 and I've always had her there. That's something that's important to me.

When talking to Mike Blair I found a charming, refreshingly honest young man who speaks with intensity and enthusiasm when talking about the important things in his life. In the Statistics given at the end of the chapter he didn't have anyone he would most like to meet or least like to meet because 'I am not good at speaking to new people.' I am not sure about that as I found him very good company and very easy to talk too.

After his current contract expires at Edinburgh he has expressed an interest in playing rugby in France as his friendly rival for the Number 9 shirt in the Scotland squad, Chris Cusiter, has in Perpignan. I could be wrong but I get the impression that, in the same way as you can cut through a stick of Blackpool rock and see the word 'Blackpool', if you cut through Mike Blair you would see the word 'Edinburgh'.

I think that the captaincy of Scotland is in very capable hands.

2008–2009 Season Update

It was a great surprise to me that the Scottish captain did not make the original British and Irish Lions squad, but the unfortunate injury to the Munster scrum half, Tomas O'Leary, led to his inclusion.

Mike Blair: Statistics	
Date of birth	20 April 1981
Birthplace	Edinburgh
Height	1.81m
Weight	85kg
Position	scrum half
School / university	Edinburgh Academy; Edinburgh
Present club	Edinburgh Rugby
Previous clubs	Edinburgh Academicals; Boroughmuir
Nicknames	Blade
Favourite TV show	*Friends*
Favourite film	*Blood Diamond*
Favourite music	anything on the radio
Favourite book	James Patterson books
Favourite food	Viv's macaroni cheese; Mum's roast
Most like to meet...	nobody
Least like to meet...	nobody
Best moment in rugby	Calcutta Cup 2008
Favourite place to visit	Caribbean
I love...	my family
I hate...	fresh tomatoes

TOBY FLOOD

England; Leicester Tigers

In rugby your First Team debut is a massive point in your career. It is a step into the unknown and the opportunity to test yourself both physically and mentally for the first time as a professional player.

I had seen the gangly youth in training and Development Team games and heard John Fletcher, the then Academy director at Newcastle Falcons, talk about the promise that Toby Flood showed, so it was with an anticipation that comes from wanting someone to grasp the moment that I took my seat in the press box at Kingston Park, home of the Newcastle Falcons, to witness the 19-year-old's first start in Premiership rugby against London Wasps in February 2005.

Grasp the moment Toby certainly did as he dropped a goal and kicked two penalties in Newcastle Falcons' 29–28 win. The points were massively important to the outcome of the game but they came off the back of a very assured performance which demonstrated the young man's abilities to cope with the pressures at Premiership level.

He was playing in a position that was alien to him against one of the most powerful teams in the Premiership, but it was one of the most impressive debut performances I have seen. 'I was lucky to get a place in the team, I can't lie. It was four weeks after my second knee operation and Rob [Andrew] asked me to come into the squad. I did a fitness test at 4 p.m. the day before the game which went OK and I was in the team. It was probably a blessing in disguise to be just chucked in at the deep end.

'My first couple of starts were the result of a lot of the First Team squad being injured – Burkey [Matt Burke], Dave Walder and others – but once I'd been given the opportunity, the chance to have a go at becoming a professional sportsman, that was something I couldn't relinquish and realised I had to give it everything I had. Ambition and the desire to achieve that goal became even more important to me because I really, really wanted to be a professional rugby player. I saw the lifestyle these guys lived, the camaraderie they have through playing professional sport and wanted to be a part of it.'

Toby originates from Frimley in Surrey, the same town as Jonny Wilkinson, but moved to the North-East of England where his rugby was shaped initially at Alnwick Rugby Club and then latterly at King's School, Tynemouth, and Morpeth Rugby Club. The Flood family have their heritage rooted in the theatre rather than sport. Toby's grandfathers, Albert Leiven and Gerald Flood, were both professional actors with significant roles to their name; his mother, Anna, trod the boards as an amateur and his father, Tim, managed the Whitley Bay Playhouse. However, sport was an important part of his upbringing.

'Mum tells the story that she used to play a bit of hockey, ran and was school champion at Friendship Heights, though I find it hard to believe! Dad played just local rugby. He loved it, played Alnwick Seconds or Thirds and then Veterans, as he was getting on. His team won either the Thirds or Veterans Cup and he was over the moon with that. I remember him breaking his jaw playing against Morpeth; I think he had it all wired up with elastic bands and had to eat through a straw for about four months. Luckily that didn't put me off!

'He was also my coach as a kid. He dragged me out of the house to the rugby club in Alnwick when I was about six and I played there for a few years. He stopped coaching when I moved out of the juniors but now he's back doing it at Percy Park at the weekend. It gets him out of the house and he enjoys it.'

I think that one of the pressures of the systems put in place to identify talent and nurture it in specific sports is at odds with youngsters simply enjoying growing up. Certainly, I always tried to encourage my own children to participate in as many sports as possible. This rounded sporting exposure and participation were also important in developing Toby during his younger years. 'Now I realise that, I'm so pleased to have been allowed to do different things. I know I could have put my hand up to my dad and played water polo or whatever and that he'd back me up 100 per cent.

146

'I have tried athletics, volleyball, football, tennis and all sorts. I've always been that sort of kid wanting to be outside rather than sitting indoors at home. I played cricket to County standard but never really enjoyed it too much. I could bat and bowl a little, a reasonable fielder, but was never an opener with either the bat or the ball.

'I actually left rugby at about age of nine and played football in the Newcastle United School of Excellence for three years. It was great for a while but by the end I did not enjoy the coaching and lost the passion for the game. My dad was great and very supportive but put the responsibility on to me by insisting that if I wanted to leave I had to speak to the coach myself. He wanted me to act in a certain way by taking responsibility. He was trying to get me to understand how you have got to act and how you've got to behave to be a good person. So I thanked the coach for his time, that I really appreciated it, but told him I was not enjoying it any more. I didn't get upset but got emotional.

'I've often wondered, though, if I'd cracked on with it, would I have made it as a professional footballer?'

It is this emotion that to this day makes Toby the person he is. He wears his heart on his sleeve, cares deeply about what he does and has difficulty in hiding his feelings, but it says a lot about his upbringing in terms of making decisions and standing by them. 'I was a bit of a nightmare as a child when I was very young but my parents did bring me up with the belief that if it's right then do it but if it's not then don't.'

He attended Chancery Middle School in Morpeth up to the age of 14 and then, when the family moved to Tynemouth, attended King's School, which was a rugby-playing school, and enabled him to train and play regularly as part of the school curriculum.

By the time GCSEs raised their ugly head his interests were not in the sciences but it was History and Sociology that captured his imagination. 'With the sciences I could get by and managed to get good grades for my GCSEs, but I never really had the bug for science... One of the best things I heard was that history is fun stories with dates. That was how a teacher described it. It's very true, I think, and I love learning about what's been and gone.

'As a kid I possibly wasn't the best studier – my mind would wander and I was never the swot of the class. When I was very young I'd always be pining to be outside playing sport. I felt comfortable because I could beat someone at football and could throw the ball further than most. I'm not saying I was the best because there were others quicker, faster and with better skills than me but I could cope with these kids and did all right.

'In schoolwork I would do my best but in sport I found a way to unleash my energy. At that time I never had dreams of professional sport as a career. I just wanted to go out and play.'

Toby represented Northumberland County at all age groups from age 13 onwards. As he got older it was rugby that became his major sport as he developed as a player. There are many memories that Toby has of his early years but two things that stand out for him both relate to his time at Alnwick Rugby Club. 'I have good memories of winning the Under 9s mini's trophy with Alnwick. We beat Northern in the final and it was fantastic. I don't know why it was so good but it was. We had a good team – a lot of the guys still play rugby today and it was fantastic to win something at that age. It still means a lot.

'Also very vivid in my mind is the great times I had watching my dad playing rugby … well, not really watching. Going along but then getting bored after 30 seconds to a minute and playing football with the other kids. On international days they played at 11 a.m. so that they could go and watch the Six Nations on the television in the bar. I remember the guys sitting or standing in front of the big television in the corner watching the game. Of course I'd meet up with all the other kids and fool around.'

On leaving school he joined Morpeth Rugby Club and as an 18-year-old played First Team rugby and represented Northumberland in the County Championship. It was at this point, after tracking his progress as a junior, that Newcastle Falcons made an approach to bring him into the club. 'I was 18 when Fletch [John Fletcher] called me and asked me to join the Newcastle Falcons Academy. That was the first time that I thought that a career in sport might be a possibility. Then again, I knew that to study would be important and that I'd have to go and do that as well.' The decision was taken that he would take the opportunity provided by Newcastle Falcons but recognised the need to put the safety net in place in terms of his studies.

Toby was accepted on to a Management degree in the Newcastle Business School at Northumbria University and became a student in September 2003. His choice of subject may have been rather random but with hindsight it proved to be a good decision as he loved the course. 'There were times when I thought I should have just done History, but a business education will give me a lot more options when I eventually finish playing and the course was great.'

Getting the balance right between rugby and education was difficult. After Toby excelled in his debut against Wasps the focus shifted from being a student and potential rugby player to being a rugby player who was also a student. As Toby's rugby developed, it was clear that we were dealing with a special talent and the emphasis changed yet again to rugby player who studied part-time.

This change in emphasis presented certain challenges to me in my role as Education Advisor at Newcastle Falcons in trying to build flexibility into his study programme. Class attendance, assignment hand-ins and examinations are all things that are difficult for elite sportspeople to balance with the demands of their sport and would have been impossible for Toby without the magnificent support of Northumbria University's Business School.

For a young man developing academically, socially and as a sportsman, keeping things on an even keel whilst growing up amongst peers who do not have the same goals in life can be difficult. 'I think there are a lot of people who could end up taking the easy option, thinking I'm 18 years of age, at university, I want to be out with my mates and all that sort of stuff, but it never really appealed to me. I was never a big socialite and did not go out often. I'd probably go out a couple of times a year and blow the cobwebs away.

'For me it was a case of realizing that I'd been given this opportunity or this chance to have a go at becoming a professional sportsman and that I had to give it everything. I wouldn't say I sacrificed a lot, but I have a lot of close friends who would go out as normal 18-year-olds do, going to town, whereas I wouldn't. I would stay in and concentrate on achieving what I was hoping to achieve.'

A word or phrase to describe yourself at 21 years of age?

Desperate...

'Determined' is such an obvious word to use but there is a kind of desperation for something that wants me, needs me, drives me to achieve what I want to achieve. If I don't make it then I don't make it, but at 21 I was working as hard as I could and doing as much as I could to hopefully achieve my goals.

Since his debut for Newcastle Falcons in February 2005 Toby has established himself not only in Premiership rugby but also on the international stage. He has represented England at 18 Group and was a part of the 21 Group Grand Slam-winning team in 2006. The 2006 November international against Argentina at Twickenham gave him his first full cap when he came off the bench as a second-half replacement for Charlie Hodgson.

It was maybe not the best of starts because, when trying to force the play, he gave a pass that was intercepted by the Pumas and led to their winning try. However, the self-confidence that has typified his development enabled him to get over the disappointment and learn from the experience. 'If I could take that pass back I would. It hung around in my mind for a while but I had to put it to bed and get behind the team. I couldn't be selfish.'

Toby has established himself on the international stage very quickly and not only in his favoured position at fly half but at inside centre. He was involved in the 2007 Six Nations campaign, making his full debut against France, and, although originally not selected for the 2007 World Cup, after an unfortunate injury to Falcons colleague Jamie Noon, he was flown to France to join the squad. His impact on the tournament was significant as he played a role in the quarter-final, semi-final and final, coming off the bench in all games as a second-half replacement for Mike Catt.

Toby has continued to be a presence on the international stage, starting in all of England's 2008 Six Nations games and being a part of the 2008 touring party heading to New Zealand and two test

Above: Mike Blair © Edinburgh Rugby. Below: Rory Best © Inpho Photographers.

Matthew Tait © Clint Hughes.

Above: Mike Blair © Scottish Rugby/Press Association. Below: Rory Best © DicksonDigital.com.

Above: Martyn WIlliams © Huw Evans Agency. Below: Steve Borthwick © England RFU / Russell Chyne.

Martyn Williams © Huw Evans Agency.

Jamie Roberts © Huw Evans Agency.

Hugh Vyvyan © Saracens Rugby.

Chris Paterson © Scottish Rugby / Press Association.

Above: Chris Paterson © Scottish Rugby/Press Association. Below: Andrew Sheridan © Clint Hughes.

Shane Horgan © Inpho Photographers.

Above: Martin Corry © Tiger Images. Below: Toby Flood © Tiger Images.

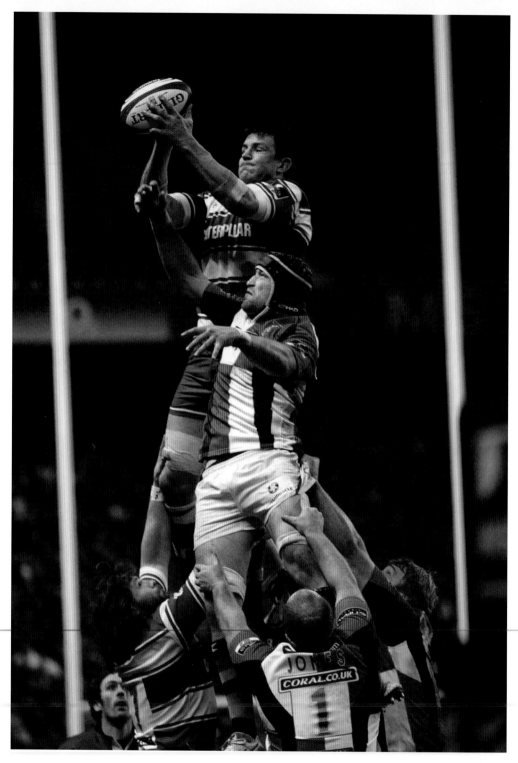

Martin Corry © Tiger Images.

Toby Flood © Tiger Images.

Above: Geordan Murphy © Tiger Images. Below: Andrew Sheridan and Nick Easter © England RFU / Russell Cheyne.

Above: Nick Easter and Steve Borthwick © England RFU / Russell Cheyne. Below: Carl Hayman © allblacks.com.

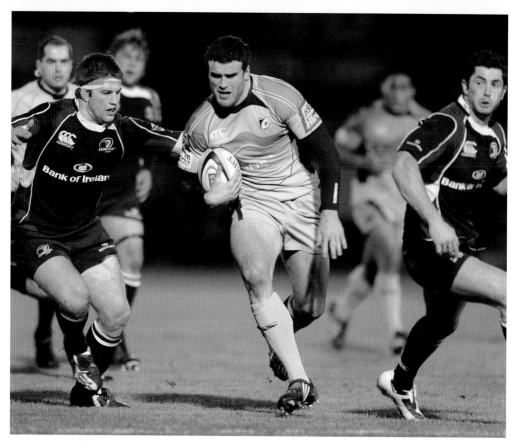

Above: Jamie Roberts © Huw Evans Agency. Below: Carl Hayman © allblacks.com.

matches against the All Blacks. Exposure to top-level competition is important as he continues to develop his game. 'I think experience is talked about as being a vital thing but I don't think it is just about being there; I think learning quickly from the experience is more important. If you have three or four starts you will become experienced, but simply because you've seen it all before does not mean you now know how to react. You need to reflect on the experience to grab learning from the situation.

'A big thing for me is the fact I've played reasonably consistently now for two to two and a half years and this has allowed me to understand what's needed from me. I better understand how I need to perform, how I need to play, reading a game as it develops, when a situation demands going from slow ball to fast ball, how to overcome a blitz defence, and all the other things that happen in a game.

'When you first go into sport you're very naive but you have to learn quickly. I think it is then a case of applying that learning and trying to improve to become more consistent. If you look at elite players, say Jonny [Wilkinson], Dan Carter, Martin [Corry], Phil [Vickery], these guys are consistently performing at a high level and there are very few occasions where things go badly or things drop off. The more I play, especially at international level, the more exposure I get and exposure I think is a vital thing.

'If you look at a lot of very young players whom you know potentially could be up there amongst the elite, poor decision making and execution can lead to things going wrong and inconsistency. These players have talent and can cover their shortcomings by doing something completely unexpected. They have not had the exposure that enables opposition players to fully know their game.

'Games are analysed to incredible levels of detail and this enables competitors to know what you are about, how you play and limits your ability to do things that are unexpected. This is why I think consistency at the highest level is so difficult and where players should be aiming in their development. This is something I am working, striving towards and hopefully I am on my way there but I still have a way to go.'

In preparing players to perform at the highest level great advances have been made in fitness and conditioning to give players the physiological make-up to enable them to maximise their physical potential in competition but the psychological make-up of the player, their ability to use the 'top two inches' under the pressure of high-level competition, singles out the great from the good.

Toby is a very confident person both on and off the field, mentally strong and arguably emotional, giving everything and expecting others to do the same. Whilst desire and emotion are important attributes, they do need to be controlled. 'I get frustrated when things that I want and need to see happen from other people don't happen. I'm just desperate for things to go well and admit it does get a bit frustrating when they don't.

'It might look like I'm really wound up but it's actually just for a second, then I'm off thinking about something completely different. I think that as I grew up I was emotional about sport and always had that desire to win. I find it hard to hide those feelings. I am working on it and feel I am getting better as I get older, but I still have a bit more to do. It's just the burning desire to always win. I do not think I'm a bad loser; it just takes me a while to get over defeat.

'The difference between winning and losing in professional sport is so minimal – a knock-on or a pass goes to hand; a kick that goes one side of the post or the other; a missed tackle, or bringing a player to ground and the referee views a situation differently than you. I think that these sorts of things that are outside of my own control are the hardest things I have to deal with, but they have to be dealt with as the game is very much about the collective effort and your part in it.'

In a short career to date there have been a lot of memories and experiences, of which the final of the 2007 Rugby World Cup is obviously one, but leaving a significant impression was the 2007 Six Nations game against Ireland when rugby was taken to Croke Park, Dublin for the first time. Although Toby did not actually get on to the pitch, the noise, the history, the tears have all left a lasting and abiding memory. 'It meant a hell of a lot to a lot of people, all that history and the feeling around it – it was huge. The strength of the memory comes probably from my love of desire and emotion but witnessing that emotion, guys in tears, the noise and the depth of feeling of the crowd was really special.

'I don't actually think the crowd affected our performance on the day but I think we probably gave Ireland a bit too much respect. Having said that, I don't think we would have won that game no matter how many times we'd played them. The script was written – Ireland would win that game but we know we didn't help ourselves.

'Club-wise probably my first ever start at 10 was a special moment. It wasn't Premiership; it was an EDF Cup match against Sale Sharks and the game went well. I absolutely loved it. It was fantastic to be involved in my first start at 10.'

Emotion and desire are important parts of Toby's make-up. He gives everything to what he is doing and expects others to do the same. Whilst he came through the Academy system, he feels that the approach is a little soft in that it's all about the individual, the player and the player's development. When you reach Premiership and international rugby the focus changes from the individual to the team and what they want to achieve. This leads to a very focused and necessarily honest relationship with yourself and your teammates and the need to recognise the fact that in a results-driven business there are going to be people making decisions about individuals that will impact on you and the team. There may be casualties and it may be you or someone close to you.

'It is inevitable that this environment changes you as a person; it makes you harder. Guys have to achieve results within timeframes. If they don't you know they are gone and that should not really startle you. This reality kicked me into understanding that you have to be a harder character. In 2008 both my club and international coaches have had their problems and moved on and it has been a lesson to me on how the world works.

'As professional sportsmen we have to recognise that maybe 90 per cent of the time we relate to each other in a way that recognises the need to develop the team bond and ethos. Maybe our behaviour is softer than in the real world, but the other 10 per cent of the time when difficult events are taking place you realise that there's not much given and it toughens you up in the sense that, when things need to be said or done, then you yourself just need to be as cut-throat as everybody else.

'I am not saying there's no loyalty because there has to be loyalty.

I think loyalty is just so important in this sport, but then you know you have to understand that loyalty can get you so far but then there needs to be big decisions at times. It is great to play for a team that you love playing for but then you look above you and the likes of the coaches leaving and that sort of stuff makes you realise that you're inside a bubble and that decisions are being made beyond your control and that is tough.'

It is a reality of professional sport that careers are short and that being focused and looking after your career needs are important for players to maximise their income potential whilst they still have the ability to do so.

A word or phrase to describe yourself now?

It's still the same for me as it was when I was 21 – desperation/determination. I have had some great standout moments but there is still a huge amount I want to achieve in my career. If I lose that determination and desperation to achieve what I want to achieve then I might as well pack it in.

I think there are days when I could just do with being on a beach in Barbados to be away from it all but then if I get there I know it would be two days before I'd end up doing exercises and constantly working. As I get older maybe that may change but I hope it never does.

At the present time rugby is at the forefront of Toby's mind as his career develops but he does recognise the importance of engaging in activities outside of rugby. He is convinced of the need to do things that are not rugby related to keep mentally alert. 'French, German, a cooking course or whatever, just go out and do something.' Currently his non-rugby time is spent fly-fishing with England colleague Jamie Noon and friends from school as well as learning to play the guitar, a pastime which is great fun and an easy way to lose time.

Having obtained his Business Studies degree he is determined at some point to undertake a master's degree but currently is taking timeout from academic study. Juggling studies and rugby was always a challenge but writing his undergraduate dissertation during his first Six Nations' campaign, he says, was 'interesting'!

The summer of 2008 saw the young international switch allegiances and Newcastle Falcons' loss is Leicester Tigers' gain as he moved to the East Midlands for the start of the 2008–2009 domestic campaign.

It comes as no surprise that the likeable character has fitted into the Leicester way of things easily, with strong performances that have helped his team head their Heineken Cup group and hold their position near the top of the Guinness Premiership. These performances have also kept him in the England picture and, after Danny Cipriani's difficult autumn international series, Toby's start against the All Blacks put him top of the current fly-half pecking order. Injury prevented him starting England's 2009 Six Nations' campaign, with Brive-based Andy Goode brought into the fold, but as soon as was possible the Leicester Tiger was again starting at 10 and playing with a fluidity that has him very much in the mind of Lions selectors.

Personal desire and ambition keep him focused and moving forward with his game. 'To be honest I want to be best I can be. I know it sounds stupid but the only thing that's going to limit me is me. It's that desire to go out and achieve the most you can. Whether that best of me is now with 21 caps and it's finished, or it is that I can go on and play for England for the next ten years and get on a couple of Lions tours and all that sort of stuff ... that would be unbelievable, but who knows? The desire is there.

'There's been great support from the people in the England squad as well as at Newcastle Falcons to help me be the best that I can be. Blackie [Steve Black] said, "Do the best and be the best you can be." I can only give the best of me and see what happens. You know, if that is good enough to play international rugby and do these things, then fantastic. But if it's not, then I can totally deal with it. If I have disappointments I'll go and work even harder, keep putting my hand up and try to perform the way I want to perform.

'I'm ambitious and want to be in a place where I can enjoy rugby, develop as a player as well as a person and surround myself with good people. I have no real ambitions outside rugby. I am very happy to do what I'm doing and at the right time crack on with a master's degree but I have no idea as to the subject.'

The advice Toby would give aspiring young rugby players is to enjoy growing up and be what you want to be. 'I believe that cream rises to the top and if you're desperate to do it, then get cracking and work hard. However, we are all different and you could be the guy who recognises that you enjoy rugby but excel in other things. You may be fantastic in class so just allow yourself to be whatever you want to be. Work hard at whatever motivates you and see where it takes you.'

2008–2009 Season Update

I really felt for a young man that I know very well at the end of the season. As he left the field injured near the end of the Heineken Cup semi final against the Cardiff Blues, he had guided his team to a winning position. He would have hoped to shake off the injury and take his place in the Leicester team in the upcoming Premiership and Heineken Cup finals but it was not to be. The shattering news soon came that the injury was a major problem requiring surgery that will keep Toby out for a significant part of the 2009–10 season. It is the nature of the sport but two major finals were missed. There must have been tears!

Toby Flood: Statistics	
Date of birth	8 August 1985
Birthplace	Frimley
Height	1.88m
Weight	92kg
Position	fly half; centre
School / university	King's School, Tynemouth; Northumbria University
Present club	Leicester Tigers
Previous clubs	Newcastle Falcons; Morpeth; Alnwick
Nicknames	Floody; Pob; Girls Legs
Favourite TV show	*Entourage*
Favourite film	*Gladiator*
Favourite music	Red Hot Chili Peppers
Favourite book	*The Godfather*
Favourite food	chicken salad
Most like to meet...	Ben Woods (Leicester Tigers player) girlfriend
Least like to meet...	Geoff Parling (Newcastle Falcons)
Best moment in rugby	Newcastle Falcons and England debuts
Favourite place to visit	The Peth (Morpeth)
I love...	watching Geoff Parling run
I hate...	mushrooms

CHRIS PATERSON

Scotland; Edinburgh

To stand at Carter Bar on the Anglo-Scottish border looking out over Carter Fell and the Cheviot Hills is simply breathtaking. It is one of the most beautiful places in the United Kingdom but this rugged landscape provided the backdrop to a period of history from the late thirteenth century to the sixteenth century that was characterised by frequent warring between England and Scotland. The families on both sides of the border were caught up in the nationalist feuding as passing armies created havoc. Crops were destroyed, livestock stolen, dwellings torched and people murdered or dispersed.

It was the time of the Border Reivers, people who had a strong affinity to clan or family and raided cattle and sheep to survive these troubled times. Border people clung on to their sense of identity and culture and still today retain a strong-willed independence and distinctive character borne out of the determination to preserve their lands during this 300-year feud.

This heritage and strong sense of community is seen today in the Common Ridings – annual mounted processions around the Border towns' boundaries to commemorate times past when local men risked their lives in order to protect their town and people. Over the years local poets and writers have used their daily encounters and experiences to write stories and ballads inspired by every aspect of Border life, from the shepherds, supernatural folklore, love and romance to the plundering and pillage by the Reivers.

In the Border town of Galashiels the Braw Lads Gathering is the town's Common Riding celebration, the name being taken from 'Braw Lads o' Gala Water', a poem by Robbie Burns. The poem is the story of a lass who doesn't think that the men from other towns match her lad from Gala Water!

The first recorded reference to the town was in 1124, during the reign of David I, and from its long history the town can boast some famous sons, but in relation to rugby it is Chris Paterson, the current Scottish record cap holder and points scorer, who could be considered the current Braw Lad o' Gala Water.

Galashiels holds a special place in the heart of the Scottish international who now plays and lives in Edinburgh but can be seen scuttling back to his Border roots whenever possible. A trend started at the time of his birth. 'I was actually born in Edinburgh. At the time the Borders only had a small military hospital, basically a wooden shed built during the war so for mums-to-be it was either Peel Hospital or, if you had time, Edinburgh. Mum had time so I was born in Leith but taken straight back to Gala.

'We lived in Galashiels and the whole family is from there. Dad was a lithographer and ended up manager of a printing company. Mum worked for granddad, who had an engineering firm, Morrison Murray. She was the accounts person and was a Morrison before she married Dad.

'Mum and Dad built a house on my grandparents' land, in their garden. When I came home from school my gran would look after me and I would go out to play in the garden with the rugby ball. My parents are still there. It was a great time. I absolutely loved school and had loads of friends. I would get upset or take the huff because I did not want to go back after Christmas or the summer holidays, but looking back I'd take that over going into work on a Monday morning after a defeat!'

Rugby is a big part of Border town life and community and it is no surprise that the sports-mad youngster gravitated towards the town club. It was the world-renowned Melrose Sevens of 1996 that marked the beginning of Chris's playing days with the senior Gala side. Gala Wanderers, the town's youth team, had provided the rugby for the recently turned 18-year-old but a Monday-evening phone call set him on the road to the top of the sport.

'It was Sevens time up at the Borders and the phone went. It was the senior Gala side and they asked me to come into training as they'd like to look at me for the weekend. So I went to training on the Tuesday and Thursday and, lo and behold, here I am just turned 18 in the first-round game for Gala against Hawick. I played at standoff and I absolutely loved it.

'Tony Stanger was playing for Hawick, and other players like that were in the tournament, so here I am still at school on the Friday, playing Sevens on the Saturday and school on the Monday! At the time I actually had a part-time job washing dishes and making starters in a restaurant at Gattonside, which is right next to Melrose, over the River Tweed. So I am playing in the Sevens in the afternoon and then across the road four hours later behind the sink washing dishes. If we'd have made the final I'd have been sacked!'

Two seasons of senior rugby followed in Scottish Division Two but it was the third season in 1998–1999, the year before he signed a professional contract, that was a significant time in the development of the Scottish international. That season is packed full of happy memories and success. From talking to Chris it strikes me that the thirst for success and a strong sense of personal responsibility for individual performance come from this pivotal season. Something clicked that gave the confidence that said: I can make it to the top.

'In the 1998–1999 season Gala was getting quite serious. They had a good team and we were really going to go for it this year. At that time the super districts didn't have many fixtures so the international players were going back and forwards and playing every now and again for their clubs. Gala were still in Division Two but we had a great bunch of blokes and we just knew something great was happening up at the club that year. We'd signed Nathan Hines from Australia and he was world-class and only a year older than me.

'The first game of the season was against Dundee High School at Netherdale. Nathan had flown in on the Friday morning from Australia and then played on the Saturday. The very first kick went up and the receiver missed it as this guy came in for a one-handed catch and we thought, crikey, we've got a good one here!'

'That season we played some brilliant stuff with Gala and won the Division Two Championship. We also got to the final of the Scottish Cup with all of the First Division clubs involved. There was a real buzz and the whole town was behind us.

'We played Kelso in the final of the Scottish Cup and we were three points down pretty much the whole game. I'd played OK but, because I'd played for Scotland Under 21s, I sort of knew people were looking to me and I remember thinking, "It's your stage." Although it was pretty much a dull game, with two minutes to go I scored a try. There were 10,000 up from Gala, so it's 5–3 and it's bonkers at Murrayfield. The game kicked off again, we got back up the field and I dropped a goal.

'From not playing that well I'd scored a try, dropped a goal and been made 'Man of the Match' with all the hoo-ha that goes with it, but I knew myself that I could have played better.

'The following week there was a dinner in Edinburgh where Gala was honoured as 'Team of the Year'. A few of us were there, Gary Parker, Craig Townsend, David Gray, Tom Weir and Nathan Hines, but the dinner went on for ages. The next day it was the Melrose Sevens tournament and nobody was drinking, but it was Gary who turned round and said, 'What a great year but wouldn't it be funny if we won tomorrow? We all burst out laughing because it was very late and we were the first tie on. I don't know what happened that day but we just clicked.

'I still like to think of it as one of my favourite days because everything just went so well. I don't know how I played like that. I think it's the best I've ever played in my whole life. I scored a 100-metre try in the final and all this sort of stuff. We won the Melrose Sevens and I was just thinking, "What the hell's happening?!"

'I remember walking down the road to college in Edinburgh on the Monday and my whole world had changed because I had finally agreed to turn professional. I was just so happy.'

The Borderer's time with his home-town club had started with the Melrose Sevens and ended three years later at the same tournament and a startlingly successful professional career was just beginning. The upbringing in that close-knit Galashiels community and the sibling competition in rugby brought out the strong-willed independence and distinctive character typical of Border folk and also gave him his nickname that sticks to this day – Mossy. 'My brother David thought I looked like a cartoon character from the TV, a dinosaur called Mosschops. I don't know but it's stuck with me ever since.'

A Gala man called Johnny Gray became Mossy's first rugby coach. There was not much rugby at Langlee Primary School but each year there was a sevens tournament where each ward would enter a team. Chris's brother David, who is three years older than him, wanted to enter a team and this led to the contact with Johnny. 'A Gala man, Johnny Gray, was a bit of a local favourite. He's a rugby man within the town. He played for the South of Scotland and his son is Richie Gray, the former Scottish international. So Dad told my brother to see Johnny and he took the Under 12s and Under 10s sessions. We trained every Saturday morning for the one tournament of the year. It gave you a focus and that's how I got started in the game.'

The Patersons were a sporting family with dad, Dave, playing rugby for Gala and uncle Duncan being capped by Scotland. Rugby is an important aspect of Border life and Chris and his brother grew up around Netherdale, the home of Gala RFC. They would go along with mum, Lynn, to watch their dad play and as the brothers got involved in youth rugby Mum did the teas.

Although it was Dad that played rugby the competitive edge in the young Patersons came as much from their mum as their dad. 'Mum was a competitive and keen hockey player. When I got my first cap for Scotland it was also Paul Burnell's 50th cap, which was a nice touch. Mum was at Murrayfield and, as it happens, was sitting next to Paul's wife, who didn't know her from anyone else. So for the first half of the game Paul's wife suffered my mum digging her arms into her and pushing her as she lived the game! She was safe in the second half when we changed ends and some other unfortunate on the other side got the treatment ... probably my dad!

'I was very lucky; I grew up in a sporty family. In the Borders it was mainly rugby; it was just what people did but I'd play anything. I'd pick up a racket when tennis was on the television and pick up the darts at Christmas when that was on television. I played cricket and I loved a game of football with my mates, but football wasn't really a big part of Borders life. I'd play anything though, as long as I was active and outside.'

As Chris moved into high school at Galashiels Academy, schools rugby became more structured with first- and second-year teams, an Under 15 team for the third and fourth years and an Under 18s team for the fifth and sixth years. Once players got to the Under 18s team there was also the possibility of playing for Gala Wanderers, the town's Under 18 youth team.

It was usual for the players to turn out for the school in the morning and then the club in the afternoon, something that would be frowned upon in today's world, but having done exactly the same myself in the North-East of England it was certainly character building and great fun.

'When you got to 17 or 18 you played for the school Under 18s in the morning and then you played for the Gala Wanderers' Under 18s in the afternoon, which Johnny Gray also coached. They played in the South District League against the likes of Hawick PSA, Hawick Wanderers, Kelso Harlequins, Selkirk Youth Club and others. It was completely different to school rugby even though you'd play the same players give or take three or four who had left school early.

'The school team was always good rugby; you were well looked after and it was nice. Then an hour and a half later you'd play Under 18 club rugby against basically the same players and you were fighting and scrapping. It was really hard Border youth rugby. To compare the two was like comparing night and day but the combination of the two was brilliant, and now I think that's missing.

'You always had the discipline at school and you had it at the club, too, but at the club the guys were 18, there was drink on the bus and we were fighting and battering each other in the games. It was hard Borders rugby with a hard ethic to win. The town would come out to watch. If Gala senior side weren't at home then the locals would come and watch the Gala Wanderers. It was real, meaningful rugby.'

Representative rugby in those days was also complicated with dual school and club systems operating but this broad base gave a lot of opportunities for players to be seen. The young fly half gained representative honours through the schools system when in his final school year he made the South of Scotland Under 18s side and then Scottish Schools, where an enduring friendship with Gordon Ross started. Gordon at that time was ahead in the pecking order, with Mossy playing understudy, but due to injury it was not long before the opportunity to play came along.

That opportunity came in a Scottish Schools game against Scottish Youth and following that his first cap came against Irish Schools in Cork. This was a very different environment to be in and a one that massively excited the 17-year-old. 'I just wanted to represent my country, to play at as high a level as I could. I mean even then I was setting myself goals. When you reached a goal it wasn't as if that was it; I would set myself higher targets. I wanted to play Scottish Schools... Well, right, I have done that now – I want to try to be the best player in the Scottish Schools.

'I can't remember many nerves; it was more excitement but perhaps it's being 17 years old and half daft! I was massively excited.

'When I played for Galashiels Academy there was obviously a huge spectrum of ability and desire to play because there were a lot of good players at school but also players who felt they had to. If you did not play you would not go on the school's Canada tour! But the first thing I noticed when you came to play for Scottish Schools was that everyone had the ability and the desire to play so the whole thing had a totally different aura about it. We had the likes of Jason White, Marcus di Rollo, Gordon Ross in the squad so a lot came through together. I remember Jason being absolutely massive and thinking how the hell could he be 17 years old!

'At that time rugby wasn't over-coached and analysed. You just went out and made decisions on your feet and the guys around you just reacted to that. You had a pure game and in many ways there was less to worry about. The questions were out there but so were the answers and you just played the game.'

The second cap was a match to forget against a massive England side at Hawick where Scotland were to all intents and purposes blown away by a much bigger and more physical England pack with the likes of Lewis Moody and the future Scottish international Ross Beattie in its ranks.

At the end of that 1996 season Scottish Schools embarked on a tour to South Africa and the young fly half had a fantastic experience of intense rugby and seeing professionalism up close as they followed the All Blacks and played curtain-raisers to their international games. 'I managed to get selected for that tour and that was a brilliant experience for many reasons.

165

One was the touring experience of being in South Africa. The rugby was so intense and totally different to anything I'd experienced before, but I think the most important thing was that we shadowed the All Blacks as they were touring in 1996 too. We played curtain-raisers to their four Tri Nations games. We played at Newlands, Loftus and Kings Park and so there were big crowds at these games.

'We were rubbing shoulders with these guys. From the World Cup in 1995, watching Jonah Lomu on TV to ten months later, we were with these guys in the airport and warming up and playing on the same field as them. It was a brilliant experience. It was a really successful tour. We played Bowland and then South Eastern Transvaal at a place called Whitbank. We were an Under 18 Schools team and they put out an Under 23 side against us so it was just fighting, getting on with it, and we won. Gogsy Ross kicked a winning penalty.

'Gogsy was the captain and he was outstanding. I played fly half in the midweek games and then sat on the bench for the Saturday games when Gogsy played. He was definitely the pick of the bunch and a really, really good friend. We were young lads living together on tour for six weeks or so, then beating this big South African side who were men and just wanted to kill us, it was great. I think that tour gave a lot of us the desire to move forward with our rugby. It was a highlight for me.'

In this period when Chris's representative rugby was taking off he was a pupil at the Galashiels Academy and a very happy pupil surrounded by staff that were as sports-mad as he was. Rob Moffat, who was his PE teacher and now a coach at Edinburgh, Davy Wright and principal teacher, Bill Noble, were all big influences on the young man. 'I just loved secondary school. It was one of the happiest times of my life; I just loved it because it was sport mad and I was being active. We'd train for rugby at lunchtime and after school and then when we'd get to the athletic season there would be speed work at lunchtime and then long jump etc. after school and javelin or whatever we wanted to do.

'You could choose not to do this if you weren't active or heavily involved in sport but it was there if you wanted it. Thinking back it was quite cruel for the people who didn't play sport you know; they might want to do English or something but it was a popular sporting culture that drove the school, which for me was great.

'I was quite quiet at school and studied pretty hard, but sport did get in the way sometimes. If I had homework to do I'd do it but it was different with sport. With my rugby I wanted to be the best and that's it, but with homework I'd want to do it as quickly as possible and get it out of the way! It was totally the opposite. I'd run home from school and get my homework done and then be out. Whether that's right or wrong I'm not sure but that's what I did!'

For his Highers Chris took Maths, English, Geography, Chemistry and Biology and got them all with varying grades – A for Geography, Bs for Maths and Biology and Cs for English and Chemistry.

The summer of 1996 was an important time for Mossy but, with his debut for Gala in the Melrose Sevens, his Highers safely under his belt and a successful Scottish Schools tour to South Africa completed, he moved to Edinburgh to start life as a PE student at Morray House College with his big pal Gogsy Ross in the same class.

To many who suffer the trials and tribulations of difficult daily commute a journey of 75 minutes or so may seem inconsequential but the characteristics of a Borderer were evident in the feelings of the youngster as he moved to the big city. 'Although Edinburgh's close to Gala, about an hour and a quarter in the car, in lots of ways it seemed very different; there were just totally different values being a Borders and a city person. You grow up disliking each other. Every time a city team came to play at school in Gala there was a real difference. Excepting all of that it was brilliant. I loved the college and the course and had a great time.

'With my rugby at Gala I was travelling up and down the road every week for training Tuesdays and Thursdays and then back at the weekends for games. So it was really funny when my mum and dad dropped me off the others were saying, 'I'll see you at Christmas' and I was saying 'I'll be home for tea on Tuesday, Mum!'

The next three years were a busy time as Chris's studies went well at Morray House but his rugby had him clocking up the miles between Galashiels and Edinburgh. Chris was establishing himself in senior rugby at Gala but at times it was difficult with performances not matching personal expectations. By his own admission, the young fly half was not playing well and Gala were struggling to win games against teams with international players in their ranks. If it had not been for the leagues in Scotland being restructured with no team to be relegated from Division Two it would have been Gala for the drop.

However, against this difficult background the Gala coaching staff saw potential in their young fly half and he played the full season. Getting game time was important in terms of his development as a player but Chris's physical condition was also a cause for some concern. Help was at hand, however, from a leading Newcastle Falcons player who to this day takes his training as seriously as any professional sportsman, Alan Tait.

Taity is another proud Borderer from Kelso who had made his mark not only in Rugby Union but also in Rugby League and he was big pals with the Gala coach, Gary Calendar. 'Fair play to Gary Calendar, he said, "You're in and you're playing, you'll learn." He was getting a bit of stick at that time, though we couldn't get relegated, and he looked after me quite well. He saw that I was a bit frail and clubs at that time didn't have weights rooms or fitness coaches so after one game on a Saturday he said, "Meet me on Sunday." I thought, "Oh God, what's this all about?" but I met him in the car and he said, "I'm going to take you to see somebody," and it was Alan Tait.

'Taity was brilliant. I knew of him but I didn't actually know him. He said that he had been a bit frail but had played Rugby League and done weights to build himself up. He gave me a training programme and advice on supplements and said, "Do this, this and this, and hopefully it will build you up," and it did, it made me stronger. Taity was up at Newcastle at the time and it was just before the Lions tour in 1997.

'So what a day! We've worked together with Scotland for quite a while now and know each other well but at the time I just thought, good on you, a British Lion giving his time up to talk to me!'

Although the club season was not great, representative honours still came along with South of Scotland Under 19s and Scotland Under 19s and the carrot of the Under 19 FIRA World Cup in Argentina in the summer of 1997.

Frank Hadden, the current Scotland coach, was coach to the Under 19s and it was during this competition that the young Borderer's versatility was utilised by the national side as a small squad coped with the demands of the competition. Standoff against Portugal, outside centre against Ireland, fullback against Italy and wing in the final game, which was the fifth, sixth playoff match against South Africa. 'In the Under 19 World Cup I played four games in four different positions and played the full 80 minutes in each game. Gordon Ross was the first choice standoff and he was better in that position than me and I was just happy to play. That was the start of me moving around. I'd never played those positions before.'

It was on that tour with Scotland that the first signs of a different approach brought about by the professional era started being evident. Dietary advice, strength and conditioning programmes and even the advice of a sports psychologist were introduced into the national age group set-up, with the FIRA squad of 1997 being the first to benefit. The advice was filtering down to the new crop of elite players, but that is what it was, advice, and no monitoring systems were in place to see how effectively it was being applied. It was up to the players as to whether they bought into the ideas or not.

'I took it very seriously. I was lucky because I was at Morray House with Gogsy so we'd get on with the weights and do the speed work at the back. I enjoyed the next season, which was my second season with Gala, and I took the advice from the Scotland guys into my training. I always took pride on being really fit, not carrying weight, having a good diet and not drinking. For Gala in pre-season there would be guys who were in their thirties and there were a lot of guys in the middle maybe carrying a bit of weight, who had been to work all day and were a bit tired. I was 18, wanted to work hard, do the right things and be as fit as possible. I didn't want to shout about it but I took this attitude into training and I remember taking my own water bottle to training and they're thinking, "What's he doing!"

'A new coach, Gary Parker, came on board and he said something I'll never forget. Gary sat me down in the bar at Netherdale after a Thursday-night training session and said, "I've never done this with a player before, but don't worry, we're picking you, bad games, whatever, you're starting at 10."

'He told me to just go out there and play. I genuinely felt a massive weight lift from my shoulders. I think the kind of person I am, I wanted to show him that I wasn't taking it for granted, so I worked doubly hard. I had a really good season and Gala did pretty well. We won the Border League and I felt much more confident.'

The Scotland representative system once again recognised the development of the young Gala fly half, but the harsh reality of the regional representative system is remembered with fondness and humour in equal measure. Goodness only knows what the Health and Safety police would make of it these days. 'South of Scotland Under 21s was really enjoyable. We'd kick all kinds of stuff out of each other at Hawick, Selkirk, Jed and Melrose. It was violence really on a Saturday afternoon and then on the Sunday morning you'd all be training together. I remember Derek Turnbull, a former Scottish back rower, was one of the coaches and he'd save his empty milk cartons from during the week and fill them with water for the training session!

'We were a strange mix, with some of the guys on the bevvy the night before! You'd get to training and the majority of the guys would be saying, "Oh I don't feel like training. I feel rough!" Bearing in mind half the guys were feeling rough, training, then drinking water out of stale milk cartons, that sort of thing made us stick together and have that Border attitude. We won the Under 21 Championship that year and, the following year, we beat everybody.'

For the National Under 21 side it was again injury to Gordon Ross that gave Chris his opportunity when aged 19 against Wales. Gogsy had started against France and Ireland but the Wales game proved to be a memorable occasion for Chris who scored all of Scotland's points in the first away win by the Under 21s. The game was played at Langwern Steelworks after Caerphilly was deemed unplayable after horrendous rain led to a waterlogged pitch.

The game was also an important marker in the sibling rivalry between Chris and his brother David and reinforced the belief that being a professional rugby player was within his grasp. 'My brother played a lot of rugby and he was, and still is, the youngest player to play for Gala at 16 years and so many days. He played Scotland Under 18s, 19s and 21s and I had always wanted to better him, so I thought I have to at least be an Under 21 international.

'I was more nervous playing in the 21s than in the 19s. I was desperate to play well, to prove to David Leslie and Roy Laidlaw, the coaches, that I could do it. It was the first time ever that I thought of the possibility of rugby becoming a job. It was a whole close link, a short jump between the 21s and the full national side. Some of the guys I played with the previous year at Under 21 were now playing international rugby, like Scott Murray,

'After the Wales game I kept my place for the last game in the championship against England up here. We were beaten but it was a close game. Scotland A won the Grand Slam that year and we were the curtain-raiser to that game at Stewart's Melville's ground. I was really, really happy with the way we played and it was very close but Michael Horak scored an interception try to win the game at the end.

'I was playing 10 and was meant to play against Jonny Wilkinson. We'd heard that he was exceptional but he was pulled out of the game and put on the bench for the senior team against Scotland. The goal was no longer wanting to be the best player at Gala, it was to get a job. The Under 21s offered the chance and you worked hard. For me being a professional player became a bit of a target.'

The following season again brought Under 21 representation and the pleasure of steering Gala to the Division Two title, winning the Scottish Cup and the Melrose Sevens, but that season also gave him the opportunity to sample professional rugby with the big boys as he made two appearances for the newly formed Glasgow Caledonian Reds with a debut against Ulster in September 1998.

This season was a pivotal point in Chris's life, with important decisions to be made. However, the reality was that the decisions were easy. The Edinburgh Reivers coach was Ian Rankin and he had talked to the young fly half a couple of times and put an offer of a professional contract on the table but no decisions were made. Edinburgh came back after the Melrose Sevens and that offer went up. It was decision time.

'The course at Moray House was a four-year Honours course and it was quite different to any other course because you'd get nothing unless you did your four years. I got the chance to go professional after three years and I had a difficult decision to make. I spoke to the Principal at the University, Arwynn Williams, a keen rugby man whom I've kept in touch with, and I asked him what I should do.

He shook his head and said, "Go for it." He said, "If you've got a chance to be a professional sportsman then go for it and never, ever look back." So I walked in his office and then walked out a minute later and said, "right, decision made."

I knew that the format of the course was changing and that if I wanted to finish it I would have to come back within three years. It wasn't like I could wait ten years and go back to my degree, so that added a spanner to the works, but I was delighted. I knew deep down that's what I wanted to do.

'Not long after that, maybe two weeks, the Scotland squad for the pre-World Cup South Africa tour was announced. I'd never really considered it but the manager, Dougie Morgan, phoned me and said, "You're coming on the tour." It was an uncapped tour, though it was a full tour except for a test match against the Springboks.

'At that time I was living with my flatmates. We were all in our third year and they were working flat out for their course. I thought, well, you don't know what's going to happen, even though they were drawing up the contracts and stuff, so I sat down and finished all my assignments and essays after I'd made my decision to leave. For the sake of my flatmates and also for the sake of not looking a fool if it all went wrong, I sat down and finished all the work at the end of the three years, then just walked away.

'A week later on the day I flew with the squad to South Africa I signed for Edinburgh.'

> **A word or phrase to describe you at 21 years of age?**
>
> So happy...
>
> It sounds really twee but I was just so happy. Everything was just going so well.

As the newly contracted professional took his seat on the plane to South Africa his only exposure to professional rugby had been two appearances for Glasgow Caledonian Reds but on that uncapped tour he got his first Scotland start as a fullback against Mpumalanga.

On his return to Edinburgh pre-season training made the new

professional realise that his game needed to step up a level if he was going to be successful, as he again became a little fish in a much bigger pond. Pre-season culminated in a couple of warm-up games – one being against Gloucester at Kingsholm. Mossy was playing reasonably well and scored all of Edinburgh's points that Saturday but the events of the following Monday held further surprises.

'I was staying at Gala at the time – I was actually down at Netherdale when I got a call from Mum. She said that Dougie Morgan had been on the phone for me. It was that night that the Scotland players were going to be told if they were in the World Cup squad but I did not know that. I remember I was thinking, that's strange, but my dad must have had an inkling because he kept saying, "phone him back, phone him back!"

'I tried and tried, but obviously he was phoning around because his phone was engaged all the time. My dad was saying the World Cup squad's being announced so you must be on standby, but I am sure he was thinking why would he be phoning on a Monday night. Sure enough, I was in the squad and thinking what ever will happen next!'

With only two practice games for Edinburgh under his belt the youngster went on the pre-World Cup Canadian tour, was involved in two warm-up games against Romania and Argentina, and was included in the actual World Cup squad. Scotland's first two games in the tournament were against South Africa and Uruguay, but it was a rather nervous fullback who made his international debut against Spain.

'I was a wee bit nervous as the circumstances were a little strange. The games against Uruguay and Spain were so close to each other. I think one was on the Tuesday and the other on the Saturday. So the week before, the team management decided to announce to the players two teams, one to play Uruguay and, if no injuries and all went OK, then the team that will play Spain. They told us both at the same time.

'I was named for my first cap for the second game against Spain. I knew a fortnight before the game and, of course, you're not allowed to tell anybody else except your mum and dad. So that probably made me a bit more nervous because it was a long time coming and I was picked to play fullback. It was only about the fifth time I'd ever played there.

'I thoroughly enjoyed the game and we won 49–0. It wasn't hugely intense but it was my first cap.'

With that first cap tucked away, the focus changed to Edinburgh and the newly formed Scottish-Welsh League, an environment that was tough in lots of ways. 'We'd be on the bus every fortnight to Cardiff, Swansea, Llanelli, but also to the likes of Dunvants, Caerphilly, etc. To be honest we weren't very good and we didn't win away from home, probably because of the long bus journeys, but it gave us regular games and spawned the Celtic League. We did that for two years and it was a hard time but we felt we had to do it to be accepted, I suppose, by the Welsh guys.'

With Edinburgh, Chris was still playing fly half but Ian McGeechan, the Scotland coach, wanted him to play fullback, and the Edinburgh coaches at the time, Ian Rankin and Bob Easson, went along with the request.

His performances at fullback were catching the eye and further international honours were not far away. The Borderer played for Scotland A against Italy and Ireland as the full national side stuttered in the Six Nations campaign of 2000, actually losing for the first time to Italy. Next up was a Murrayfield encounter against France and this provided the opportunity for Chris to feel he had actually arrived as an international player. 'It was my second cap and was a big game against France in the Six Nations at Murrayfield. Although it was my second cap, I treat it mentally as my first cap. Scotland had not been doing well and I think they thought, we'll give Chris Paterson a shot, so I was called up.'

It is at these emotionally intense moments that top-level performers step over the line. The inner resolve and determination of the young fullback gave him the confidence to prove to everyone and most especially himself that he could do it at the top level. 'In the tunnel I was just so excited. I think as I have gotten older I get more nervous before games but back then it was pure excitement. As a young player you can get away with a lot more; there is less pressure and expectation. I remember thinking I am going to do it, to prove that I can be the best player out there.

'We lost but not badly, by two or three tries, but I got "Man of the Match", took over kicking duties and I thought, I can do this. It was just so exciting.'

The next week it was Wales in Cardiff and, although reasonably happy with his own performance, it was another loss that set up the Wooden Spoon encounter against the English going for the Grand Slam on Sunday, 2 April 2000 at Murrayfield. I remember that weekend very well as I coached England Students Under 19s who beat their Scottish counterparts at Edinburgh University's playing fields on the Saturday lunchtime. That game was played in brilliant sunshine but the weather forecast all week had been indicating that a change was on the way. That change came on the morning of the full international and it lashed it down!

'We beat them 19–13 at Murrayfield but I didn't touch the ball; it was lashing down, flooded. I didn't play well but it didn't matter – we beat England! It was the usual 15 Braveheart heroes stuff. I knew I hadn't played well and I was at fault for the try because I went on the wrong side defensively from a five-metre scrum. Dallaglio probably saw it and picked up. I should have been in that side.

'In a lot of people's eyes all that mattered was we won, but to me I knew I hadn't played well and I didn't enjoy it... Well, I did enjoy it but I could have done better.'

That game was Mossy's fourth cap and a lot of rugby has been played in the intervening years for Scotland, Edinburgh and a year in the English Premiership with Gloucester. However, one team missing from that list is the British and Irish Lions, and the fullback's omission from Sir Clive Woodward's squad in 2005 certainly raised some eyebrows and for the player was extremely disappointing.

How players cope with disappointment is a very individual thing but the Borderer has his own personal coping mechanism. 'I only have two emotions basically – I'm either happy or angry. I'm not an emotional guy as in teary or affectionate – I'm either happy or angry – so, if I play badly or am disappointed, I get angry. I keep it to myself but it inspires me to do more and work harder.

'Thinking about the Lions there was the 2001 tour; I was playing for Scotland at the time so you know you're in with a shout. I got into the extended squad but I knew I wasn't good enough. Basically I played well in the first season for Scotland but in the second season in 2001 I struggled a wee bit. The Lions were to tour Australia and Scotland played Australia at Murrayfield. They were way ahead of us and we were beaten heavily. They had the likes of Joe Roff, Stephen

Larkham and Chris Latham and you felt these guys were pretty good. Obviously you check the announcements because you're an international player, but even if I'd gone I knew I would struggle to get into the test team; I'd play and do my best but it would be pretty tough.

'2005 was a real disappointment because it was probably the best I've played in the Six Nations. I had a run at fullback in every game and I felt I'd played really quite well in a team that wasn't winning. I was happy with my performances and that's why I felt I had a chance because sometimes it's easier to play well in a good team, a winning team. I didn't take the huff... I was just really angry. Angry with myself – thinking, what else could I have done? Did I do something wrong?

'The day the squad was announced I had a player appearance for the SRU at the airport and the media were there congratulating me, just taking it for granted almost that I'd been selected. That was tough but at the time the anger drove me on and I went on tour to Romania with Scotland and played pretty well too.'

That major omission aside, Chris's achievements have set the bar at a level that few will even aspire to, let alone pass:

- On 27 November 2004 he became the youngest ever Scottish player to earn 50 caps when aged 26.

- In 2005 he was named the BBC's 'Fullback of the Six Nations'.

- Statistically he is the best goal kicker in international rugby, having successfully kicked an astonishing 107 penalties and conversions from his last 120 attempts.

- On 7 June 2008, in the tour game against Argentina, he overtook Gavin Hastings' longstanding Scotland points record of 667. His current total stands at 687.

- The following weekend he became Scotland's most capped player when, on 14 June 2008, he won his 88th cap and was 'Man of the Match' in Scotland's 26–14 victory over Argentina in Buenos Aires.

Some would be happy to dine out on this list of achievements, but again the determination and inner strength so typical of Border folk comes to the surface. Chris still thinks he has much to achieve.

A word or phrase to describe you now?

Frustrated...

As I get older I get more frustrated. It's difficult to explain and I don't want to get too deep, but with rugby there's no end point to improved performance. You play in order to get better and you aim for this perfect game, which is unrealistic but sometimes you almost get there. You get a great result, you play well and you'll be 'Man of the Match' but then you know the next goal needs to move you on. It's frustrating because you are always pushing yourself further, knowing that you can never get there.

I have always set myself goals that I have worked hard to achieve but I always want more. I wanted to be the most capped player and I am, but you want more. I wanted to be the highest points scorer and I am, but now I want more.

You would have thought I would have been absolutely delighted to have reached the caps and points record and I am, but because I want more I can't enjoy it.

It's all frustrating.

Maybe for the most capped Scottish international it is the ever-increasing expectations he places on himself that characterises the man. People who are successful in all walks of life tend to be their own biggest critics and at times maybe the simplicity of times past offer refuge from and possibly inspiration to embrace the demands of performance at the highest levels. 'There is such a lot of pressure surrounding games these days that sometimes I think it would be great to get back to how simple it was ten years ago.

'The pressures are obviously different and I've been through a lot since I was 21. There have been good times and there have been bad times. Sometimes it doesn't go well and maybe, because you're

177

older, more experienced and reasonably high profile, you're a target. I find I can play really well and have one mistake and I've had a bad game.

'When things don't go so well people want change and sometimes people just automatically assume because you're older and been around for a while that it's time for someone else to come along. That frustrates me because I'm still driven to improve and I've never been fitter, all of my test results show that.

'As I'm getting older I recognise that I'm putting more pressure on myself. I'm not sure if it's because the clock's ticking or if it's that my self-analysis is changing, but if I play badly, or if I play well but make one or two mistakes, I lie awake and think about the mistakes but at the same time I'm also thinking, what am I doing? –this isn't doing any good.

'I suppose it would be great to get back to my happiest times in rugby and I'm trying to adopt the mindset I had when I was 21.'

As I write this Chris is at Scotland's training camp in La Manga, Spain, ahead of the 2008 autumn internationals. New Zealand are the first visitors to Murrayfield on 8 November and the game will give Chris the opportunity to push the bar to even higher levels in terms of caps, points and tries. His next target is two more tries to equal the current record of 24, jointly held by Tony Stanger and my namesake, Ian Smith. At 30 years of age there is a lot of rugby left in that Galashiels body together with a lot of ambition and desire.

'I do have an ambition to reach the highest level I can. If I think back to how I was feeling during my time at Gala, how I improved from my first to the third season. I think I achieved what I could achieve, being the best I could in that environment, and then moving to Edinburgh and starting again and then up to international bracket and starting again.

'I still don't think I've reached my best yet and I hope that doesn't sound big-headed, because that's the last thing I ever want to be, but I have just a huge desire and work ethic. It's something I desperately want to do, to play better for Scotland. I've had good games and had bad games, but I want to play better than I've ever played before.

'I'm not sure it is attainable – perhaps you're always chasing that perfect game – but I think I can play better, contribute more. I suppose if the desire is there and you're working for it you might get there but if it's not there then perhaps it's time to move on, to go. You've given it your best shot, done your best, but if it stops happening you have to move on.

'Every time I go out I want to prove to everybody I'm the best I can be, and if I stop doing that I'll not be able to live with myself!'

Chris married Claire, his 'braw lass o Gala', in the summer and time outside of rugby is precious. The travelling, tours, training camps and so on all take chunks out of the clock, but family is important to the Patersons. 'One of the things that has changed massively through the years is the time you spend at rugby. These days I'm out the house half eight and back half four to 5 p.m. every day and it's only ten minutes to Murrayfield. The day after a game it's recovery and there's training and a lot more analysis now and travel. You're not just turning up on the bus; you're flying the day before. What I'm trying to do is switch off when I'm away from it.

'You try to get away from rugby and not think about it but it's difficult because our day off may be a Wednesday or Thursday and your mates, the guys I played rugby with at Gala, they all work and they get Saturday off, so it's hard. We try to stay in touch with our families. My brother is married with a family. They have a daughter aged two and live in Glasgow, so we see them as much as we can. My mum and dad and Claire's mum, dad, brother and sister all live in Gala. We're all pretty close.

'In the summer I play golf and try to get out and be active. I sound boring but I don't really have any hobbies... I probably need one! I'm a guy who likes to devote myself to one thing. Some guys study but I'd feel I was cheating my rugby.'

For someone who is so obviously committed and enthusiastic about his sport the thought of coming off the Murrayfield turf for club and country for the last time is a reality that will need to be faced up to but, for the present, the focus is still on playing. 'I suppose I want to be able to finish in three or four years' time and say right, draw a line under it. You've done all right and can be happy with what you've achieved. I mean, if something happened to me now, I can say I've been so lucky that nothing bad happened when I was younger, a serious injury or whatever. I managed to get the lucky break to turn professional and I do appreciate that and what I've achieved.

'Over the past year or so I've been thinking a lot about what I'll do when I finish playing. I had all sorts of ideas but I've not nailed anything down. I'd like to be involved in sport because I studied PE teaching at Murray House, even though I never took my fourth year. It seems stupid to throw away ten years' professional experience to take up something else.

'I think it's important to help others with your experiences. I'd like to work with young players, not just elite players but young sportspeople face to face ... specialist coaching. I'd not like to coach a team, but I'd like to work with kickers or get an academy thing set up and work with youngsters where you can really make a difference individually one on one without the stresses of working with a team. I could be interested in that in later years but it's something you build towards.

'Hopefully when I finish I'll savour what I have achieved in the game and be happy knowing I gave it all I had to give.'

I saw Chris playing for Scotland in the very wet Calcutta Cup clash in 2000 but it was playing for Edinburgh in a Heineken Cup match against Newcastle Falcons at Murrayfield in December 2004 where he caught my eye. It was not a good game, apart from the fact that Newcastle won, but my abiding memory was of the winger who really looked a class above anyone else on the field. I was so impressed with him as a player and my feelings for him as a person are exactly the same after having met the man and had the thoroughly enjoyable experience of chatting to him at his Edinburgh home.

Scotland have been very lucky to have had the Borderer within their ranks since his World Cup debut against Spain in 1999 and the records he already holds will undoubtedly be taken to even higher levels – his ambition and desire show little signs of abating. I know there is no place for sentiment in professional sport but it would be a crowning achievement to a fantastic career if the British and Irish Lions left these shores in 2009 with the versatile skills of Christopher Douglas Paterson available for selection. My fingers are crossed for the 'Braw Lad o' Gala Water'.

2008–2009 Season Update

By the end of the 2008–9 season, Chris had taken his Scotland points total to 738 and his number of caps to 95. However, it must have been a frustrating year for the man of Gala. Injury curtailed his efforts in the autumn internationals and the recently departed Scotland coach, Frank Hadden's belief that the skills of the most capped player and top points-scorer in Scottish rugby history would be best utilised coming from the bench I found hard to understand.

Not being a regular starter for Scotland must have influenced the Lions' management team's thinking as Chris did not make the tour.

Chris Paterson: Statistics	
Date of birth	30 March 1978
Birthplace	Edinburgh
Height	1.83m
Weight	78kg
Position	fullback; fly half; wing three-quarter
School / university	Langlee Primary School; Galashiels Academy; Moray House College
Present club	Edinburgh
Previous clubs	Gloucester; Gala RFC; Glasgow Caledonians
Nicknames	Mossy
Favourite TV show	*Strictly Come Dancing*
Favourite film	*Batman Begins*
Favourite music	anything
Favourite book	Ian Rankin novels
Favourite food	Thai
Most like to meet...	Roger Federer
Least like to meet...	nobody
Best moment in rugby	Rugby World Cup quarter-final 2003 v Australia
Favourite place to visit	South of France
I love...	being happy
I hate...	being frustrated

JAMIE ROBERTS

Wales; British and Irish Lions; Cardiff Blues

Sitting in the Sports Bar of the Vale of Glamorgan Hotel having a coffee with Martyn Williams was the first time that the name of Jamie Roberts had engaged me in anything other than passing interest. I knew that the Cardiff Blues youngster had made his international debut the previous season for Wales against Scotland in that magnificent cathedral of rugby that is the Millennium Stadium but that was the extent of my knowledge. However, when someone you respect as much as Martyn starts talking with such emotion about a kid who is going to be a fantastic player but is also mentally strong enough to make difficult decisions at such a young age you have to take notice.

We were chatting about life after rugby and the things Martyn was now doing to ease his transition from the rugby-playing world to the world of work inhabited by most of us. 'I'm lucky now because I think my profile's quite high and people are maybe more willing to help with things that I want to try and gain experience of, but looking back I know that I should have been actively doing it when I was younger.

'There's a young boy at Cardiff, Jamie Roberts, who just got his first cap for Wales and he's going to be a doctor. I know that Cardiff have been on at him for the last couple of years to go full-time but he's insistent that he wants to combine his rugby career with finishing his studies to be a doctor. I'd definitely recommend that way of doing it; get the studying done. I mean looking back I was determined that nothing was going to detract me from getting on with the rugby but you know it's all about getting the balance right and I really admire Jamie for what he is doing.'

With my curiosity engaged it did not take me very long to realise that the youngster originally from Newport was a real talent in lots of ways and, with the help of Gwydion Griffiths from the Cardiff Blues, I met with Jamie in one of the sponsors boxes overlooking the pitch of Cardiff Arms Park.

The perceived wisdom is that the first three to four minutes is a critical time as we generate our first impressions of someone. Goodness only knows what Jamie was thinking about me but I was thinking what an ordinary, pleasant kid. Not necessarily the expectation generated by Martyn's description of a driven and extremely motivated individual. However, by the end of our chat I fully understood what Martyn had meant and I was trying to reconcile the two extremes of a very ordinary, but at the same time very extraordinary, young man.

I don't think they are contradictions but simply part of the make-up of the individual that enables him to relate the experiences of living with his non-rugby-playing mates, shedding a tear as he left school and trying to gain entry to the nightspots of Cardiff when not quite 18, in the same way as he describes playing for Wales Under 18s, Under 19s and Under 21s in the same year, getting up in the early hours of the morning whilst at the Under 21 World Cup in Argentina to do his A-level examinations, with three grade As being the result, and currently balancing the demands of professional rugby with studying medicine.

Jamie was born in the Royal Gwent Hospital, Newport on 8 November 1986 and lived for the first year of his life with his parents, Jackie and Norman, and older brother, David, in Allt-yr-ynn, a quiet suburb of Newport. The family then moved to Draenen Pen-y-graig (Thornhill) under the shadow of Caerphilly Mountain in North Cardiff where his parents live to this day. Jamie only moved out of the family home in November 2008, having bought his own place in the Pontcanna area of Cardiff where he has adopted the high-risk strategy of allowing friends to move in. 'I've just moved out of Mum and Dad's house in November! I live with three mates who are all rugby lads and the house is still in one piece! Tom was one of my best mates at school and is a scrum half with Newport and the Dragons; Scott is a fly half with Glamorgan Wanderers and Owain who I also went to school with plays for Barry – more towards the social end of the spectrum! It's awesome and I really enjoy it. I would hate living on my own and I think I am too young to do it. I'm still at university and want to hang around with my mates, so there's no chance of a girlfriend moving in quite yet!'

Participation in sport did not play a large part in the lives of Jamie's parents but, whilst they did not play sport themselves, Norman was a keen rugby supporter and it was the Newport club that grabbed the attention of the Roberts kids and their dad. 'I think my dad's uncle was captain of Newport back in his day but my dad didn't really play any sports; he was more of a watcher and was a season ticket holder for years at Rodney Parade. Mum isn't sporty either. With my dad going to watch Newport, my brother David and I were also taken along and were Newport fans even though we lived in Cardiff. That changed when I was 15 and started playing for Cardiff: Dad swapped over and he's Cardiff through and through now. I played rugby all the time as I grew up but David only played for a while, until he was about ten or eleven when he broke his collarbone. That put him off for life.

'He's a trainee cameraman for OMNI, a company which does camera work for the BBC and S4C now. Funnily enough we were to play Pontypridd here at the Arms Park and it was called off but we still had to do an interview. We had a ten-minute slot to do and that was the first time he was in the studio at the same time as me. It was funny being in the studio with him.'

As the Roberts kids grew up in Thornhill it was the emergence of the Welsh medium education system that offered their parents the preferred option for the two brothers. Although not Welsh speakers themselves, Jackie and Norman wanted the boys to use the language in their studies, and schooling was undertaken with all classes in Welsh at Ysgol y Wern Primary School in Llanishen. 'I started at a local Welsh-speaking school, Ysgol y Wern and that fed into the only Welsh-speaking secondary school in Cardiff at the time, Ysgol Gyfun Glantaf, though another one, Ysgol Gyfun Plasmawr, has opened since then. I went to Glantaf by the river.

'My parents weren't from Welsh-speaking backgrounds but they felt it was best for my brother and me to go to the Welsh-speaking primary school. My mum tried to learn Welsh at classes but it was so hard for her. She picked up some of the language but it's such a hard language to learn when you are older; for us kids it was no problem really but it was a bit easier for kids who were going home and speaking Welsh in the evenings.

'All of the lessons were in Welsh and we did our GCSEs and A levels in Welsh. Sometimes it was hard for us turning up at school after having spoken English all the time the night before and then having to switch over. Often during courses we'd answer in English and get into trouble. It's a bit of a strange thing that we did all of our schooling in Welsh and then we go to uni where all of our classes and assignments are not in Welsh but in English. I still think it's a good skill to have and I find it really useful.'

Jamie's obvious pride at his 'Welshness' is encapsulated in his school's motto 'Coron Gwlad Ei Mamiaith', which translates as 'A country's crown is her mother tongue'.

Ysgol Gyfun Glantaf school celebrated its 30th year in September 2008 and holds a lot of good memories for one of its high-profile alumni. 'I really enjoyed my time at school and, if I could be young enough to do it all over again, I would want to go to the same place. I have a lot of good memories.' Jamie's time at school enabled him to demonstrate his academic talents as he successfully overcame the challenge of firstly his GCSEs and then his A levels. At GCSE level the school had a core curriculum of Welsh, English, Maths and Science, with his optional subjects being PE, Geography, Business and IT, and it was no surprise when the results of August 2004 brought straight passes with A* and A grades for all subjects with one exception – a B for RE. 'I did enjoy all my classes apart from RE, which I hated! I'm not really a religious person and don't go to church; I'm not a strongly devout Christian and it just didn't really appeal to me. I was quite science-orientated and the fact that it's learnable, there is a right answer, and that's something that gets me. For my A levels I chose Maths, Chemistry, Biology and did an AS level in PE, which I dropped after the first year.'

The youngster from Thornhill was also very active in organised sport from as early an age as seven when he went along with older brother, David, to Cricc Rugby Club. 'I started at seven playing rugby with my brother. He started at Under 8s and I went along, too, even though I was 18 months behind him. We played at Cricc Rugby Club, which was really brought together to promote the medium of Welsh. It was not really games; we would turn up on Saturday morning for training but we might only have a game once a month. Back then they weren't very competitive – it was more social – but they've grown and are much stronger now. I've been back to do the youngsters presentations and it's awesome seeing the guys who coached me.

'I stayed with Cricc until I was an Under 12 but they did not really run teams from Under 13 onwards and so it was in Year 7 or Under 12s that I started playing rugby at school for Glantaf. They have a massive reputation and played week in and week out in various leagues. At the same time I went to another club, Rumney, and played for them from Under 12 up to Youth. I played both club and school so was playing twice a week, but at that time you don't mind – you just want to play.'

Rugby was not the only sport to grab the interest of the talented youngster with cricket being played at county standard. 'I did badminton and athletics including a bit of cross-country, though I was not very good at it! It was more for fun really. I played U14–U15 cricket for the county and I had to choose between rugby / cricket when I was 16. Cricket training was twice a week even in the winter with net practice. Rugby was also twice a week and I kept doing well with the rugby, so I had to drop cricket, which was a shame but I'm still friends with the guys from my cricket days. At that age you feel you're invincible! You just want to try everything but rugby was taking up more and more time.

'Glentaf put a lot of emphasis on rugby tours and I went to Australia, South Africa and Dubai with the school – they were brilliant times. They were organised in the summer and the first was a sixth form trip to Australia for six weeks. I just missed out age-wise but a couple of lads dropped out, so I made it with a mate called Andrew. We went with the older boys and it was a great trip – brilliant! A year later we went to South Africa and, in my last year, to Dubai.

'In representative terms I captained the Cardiff Schools Under 15s and then played for Wales Under 16 A. I was selected for the Welsh Schools Under 18s a year young in my first sixth-form year. For the following season the Welsh Schools/Youth System was revamped to make it Wales U18, U19 and U21 and so, in my last year at school, I captained Wales U18 but ended up playing Wales Under 18, Under 19 and Under 21. After I captained the Under 18s I was selected for the Under 19s and went to Durban in South Africa for the World Cup. After that I was selected for the Under 21s World Cup in Argentina.'

Playing for your country at three different age groups in the same season is a big ask for anyone, but in your A-level year at school the emotional engagement of playing for your country when you are captaining your age group and then taking part in two World Cup tournaments in far-flung parts of the globe whilst one and three years young would completely faze most people. Whilst I am sure that there will have been lots of discussion and several sleepless nights in the Roberts household, that year sent the signals that rugby and medicine had a rare talent on their hands with an inner resolve and work ethic that would enable him to achieve whatever he wanted to achieve.

'Particularly the last bit of that year, oh it was crazy! Chris Davy was the coach of the Under 21s and is a university lecturer who is now up at UWIC. Being a university lecturer meant he could invigilate my exams so we were up at about 6 a.m. in a room in the team hotel. I had four exams to do and I downloaded passwords and exam papers from the internet to let me sit the exams in Argentina at the same time as they were being sat in Wales so that there was no chance of me finding out what was on the paper. Chris then brought my answer papers home to be marked.

'I missed out on a few of the activities that the other guys did like white-water rafting and shooting but I just had to be strict, stay in and revise. It was hard but in hindsight I'm pleased I did. When you want to achieve what you want to achieve you have to do this sort of thing and be determined to achieve your goals.

'I was really worried about going to Argentina beforehand because your A levels are big exams. I had my place at medical school but I needed two As and a B; it was a big ask. My mum was concerned, quite rightly, that I'd go and not concentrate on my exams but as it turned out I got three As.

'At the moment I'm reading a book called *The Man Who Sold His Ferrari* and it's about a guy who had everything, riches, etc. but no goal in life. If you have no goals to achieve, no direction, it becomes a very sad life. I need that focus: in rugby terms it's playing for Wales, playing the best you can. It's the same with uni; I want to be a doctor, a consultant surgeon. I believe you have to have goals to drive you.'

The day of A level results brought to an end a pivotal year and closed that chapter of Jamie's life, but it is with great fondness that the big Cardiff Blue remembers his time at Ysgol Gyfun Glantaf. 'It was just an awesome environment. We would go there every day and have a laugh. We took classes seriously but at breaks and lunchtime and in your free periods there was always something to do. In sixth form you did a lot and we had a lot of responsibility and did things with the younger children. We went with them on an activity week in west Wales and generally helped them. It was just a great environment. They were great teachers who worked really hard for the children and it was sad leaving. I think I cried on my last day! It was really sad to leave.

'We just grew up together and shared all those experiences of growing up, sharing it all. Trying to avoid the drink, drugs, but trying to find out about sex; you know it's such a massive part of people's lives at that age. The first time you go out with your friends, even though you're under age. The buzz trying to get into clubs – you can't replace it with anything. I miss being under age! Doing all these things with your mates, sharing it all was fantastic.

'A level results day was special and we all went off and did different things, but we still keep in touch more or less weekly. My main group of friends now, we all went to school together; there are a couple of guys from the year above, the girls and my mates from my year, I'm still really good friends with them and they form my main social group. One of my best mates, Rhys, went to study at the LSE in London. He has now graduated and is training to be a barrister, which is awesome. A couple went off up north to uni.

'I've lived with Tom [Issaccs] all through uni and I know what he's gone through. I've seen the pressure he's been under with university work, particularly his dissertation. They can be tough times, really tough times. I think it's good to share those experiences with people, to share the pressure really. It's good to know that we're all going through the same things. For me, a circle of friends from outside rugby is crucial; it grounds you. I go home and they don't want to talk about rugby. They know I play rugby and all that but they don't necessarily want to talk about that. I'm just their mate and that makes me feel good about myself.'

In a rugby sense Jamie's last year at school was exceptional, but it was in his lower sixth year when aged 17 that he made his Wales Schools Under 18 debut against the old enemy, England Schools, at the Leicester fortress that is Welford Road. The game was a very special occasion for the Welsh fullback and, as he walked down the steps to the pitch, the emotions of the whole team were running high but Welford Road is a place at the heart of English rugby and for away teams a very difficult place to come and play. Many teams have arrived full of hope and expectation and left with those hopes shattered. On the day England took the spoils but the Glantaf pupil had taken the first steps on his international journey.

'I was excited and nervous but you have to take it in your stride, you just focus on what's going on and what lies ahead. When you're that young, playing for Wales Under 18s, it's massive and everybody's talking about it at school because rugby's a religion in Wales. Playing for Welsh Schools, it was huge. They still have a picture on the wall at school. I remember that game; I dropped the ball over the line in the first few minutes and we ended up losing, but it was still brilliant. It's great to represent your country but all that age-group stuff leads on to your first full cap.

'Once I had played representative rugby, I was thinking to myself, I'm good enough to be here, I'm here for a reason. When I was selected for the squad I thought I'm in line to play here and I guess all of the guys were thinking, hang on, I am actually in the pipeline for a full cap. At that age I had such massive admiration for the Welsh players and it's just awesome to rub shoulders with the guys now, but at the time I was simply thinking about taking one step at a time. If I play well and make a good impression I could jump up into the Under 19 squad and the goal for all of us was to go further.'

During the summer of 2005 as Jamie prepared for life as a medical student at university his rugby was progressing at a pace. As a member of the Cardiff Blues Academy he was in the minds of the coaching staff as they exposed him to his first taste of senior rugby with a pre-season game against Pontypridd. That one appearance for the Blues may have heightened the motivation of the young fullback, but nurturing and protecting young talent is as much a skill as recognising it and Jamie was placed with Cardiff RFC to develop his game in the senior ranks. The youngster who, by his own admission, was lanky but skinny started to fill out as his body responded to structured training and weights programmes.

Cardiff Rugby Club provided Jamie's playing home for two seasons before the move into the full-time professional ranks and gave him the flexibility he needed to complete his first two years of medical study full time. The 2007–2008 season was his first as a full-time professional player with a competitive debut against the Ospreys. The stepping-up in the time needed for rugby was balanced against the switch to part-time attendance at the University of Wales as he continued his studies.

That first full professional season gave Jamie some fantastic memories that most with long careers can only dream of. 'I thoroughly enjoyed my first season for the Blues and there were some special standout moments from that year. We beat Stade Français here at the Arms Park in the Heineken Cup. I was starting on the wing but an hour before kick-off Ben Blair pulled out of the game and I got put to fullback. I hadn't played at 15 for half a year but I had a solid game; we beat them and got through to the quarter-finals. Making the quarter-finals was huge for the club as we hadn't done that since 1996 when they lost to Gloucester. As a youngster, just starting out at that level, it was huge – it was the biggest game of my life. To play against big names in rugby at places like Leicester and Gloucester was fantastic. I got to play at Toulouse too in the quarters. That whole experience – there's no substitute for it, it just makes you a better player.'

Throughout his time with Cardiff Rugby Club, and as he stepped into the ranks of the professional game with the Blues, the big fullback's international career was moving on with involvement in the Wales Under 21 squad and being a member of the Grand

Slam-winning Six Nations team in 2005. The dream of a full cap came within grasp as he was selected as the only uncapped player in the squad for Wales' Six Nations' campaign of 2008.

The first game of the tournament for Wales was against England at Twickenham, a game that ended with a resounding Welsh win and the large Welsh water carrier had a tear in his eye as his beloved Wales realised a dream. The new Welsh management team headed by Warren Gatland took the brave step of changing a winning team and it was in the next international, to be played against Scotland in Cardiff's Millennium Stadium, that the former Glantaf pupil to realised his dream of representing his country at the highest level.

On 9 February 2008, at 21 years of age, Jamie took his place on the wing for Wales and he was on his way on the international stage. 'Right from the moment I got up it was such a special day but I can't remember the night! I didn't get much sleep, perhaps three or four hours' kip and I was shaking, I was so nervous. It was such an awesome experience, being in the changing rooms with the guys and everyone congratulating you. You know why you are there, you're playing for your country and you know you have to give 110 per cent. I shed a tear when the national anthem was played but the best part for me was about ten to fifteen minutes into the game when I realised, hey, I could make a difference here.

'Before the game I believe all players have their demons to deal with; they always creep in. Am I good enough? Am I only here because someone's injured? These thoughts are just human nature. For me there came a moment about 15 minutes into the game where I thought, hang on a minute, this is just another game of rugby, I can make a difference here ... just accept you're here for a reason and you're good enough. Luckily I had had a couple of early touches of the ball and did a few good things and that was it – the game flew for me.

'The next thing you know you're in the Hilton Hotel at the after-match function and then having a couple of drinks in town. It was one of the most drunken times I've had and my housemates had to carry me in at home. I got up the next day and I was a different man.

'That first cap changed me psychologically – it is such a big thing and I'd say players were lying if they said otherwise. Once you have stepped over that line you're an international player and so the next challenge is to get off and get another game. You don't want to be a one-cap wonder, but it was a bit tricky for me as I didn't play in the next game and I didn't bench either. I did not feature again in the Six Nations, so I was stuck on one and the guys were having a dig and taking the mickey but then I managed to get on to the summer tour to South Africa and get my second cap. I'm on to my seventh now and hope to get some more in the Six Nations.'

The balancing of rugby and studies was really becoming a challenge for the new star of Welsh rugby. There were significant pressures to be coped with as the demands of international rugby kicked in and, without superb support from the University of Wales and his tutors, his education could easily have suffered. On his selection to the Six Nations squad Jamie was given an eight-week sabbatical and allowed to sit important examinations in July rather than April. Even this flexibility was tested to the limit as selection for the summer tour to South Africa meant that studying once again took prominence over enjoying the delights of touring. Three weeks after the squad's return to Wales a whole raft of examinations had to be sat and passed but the determination of the youngster to fulfil all of his ambitions was present in bundles for all to see.

'During the summer I went out to South Africa with Wales and played the two tests which gave me my second and third caps, but when I was there I had my head in the books. It was a pretty crazy time but I had ten exams in the middle part of July. It was a tough year as there was a lot of volume to studying, a lot of work, and sometimes I'd be on the pitch and thinking, have I done enough work?... And then I'd be in university and thinking, will I drop the ball at the weekend? I really had to split my mind to focus on both things.

'I think you have to look to the future and hopefully the work I did then will be worthwhile. I would have loved to have gone away on holiday after the tour but I had only three weeks to revise for big exams that combined the previous three years of work. I spent all my time during those three weeks in the library, 7 a.m. until midnight every day. I had to dig deep.'

A word or phrase to describe you at 21 years of age

Busy, multi-focused and dedicated...

I have been incredibly busy. It has just been hectic, especially last year combining professional rugby, international rugby and my third year in medicine at university. The third year of medicine is a tough time in itself with big exams at the end of the year and I was combining it with pro rugby. In the mornings I would do my weights and training, leave the training ground at midday and go to university and spend time on the wards. I'd then come home to have some food. My day off from rugby was spent at university and on the wards.

I didn't have a chance to move really but I was determined to stick at it and it will pay dividends in the end. I was really pleased I did and I passed my end-of-year exams, which I took after the South African tour, with a merit. That feeling after my last exam was amazing but revising was the worst three weeks of my life, ridiculously tough.

The 2008–2009 season is Jamie's second professional season and the pace of his life shows no signs of easing. With his challenging third-year results safely tucked away, it is the clinical practice side of his medical training leading to his graduation as a qualified doctor that is his focus for the next two years. The natural break point in his studies would have been at the end of year three but Jamie's mindset is that he wants to get his degree and then take stock of the way forward. The ever helpful University of Wales have eased the pressure by allowing him to study part-time but it is still a daily schedule that would simply be too much for normal beings.

'In the fourth and fifth year of my degree the focus is on clinical work in hospital, being on the wards, taking histories and interacting with patients. Reflection and learning is done at home in the evenings. I am trying to do those last two years part-time, so I will do my weights and gym work, then do the rugby sessions – which say finishes at 1 p.m. or 2 p.m. I will then go on the wards for a couple

194

of hours. On my day off from rugby I will also go on the wards for a few of hours. That's my daily routine.

'I want to get to the point of graduating; just to get my degree that's my main aim. Once you graduate no one can take that away from you. NHS guidelines say you can take two years out but if I took the next seven to eight years to concentrate on my rugby I know I wouldn't go back to it. I'd probably forget everything I've learnt and at that age it would be too hard to go back. I'd have to start from scratch. At this age, straight from school I can work hard and am in the right frame of mind. I just want to get it done and it'll be a huge relief when I have finished.'

The tour to South Africa brought to the fore the issue of versatility, which can be seen as both a hindrance or a help, as players, especially inexperienced players, come to terms with the demands of playing at the highest level of the game. Observers frequently refer to players who have failed to fulfil their potential because they are constantly being moved around by coaches who are under pressure to try to maximise team performance at the expense of individual development.

The versatile back made his debut for Wales against Scotland on the wing and gained his second cap at fullback against the Springboks, scoring his first try in the process. The second test against the Boks gave Jamie his third cap, but Warren Gatland pulled the rabbit out of the hat as he selected the try-scoring fullback at inside centre. Three caps, three different positions was just another big ask that former Glantaf pupil simply took in his stride.

'My position coming through the age groups was fullback but I did play at inside centre when I was under 15. My schoolteacher thought that I had the skills to make a fullback and so I played there for Wales at Under 18s, Under 19s and Under 21s all at fullback. With the Blues I have played mainly on the wing, as Ben Blair has been the starting fullback, but then for Wales have played wing, fullback, inside centre and was actually named at outside centre for the autumn test against South Africa but Gav [Henson] pulled out and Shanks [Tom Shanklin] came in, which meant I was moved back to inside centre.

'At this age position doesn't really bother me. I see being versatile as one of my strengths and I think it's good to hone your skills by moving positions. I'm still learning the game and am picking up a lot of things off the senior players. There is a big difference between the different positions – inside centre, fullback and wing – and I am still learning.'

It may be that the things Jamie brings to the inside-centre position have overtaken his other strengths in the mind of the Welsh coaching staff, because selection through the 2008 autumn internationals and the 2009 Six Nations saw him make the Number 12 jersey his own with a series of powerful performances, including being made 'Man of the Match' in the opening Six Nations match against Scotland at Murrayfield.

I am sure that, after a stuttering team performance against Italy in Rome, Warren Gatland made changes that saw Jamie warming the substitutes bench but his position in the minds of the coaches became clear as injury to Lee Bryne saw him leave the field. As the fullback left the arena Jamie entered the contest but was slotted in at inside centre as Gavin Henson was moved to fullback. The physical presence and running skills of the powerful youngster are well suited to inside centre as he confronts defences and generates the go-forward ball that teams thrive upon.

The autumn internationals saw Jamie line up in the Millennium Stadium against South Africa, Canada and New Zealand, but it was the last of the games that put a halt on the young centre's progress. On 29 November Jamie lined up against Australia but in only the second minute of the game two very committed players clashed heads. Stirling Mortlock, the Aussie fullback, left the field immediately but Jamie played on for a further 15 minutes, playing a major part in the move that set up Shane Williams' opening try for Wales. Ultimately Wales gained a superb 21–18 victory but Jamie missed the euphoria that erupted at the end of the game. After 18 minutes he was helped from the field with a fractured skull, an injury described by Professor John Williams, the Welsh team doctor as an injury he had never seen before. 'I have never seen anything like this before and I was talking to some of my colleagues and they have never seen anything like this. It was a collision of heads at a certain angle with a certain momentum causing a crack.'

The freak injury led to a frustrating six-week period away from the game. 'I've missed playing and it's really frustrating watching the boys play and watching other players doing well when you're not on the park. Gav's [Henson] come back and is doing well, Andrew Bishop is playing well, Shanks [Tom Shanklin] is playing well here, Jamie [Robinson] is playing well, young Jon Davies at the Scarlets is doing well, and it is desperately frustrating.'

The period of frustration came to an end when Jamie came from the bench to play a part in the Blues narrow 20–21 defeat at the hands of Leinster, but as we chatted overlooking the green of the Arms Park he was relishing the game to take place the following Sunday in the Heineken Cup at Kingsholm, the home of Gloucester, where he was selected to start at inside centre.

The game turned out to be a hard fought affair made even tougher as the Blues had wing Tom James sent off in the 28th minute for a head butt on Gloucester's French hooker, Olivier Azam, and, whilst James can have no complaints about the decision of referee Alan Lewis, Azam's descent to the turf was worthy of an Oscar. Despite this setback the 14-man Blues dug deep and managed a fantastic 16–12 win to secure a quarter-final spot and it should come as no surprise that the returning star was made 'Man of the Match'.

Solid performances for the Blues gave Warren Gatland the confidence to keep his developing centre in the team for the 2009 Six Nations. The competition ultimately proved disappointing for Wales as they lost the thrilling finale to Ireland to give the Irish a well-deserved Grand Slam and push Wales down the table to fourth, but as the scribblers fill their waking hours with the 'pick the Lions squad' game every list has the versatile Roberts in it.

'As a player your goal is to play for your country and I've done that so I want to keep pushing forwards. The Lions is at the next level and is massive so that's something you have to think about; it should be a goal but it would be a huge achievement. It's like all aspects of life; once you get to a certain point you have to set new goals, you accept you're where you are and then you push on, but you've got to perform well for your club, that's the key thing. You do your talking on the pitch and the sponsorship and other stuff comes after that. It starts with the training at the gym and having a good lifestyle. Getting up at the right time, eating the right stuff, all the little things you do every day, that's what it's all about.'

A word or phrase that describes you now?

Still hectic and focused but more mature.

With my studies and rugby I am so busy, and things get hectic, crazy at times. With all that's happened in the last two years I've grown up a lot and I think I'm more mature really.

As a young player you mostly mix and socialise with people who are older than you – the guys are generally mid- to late twenties. That sometimes makes me feel a bit older than I actually am. I've just bought my own house, I'm studying hard and a lot has happened really quickly. All of these things have helped me grow up.

Life is very hectic; I am very focused and I feel I have grown up a lot but, saying that, I'm still ridiculously childish! I laugh at life and don't take it too seriously.

The dedication Jamie has demonstrated to achieve all he has achieved, and the admission of being ridiculously childish, may appear to be two character traits that are not easy to reconcile in an individual. All I can say is that in the hour and a half we chatted we hardly ever stopped laughing and the things I have not written are 'interesting'.

It almost seemed like the most ridiculous question to ask Jamie but he does actually have time for other things in his life. 'I play the guitar because you can pick it up anywhere. I'm too busy with rugby and my studies to have hobbies like golf. I play a bit on the Playstation with the boys but I enjoy just being with my mates and going out, hanging around with them and socialising, although obviously not necessarily drinking – I just want to enjoy life.'

For someone who just wants to enjoy life an incredible amount of effort goes in to the challenge of following his dreams, a lifestyle that few would or could commit to. 'Learning medicine is quite tricky as it's sheer volume but it's about problem-solving. I was always good at maths, problem-solving was one of my best attributes and I enjoyed it. The basis of medicine is problem-solving. You know, someone comes in the door and you're constantly assessing them trying to find out what's wrong by getting bites of history from them. It's one big puzzle that hopefully you end up solving. That's the buzz – that's why I do it. I love contact with people.'

The list of Welsh international rugby-playing doctors is into double figures, going back to Dr James 'Tuan' Jones, who was born in 1883, but the obvious comparisons are made with the legendary Welsh fullback of the 1970s and now orthopaedic surgeon of Bridgend, J.P.R. Williams MBE. Williams commented before Jamie's international debut: 'In my day most of us had other jobs and it was hard enough to fit rugby and the medicine into a week then, so I can't imagine the dedication Jamie must have. Jamie is an impressive kid and I wish him all the best for the weekend; he's got a good head on his shoulders and I don't think he will look back from here.'

Who am I to disagree with someone like J.P.R. Williams? The young Welshman is a very impressive, personable man who is just an ordinary guy who enjoys his mates and does not take life too seriously, whilst at the same time demonstrating a massive drive and desire to do the best he can in everything he does. I would take it as such a massive compliment, were the kid from Cardiff ever to come to Newcastle, if he called to say, 'Smithy, do you fancy a coffee?'

2008–2009 Season Update

What a season for the aspiring medic. A fractured skull against Australia in November, the worries of clicking your heals when injured as others perform well, a man-of-the-match return for the Cardiff Blues in their Heineken Cup group win against Gloucester at Kingsholm, a man-of-the-match international return against Scotland at Murrayfield and finally, the dream of British and Irish Lions selection. His form early in the tour has put him in pole position for the test match inside centre spot as his partnership with Brian O'Driscoll looks both solid in defence and exciting in attack. I am sure at some point his life will slow down!

Jamie Roberts: Statistics	
Date of birth	8 November 1986
Birthplace	Newport
Height	1.93m
Weight	107kg
Position	wing three-quarter; fullback; centre
School / university	Ysgol Gyfun Glantaf school; University of Wales
Present club	Cardiff Blues
Previous clubs	Rumney RFC; Cricc RFC
Nicknames	Lump Head
Favourite TV show	*24*
Favourite film	*Goodfellas*
Favourite music	Stereophonics; acoustic music
Favourite book	Neil Strauss, *The Game*
Favourite food	chicken fajitas
Most like to meet...	Eric Cantona
Least like to meet...	Saddam Hussein (when he was alive!)
Best moment in rugby	first Welsh Cap
Favourite place to visit	the Grand Canyon
I love...	my mates and my MacBook
I hate...	arrogant people and unfulfilled potential

MATHEW TAIT

England; Sale Sharks

Barnard Castle is a small market town on the border of Durham and Yorkshire and is an extremely picturesque and tranquil part of the world. This quiet backwater is the location of the independent school that takes the town's name. The school was founded in 1883 and amongst its notable alumni – or Old Barnardians – are Kevin Whatley, the Geordie bricklayer of *Auf Wiedersehen Pet*, and Lewis, the ever faithful assistant to Morse. However, it is the sporting Old Boys Rob Andrew and the Underwood brothers, Rory and Tony, who established a rugby heritage at the school that has been taken on and nurtured by the current rugby master and Director of Sport, Martin Pepper.

In the time of professional rugby a strong relationship has developed between the school and Newcastle Falcons, as might have been expected with Rob Andrew being one of the Old Boys. Several players have represented England at different levels as well as being a part of Newcastle's Senior and Academy squads. Under Martin Pepper's tutelage Barnard Castle School have reached the final of the *Daily Mail* Cup on three occasions since 2002, with the class of 2008 just missing out on a fourth final with a 19–16 defeat in the semi-finals to St Benedict's School.

Barnard Castle School holds a special place in the heart of Mathew Tait. 'I just loved Barnard Castle School and still love the place. I was a day boy and had time after school as I didn't leave until 5 p.m. I would sometimes play squash but I remember the dark winter nights and playing football in the school courtyard. The whole atmosphere there was great.' As so often is the case with areas of outstanding natural beauty, the school and its grounds were open to the elements. My first contact with Mathew and his parents was going

201

to the school to watch him play fly half against Newcastle's Royal Grammar School on a freezing cold Saturday in February 2004 on the very exposed First Team field behind the school.

It was an interesting time for the 18-year-old as Gloucester were also courting the youngster whose talent was on show for all to see. Gloucester were to play Newcastle at Kingston Park the following weekend and Nigel Melville, the then Director of Rugby at Gloucester, had offered Mathew the chance to be with their First Team squad and even warm up with the team before the match. You have to admire Nigel Melville's cheek, but Mathew Tait was a local lad from Shotley Bridge who was not going to get away. The big guns were wheeled out and Mathew became Jonny Wilkinson's training partner and a close friendship was started that lasts to this day.

With the signature on his contract Mathew did not have to wait too long for First Team action as he made his debut on 2 May 2004 in the 16–15 defeat by London Irish but did score a try with his first touch of the ball. 'I started in the London Irish game. The week before we'd played in the Peebles Sevens and I had played quite well up there. At the start of the next week Fletch [John Fletcher] said that Rob [Rob Andrew] was thinking of getting me involved in the warm-up next week so that I would get a feel for the professional environment. I think they were trying to get me involved at that point because I'd had a big sniff from Gloucester and so they were trying to hook me in to being at Newcastle.

'Then Fletch said I was on the bench, but the next day I got a call to say they were going to start me and what did I think? I said 'sweet', but I was shitting myself!

Best thing was that I got paid for it; I think it was a £250 match fee! My one big pay day of the year was doing the turkeys at Christmas and suddenly I was getting this £250 which I thought would buy me the world! That was that. It was just awesome to be involved. I think it's a good thing to hold on to those memories. It's not naivety but you're just doing youthful kinds of things without getting bogged down with trying to think too much about the game, which you can do once you get into it properly, when it becomes your job. I played against Paul Sackey that day but only lasted 60 minutes.'

Mathew was still a schoolboy and, to many individuals without the same degree of intelligence and mental toughness, sitting A level examinations so soon after your Premiership debut may have been difficult, but A-grade results in Biology, Physics and Geography are testament to the character of the person.

Mathew was born in Shotley Bridge near Consett in County Durham on 6 February 1986 and then moved to Wolsingham, where his father is a vet. As it did for my own two boys, rugby started in the junior section at Consett Rugby Club. Maybe Mathew's and his brother Alex's ability to cope with the exposed nature of the pitches at Barnard Castle School come from their early days of rugby at Consett. If you haven't been before, Consett can be cold, really, really cold! I have spent many a happy Sunday morning in the middle of winter watching the hardy souls coaching and playing mini rugby from the warmth of my car.

'I first started out at Consett Rugby Club. When I was at primary school a mate of mine, Billy Hoares, went there. His dad was a coach at the club, Roger Hoares and I just used to ride along with them and really enjoyed it. Alex came along as well. I played there until I was about 12 or 13 and eventually stopped because I was at Barnard Castle School at the same time and was playing so much rugby. I kind of got a bit bored with it so ended up doing football on Sundays. So it was rugby practice all week at school, then we a played a game on Saturday and I played a football match on the Sunday.'

Sport is an important part of school life at Barnard Castle and that gave the youngster the chance to try his hand at different things. Any sport was worth a try: squash, football, cross-country and athletics were all things that Mathew got involved with, but it was football and rugby that he enjoyed.

Mathew's siblings all play sport, their abilities having possibly been passed down the generations from his mum's side of the family. 'Dad was more the brains in the outfit! He is a vet in Wolsingham but he played a bit of rugby at university. My mum's a fairly keen hockey player. She always used to help organise the mixed women's team in Wolsingham and we would always be in there playing with the hockey sticks. My granddad on my mum's side, who has now passed away, was a football player at Sheffield Wednesday. My mum's brother was a county rugby player for Yorkshire but he had to stop because he kept popping his shoulder out. So there were a few on Mum's side who have been into their sport.

'I just played any sport I could – squash, football, cross-country, athletics – I'd have a dabble at anything really but it wasn't to any standard. I got up to North trials in sprinting at U16/U18 level but was never really good enough compared to the other guys there. I just happened to be quick on the rugby field and never really enjoyed sprinting. I enjoyed football at weekends, doing something different because I was doing rugby at Barney during the week.

'Alex and me have done OK with our sport, my youngest brother, Fin, is doing well at Barnard Castle School and my little sister, Niamh, is into hockey.'

In his time at Consett Rugby Club the ability of both Alex and Mathew was apparent and the move to Barnard Castle School enabled them to develop their skills in a very supportive environment. Martyn Lewis was Mathew's first rugby coach at the school and at the Under 14 age group the school had a good year, but since then it was Martin Pepper, currently the school's Director of Sport, who influenced him as he developed.

'At Under 14 we had a reasonable team and then Martin Pepper, who is now in charge of rugby down there, took us on at Under 15. He had a good group of players including Dicko [Lee Dickson, Northampton Saints and England Saxons scrum half]. The school hadn't been involved in any of the latter stages of the *Daily Mail* Cup before but have had three or four finals in the last five years since he's managed it. It's a testament of how good a coach he is. I'm still in contact with him now.'

Whilst it may be that his sporting attributes have come down his mother's side of the family, it could also be true that his father's role as the 'brains of the outfit' have had an impact on the make-up of the young Tait clan. Mathew is a first-class student, achieving 11 Grade A or A*s at GCSE and continuing with three A levels all at grade A. It was almost comical to be around when Mathew contacted Alex to see what results he had got for his GCSEs. Whilst congratulating him on getting 11 grade A or A*s, he was not slow to point out the fact that the younger Tait had received two less A*s. Talk about a competitive edge! 'I've always been fairly competitive and that comes from having a younger brother. There is 18 months to two years between us and we are always trying to outdo each other.'

At school it was the sciences that Mathew was attracted to and it was a mix of science, social science and sport that he focused on in the sixth form. Biology, Physics, Geography and Sport were taken at AS and then A level.

Although his current university education is unclear as he starts a new life at Sale Sharks in Manchester, he has over the last two years been trying to fit a Biomedical Science degree at Newcastle University into his hectic schedule.

In those years at school the competitive character and mental toughness were evident a lot earlier than at A level time. A memory that is at the front of his mind is the feeling of being hurt when not selected by England, an event that returned in the early days of his full international career. 'One of the big things that sticks out for me was England U16 and not being picked a year young. I was absolutely gutted about it. I just went and worked my socks off back at school. I would do extra training during free periods and things like that. I continued doing extra work in sixth form and have continued approaching training like that to this day; I will always do extra work.'

The essential ingredients were in place – natural ability, physical capability in terms of pace and power, and a good work ethic linked to a competitive, determined mindset – and the world was at his feet. Brian Ashton, the then Head of the National Academy, brought Mathew into the Junior Academy in the 2003–2004 season but he was quickly fast tracked into the Senior Academy.

The awarding of a professional contract at Newcastle Falcons in April 2004 and a Premiership debut less than a month later, during which he scored a try with his first touch of the ball, when still 18 years of age and a schoolboy, all singled out the Durham teenager as a special talent. However, after his debut against London Irish at the end of the 2003–2004 season, it was back to the books at school, but come the start of the 2004–2005 season the youngster was becoming an integral part of the Newcastle midfield and was turning in inspiring performances for his club. He was also being given a chance to show his talents on the international sevens circuit and in

December 2004 was a part of the England squad that won the Dubai Sevens. Although not yet capped by England, it was reported in the media that his form was interesting Sir Clive Woodward, in charge of the ultimately difficult 2005 British and Irish Lions tour to New Zealand.

A special moment for me as I watched Mathew's progress was the performance at Kingston Park against Sale Sharks in January 2005 when the young centre surged past the Sale standoff, Jos Baxendell, and created confusion in the covering defence with a couple of sidesteps. He then showed great strength for one so young to simply shrug off the tackle from Jason Robinson for a great try in the left-hand corner in front of the North Terrace.

Full international honours were not far away and so it was on 5 February 2005, the eve of his nineteenth birthday, that he made his debut for England against Wales in the National Stadium in Cardiff. 'I was nervous but, again, I was a bit naive as to how big a thing it was. I felt very honoured to be involved and it passed by very quickly. It was awesome to be involved though things didn't go as planned.'

England were defeated by the Welsh on the road to their 2005 Grand Slam and turned in a rather inept performance. The debutant did not really get into the game in either defence or attack and was given a torrid time in the media after suffering the ignominy of being 'dumped' by Gavin Henson. His treatment after the game by the England management left a lot of people aghast that a young player could be elevated to such a position and then unceremoniously dropped from the squad. 'Obviously it did affect me. I'd only played 11 Premiership games so in that respect I was fairly inexperienced and, yes, I did let it get to me a little but I had good people around me like Fletch, Walts [Peter Walton], Blackie [Steve Black] and my family. Looking back now and speaking to guys like Wilko [Jonny Wilkinson] that have all been through it with injuries and stuff, it's just one of those things you can't do anything about it. You've just got to busy yourself, improving not so much for the rugby but for yourself as a human being.

'I think it's human nature that we can tend to dwell on failure. I'm exactly the same now but I can look back and consciously make an effort to be pragmatic. I think that just comes with age and experience. It obviously helps when you have a good support group. I'm very close to all my family and had a good supportive network at Newcastle at the time. That was definitely a major help to getting rid of that youthful naivety. It's not just rugby; it's life in general. I think that when you're young you can walk round with your head in the clouds at little bit, thinking that everything's rosy and that nothing bad is ever going to happen. It does inevitably, though, because bad things happen!'

Whilst the events of February 2005 were difficult at the time, Mathew took stock of his position and, with support from people that mean a lot to him, he again got his career on track. Good club performances for Newcastle were followed by international recognition again but this time for England Saxons who won the Churchill Cup with a 45–16 victory against Argentina A in Edmonton, Canada in the summer of 2005. The IRB Sevens circuit enabled him to show his love of the shorter form of the game as he was named in the squad for the 2005–2006 circuit.

That season's tournament included a round which was played as part of the 2006 Commonwealth Games in Melbourne, Australia, where England finished as silver medallists, being beaten by New Zealand in the final. However, the Falcons centre made his mark on the tournament being top try scorer with nine tries. The next stop on the circuit was the Hong Kong Sevens and England managed to go one better by winning the tournament and giving Mathew his best moment in rugby. His international rehabilitation was complete when he was brought back into the full England squad for the 2006 summer tour to Australia when he played in both of the test matches.

Mathew featured prominently in the international squad through the 2006–2007 season with a try to his name in the RBS Six Nations victory over Ireland at Twickenham, and he also survived, mentally and physically, the ill-conceived tour to South Africa in the summer of 2007 which was meant to be preparation for the World Cup in France. It came as no surprise that a place in the World Cup squad was secured and, after coming off the bench in the first two games against the United States and South Africa, he made the Number 13 shirt his own after the unfortunate injury to Newcastle teammate Jamie Noon.

The young centre started the final aged 21 years and 256 days, the youngest England World Cup finalist, and it was with great joy that our dog ran around the living room as crisps and other assorted food and drink was tipped from tables as we all jumped up when he made that fabulous break that would have been the try of the tournament but for a tremendous tackle from Victor Matfield.

A word or phrase to describe you now, at 21 years of age?

That you only get out what you put in…

John Bentley [represented England and the British and Irish Lions at Rugby Union and Great Britain at rugby league] came to school to speak after a school dinner. A teacher at school got him to write it on the programme for the dinner. It's just something that stuck in my mind really as it's true.

I'm trying to improve every area of my game, good ball-carrying, my running game, my defence. It's just a case of working on everything which is a cliché but true.

At the moment I am being seen as a centre and fullback. Fullback is new for me and I'm trying to learn the position. People see it as something that I can do so I am working hard particularly on the positional skills.

Blackie used to say you've just got to turn up and be the best you can be for that day. Do what you do. I work hard so that I can get better and, being selfish, because I want to get paid better!

You only get one chance to make it in professional sport and I have been very fortunate to have the chance to do it. I suppose it would be selfish of me in a way to throw it away. It's a case of what Blackie says, the principle of Kaizen, continuous improvement, if you finish learning you're foolish. You should never stop learning, you are continuously evolving.

Working hard to improve his game is a trait that Mathew has demonstrated since being snubbed by England Under 16s a year young but, after all that has happened to him in his short but highly successful career, mental preparation for games is still something he is trying to develop. 'I just try to stay relaxed as possible. I know a lot of guys feel the benefit of banging their head off the wall but I'm not one of them. I prefer just to stay relaxed. I have a few issues with my mental preparation at the moment because I feel I should be preparing in a certain way. It's amazing that after however many games I've played that I still don't know the best way to prepare for a game. Some days you just turn up and everything clicks and you wonder why when you are not doing anything different from the previous week when you had a bit of a stinker. I'm still trying to figure out what's best for me on match day. I think it will probably constantly change.'

Mathew is a young man who has a low boredom threshold and needs things away from rugby to occupy his time. Playing rugby at the highest level he has still found time to fit in his studies at university with a dedication that is admirable. On one occasion he flew back to Newcastle from an England training camp in London for a lecture only to find it had been cancelled!

Balancing his time is a constant juggling act but it has to be prioritised with a clear view of what is most important. These things are not black and white, however, and it is almost inevitable that the different things that Mathew is trying to do will impact on each other. 'I have three things in my life and they do overlap. There's my rugby, my girlfriend and family, and my university work. It's hard to separate them and give all of them the time they deserve but my family and girlfriend understand. They know I have the next ten years or so to do as much as I can in the game and after that I'm all theirs! They are very supportive in that.

'With university I said to myself that if it impacted on my rugby I'd give it up. I work very hard to get work in and the university seem pretty happy with what I've done. I averaged 70 per cent in the first year and just got 70 per cent for an essay the other week. I do feel I benefit from doing stuff outside of rugby but sometimes it's quite tough.

'I was motivated coming back from the World Cup to do an immunology essay and exam because I enjoyed it. Whereas what I've got to do now I hate it! It's just the most boring thing and there are 60 lectures about it. At the moment I can't make lectures very much, so I've got to basically teach myself as much as I can. It's about bacteria and I'm struggling a bit at the moment. I'm supposed to start revising for an exam today but obviously because of Mr De Wet Barry [Harlequins] knocking me out at the weekend I have to wait another couple of days.'

The end of the 2007–2008 season proved to be a difficult time for Mathew in that his support network was systematically unpicked, as the Kingston Park management were moved on. First Steve Black, the club's fitness coach, and then John Fletcher, the Director of Rugby, and Peter Walton, the Forwards Coach. It did not get any better as in the settling of the dust certain players voted with their feet and Mathew's close friend Lee Dickson left to join Northampton Saints.

With all that was going on, Mathew felt that the time was right to take his career further with Sale Sharks for whom he will start the 2008–2009 season. Having achieved so much in such a short period of time, it is interesting to learn what the rugby ambitions are for the 22-year-old from Shotley Bridge. 'I'd love to be involved in and win a Heineken Cup – that is just the Holy Grail of rugby. I would love to be involved with Lions on the South African tour in 2009 and continue to be involved with England and hopefully win a World Cup. To do those things, though, I want to be the best player in my position in the world. Be the best at what you do and after that things will happen and hopefully your dreams will be satisfied.'

However, the ambition of one day being a doctor may have to be put on ice as the reality of the amount of studying is becoming apparent. 'The thought of being a doctor is now kind of taking a step back. If I get my degree and finish with rugby I'm going to hopefully be in my mid-thirties. I would need to go back to university for four or five more years. By that time I would hope to have a family and will have different priorities by then. I'm generally enjoying the degree work, but the doctor thing I just don't know. By the time I finish I might not really want to go back to university, doing all the clinical training and the late nights and miss out on spending time with my family.'

In terms of advice for youngsters making their way in the game,

Mathew's advice is very simple. 'Make sure you get your education in place first – that's the main thing. I genuinely believe it. At school I think it could have been very easy to get carried away and not study. Obviously good support at school and from your family is important. You need to have your education in place because you never know what lies ahead. You can make it to 22 and you could bust your knee, and what can you do? Rugby's not football; you're not on £15k per week.

'I am not sure about all of these academies where you get focused on rugby rather than your education. When you do so much rugby, by the time you get to 21 years of age you could have had enough of it. I think you should enjoy being young first and foremost.'

Mathew was in the National Academy system and benefited from that experience, but went straight into the First Team squad at Newcastle Falcons when he was 18 years of age. He was, and still is, a young man of immense talent that not many are blessed with. I sometimes wonder if we do not do some of our young players any favours by bringing them into the RFU academy structures when expectations are built up of a career in professional sport that, in reality, will be realised only by an elite few.

We should never stifle dreams and ambitions, but I can't help feeling that sometimes with expectation comes a neglect of the foundations needed to survive in the big wide world and education is the strongest of all foundations.

Mathew is a big miss around Kingston Park with both the supporters and players. His move to Sale has not gone as smoothly as it could, with a hamstring injury restricting his starts in the team and leading to his omission from the England squad for the autumn internationals. However, a return to fitness has seen him make a significant contribution to the progress of Sale Sharks and an immediate return to the England squad for the 2009 Six Nations. His rugby for England during the tournament was from the bench as an extremely effective impact player, but it seems likely that, as England's relatively new backs coach, Brian Smith, finds his feet the ambition shown to spread the play in England's last two Six Nations games will demand the running talents of the former Barnard Castle schoolboy.

I have many memories of 'Small Face' – from watching that school game on the cold wet hill in Barnard Castle against RGS, to sitting with admissions tutors at Newcastle University and chasing my dog around the living room to stop him eating the crisps as the World Cup final got exiting. However, the thing that I will always remember Mathew for is not really rugby related.

My wife is a nurse at the Royal Victoria Infirmary in Newcastle and works on a leukaemia ward where the joy of seeing patients get better is offset by the sufferings of those not so fortunate. A particular lady who is sadly no longer with us had a dream that her son would see England play rugby at Twickenham. A certain England centre made his complementary tickets available for the young lad and his father, and was constantly on the phone to my wife to make sure they got them.

Sometimes you see performers on the big stage and think that is all there is about them. How wrong you can be! I for one think he would make a great doctor.

2008–2009 Season Update

Mathew's first season at Sale Sharks must have been a very frustrating one as injury disrupted his progress for both club and country. However, he is still very much a part of Martin Johnson's plans as Argentina provide England's summer opponents and at long last it appears Mathew is a centre!

Mathew Tait: Statistics	
Date of birth	6 February 1986
Birthplace	Shotley Bridge, County Durham
Height	1.83m
Weight	90kg
Position	centre; fullback
School / university	Barnard Castle School; Newcastle University
Present club	Sale Sharks
Previous clubs	Newcastle Falcons
Nicknames	Taity; Small Face
Favourite TV show	*Family Guy; Entourage; Grand Designs*
Favourite film	*Harry Potter* series; *Lord of the Rings* trilogy
Favourite music	Arctic Monkeys; Coldplay
Favourite book	*Princess Diaries*
Favourite food	chicken stir fry; olives
Most like to meet...	Tony Blair
Least like to meet...	Geoff Parling (Newcastle Falcons teammate)
Best moment in rugby	winning the Hong Kong Sevens
Favourite place to visit	Thailand
I love...	relaxing
I hate...	bad manners

SHANE HORGAN

Ireland; British and Irish Lions; Leinster

When a young Kiwi left his Christchurch home for his big OE (overseas experience) he had no idea that in London he would meet and fall in love with an Irish girl and settle with her in Bellewstown, County Meath. The results of Ursula and John's happy union are the three girls and two boys that form the sports-mad Horgan family where Shane, the Leinster, Ireland, and British and Irish Lions wing three-quarter is number 4 in line.

Although of Irish and New Zealand parentage, he keeps any Kiwi traits well under the surface as I have never met anyone who is so positively Irish and immensely proud of the fact. When chatting over a cup of coffee at the top of Grafton Street in Dublin, he talks eloquently about the emotion surrounding the Ireland England clash at Croke Park in February 2007 and his feelings surrounding the event.

'An England v Ireland match always has a certain cachet and certainly when you add in all the historical links between England and Ireland and the breaking down of Rule 42 to allow the match to be played at Croke Park it was very special. For me it was more social history than a rugby event. It was a time when it was important for Ireland as a country. It demonstrated that we had matured as a nation by allowing the game to be played there. We always have to respect the past but it was a break from that past. It showed that we had grown as a nation. We could stand apart and welcome someone in after having had a very difficult history with them. We could welcome them in as an equal.

'The whole event must have been interesting from an English perspective and I would love to talk to some of their guys about it.

I thought there might have been some noise for 'God Save the Queen'. We expected a huge response, something from the crowd and we knew that that would have been a huge motivational tool for them; you know this country doesn't respect us and this team doesn't respect us, which would have given them a lift, allowed them to play at a different level.

'However, when there was such respect shown by the crowd for the national anthem the English players had nowhere to direct that anger. It was a very proud moment to be an Irishman. It was an historic moment, the biggest match that an Irishman could have played.'

I first met the big Irishman in the summer of 1996 when he came to Newcastle to train with the Falcons Academy and hopefully secure a Development Team squad place. He had come on to Newcastle's radar after playing for Ireland youth and, following discussions with Shane and his father, he flew into the Toon to train at St James' Park, the home of Newcastle United, Newcastle Falcons Sporting Club partners at the time. We had already made our mind up that we wanted him in Newcastle and were pulling out all the stops to try and impress him. Trying to create that impression nearly got me into trouble with the Dean of School at Northumbria University where I worked. While our guys trained I was standing next to Academy colleague Paul MacKinnon at the side of the pitch.

The North-East television news that night was interesting when they showed an interview with one of the Newcastle United footballers with Paul clearly standing in the background. If the shot had been a foot to the right I may have had some serious explaining to do to my sports-mad Dean!

Shane's time on Tyneside went well and he wanted to come to Newcastle to join the Academy and study Law at Northumbria University, but Ireland's desire to keep their players in Ireland and the opportunities presented by his beloved Leinster proved to be too big a pull on the youngster and Newcastle's loss was certainly Leinster's gain. 'I remember coming to Newcastle and training at St James' Park. I think it was late summer because I'd played Irish Youth internationals at the end of the season against Wales and Scotland and that's when I came on the radar at Newcastle and Leinster. I had been talking to people all of the summer about what I was going to do and I did umm and arr a bit about going to Newcastle, but the Irish RFU were adamant I stayed in Ireland.

'I could see from the Newcastle point of view that I would come into the Academy, and if you are good enough you will work your way up, but I could see a faster track at Leinster and a clearer path to representative rugby.

'Near the end of the preceding season I'd been brought into the Leinster squad to train with senior team. It was a huge jump – I was 18 years old and training with men! Men I'd been watching on TV. By the end of the summer I was actually on the bench for the senior team for one of the inter-provincial games and then played a couple of A Team games. I've been here ever since.'

With views of the Mountains of Mourne to the north and the Irish Sea to the east the village of Bellewstown sits on the Hill of Crockafotha in County Meath and was home to the Horgan children as they grew up. As well as Shane, there were his three elder sisters, Maria, Sharon and Lorraine, and younger brother, Mark. All were also into sport and, when not playing, loved watching whatever sport was on the TV.

'As a Kiwi, Dad loves all sport and Mum wasn't sporty, though she does love watching it. Her brothers played Gaelic football and rugby. She has a huge interest and absolutely loves rugby. Although my sisters and brother weren't necessarily competitive with their sport, like mum they loved watching it. I remember when we were younger watching cup finals or whatever was on. All of us sat around the TV as a family. We would watch darts and snooker together, anything really!

'At the moment it's coming up to the Ryder Cup and my sisters will all be watching that. Their boyfriends and husbands are happy that they have a girl that'll watch sport with them!'

Having five youngsters at home is a challenge for parents but Ursula and John gave fantastic support to the all-round sportsman of the family who was successful in Gaelic football and athletics as well as rugby. 'I'm fortunate that both my parents, when I was growing up, were hugely supportive in that they came to every sporting event that I did. I played a lot of sport when I was younger; I did athletics, rugby and Gaelic football, anything that was going on really. They were very supportive, both logistically getting me there and encouraging me.

'I was lucky I had a father who would kick with me nonstop, whether it was a Gaelic football or a rugby ball. When I was eight years of age I remember him running with me. It was not a pushy thing, just helping me to do what I wanted to do, whatever sport it was.

'I was always grateful for their support.'

Shane's primary school in Bellewstown was strongly involved with Gaelic football and he played for the school as well as representing his parish of Duleek. With his school's focus being on Gaelic football, rugby was played at the local town of Drogheda, which at the time boasted two clubs – Delvin RFC, situated at Bryanstown in the south of the town, and Drogheda RFC, situated at Shamrock Lodge in the north of the town. These two clubs merged to form Boyne RFC in 1997.

Over the years the future international played for the youth sections of both clubs but it started for him at eight years of age with his dad as his coach at Delvin.

Although Shane played Gaelic football and rugby all the way though his teens, it was athletics that gave the youngster his first national recognition. 'I was introduced to athletics at a very young age through a family from Bellewstown, the O'Reillys, who were strongly involved in it. Just like rugby it was not through school but at a club. I was involved on the track and did a lot of cross-country. I absolutely loved it.

'It was rewarding and in a sense very individual. I won a couple of All Ireland Cross-Country championships, but you had to put a lot of commitment in to it. As a youngster it was quite a natural thing for me to do but as I got older I had to work a lot harder. I also had commitments with other sports and it was very hard for me to find time for everything. To compete at the top of athletics, even as a youngster, I had to put a lot of miles in which took a lot of time and it was time I wanted to put into rugby and Gaelic football.

'I think it was the team thing I enjoyed a lot more; it was what

I got a buzz from. With athletics, when you win it's all about you and when you train it's all about you; but I get a real buzz from being part of a team. There wasn't a lot of camaraderie in athletics. Even though I had loved it I had finished by the time I was 14.

'It was funny throughout my teens – it was whatever I was best at I enjoyed, so that fluctuated! It probably started off with athletics and went to Gaelic football and then to rugby and back to Gaelic. I really had a soft spot for Gaelic football.

'It was when I realised at about 16 years of age that rugby was what I wanted to do then I started to get representative stuff. I did have representative games for Gaelic football as well, but for me rugby was a better fit. It was only just turning professional at that stage. I didn't know it would give me a career but I knew it was going to be the game with some level of professionalism – whatever that would be. I thought that rugby would benefit me in whatever career I chose and maybe I could do it for a living. There was also the international element that Gaelic football does not have. At about 18 years of age I played minor for Meath in Gaelic football and then later that year I retired and played rugby.'

There are parallel systems for young rugby players in Ireland. One is based upon the schools and the other the clubs and, as Shane's secondary school, St Mary's Diocesan School in Drogheda, focused on Gaelic football and not rugby, it was the club system that generated the opportunities for representative honours. At 16 years of age he was selected for the Leinster Youth a year young and went on to play for Ireland Youth in the same season. The big wing three-quarter kept his place in the squad in his age group and brought the attention of Newcastle Falcons and Leinster.

These first games in the shirt of Ireland were very proud but also nervous occasions. 'My first game for Ireland Youth was strangely enough against a Spanish Under 21 side at Valladolid not far from Madrid. They were monstrously big and kicked us right over the place. I also played against Wales and Scotland later in the year and in my second year it was Wales and Scotland again. We only played two games that year. I don't have distinctive memories of those games but I remember feeling that when I was a year young that I was almost out of my depth. I think it takes a young player a long time to shake that feeling off, the feeling of, am I going to be found out? Am I good enough to play at this level?

'I was always thinking about not making a mistake rather than thinking positively. It was more a case of not making a mistake and then being glad that positive things happened. You're passionate about playing for your country. I think it carries a lot of weight playing for your country at that age but there was a huge amount of nerves and trepidation.'

At 18 years of age Shane had won All Ireland Cross-Country championships, played representative level Gaelic football and played rugby for Ireland for two years as a member of the Ireland Youth team. Even at that age, however, he had a very rounded view of life and where he was going, based upon having to cope with a recurring injury through his mid-teens. Lifelong friendships made at school have also helped keep things in perspective.

'School was enjoyable in many ways. I never want to look back with nostalgia and it wasn't always perfect but it was certainly a good experience. I don't think school ever pushed us enough academically; we always stayed within ourselves and did what we were capable of. For my Leaving Certificate I did French, English, Irish, Maths, Biology, History and Geography. I was always comfortable enough that I was academically OK.

'What the school was good for was overall education about life and about interaction with people. It wasn't a school that was regimentally strict or wild either. The teachers' ideas were to get balance to your life. It was a very good sporting school and actively encouraged us to do sport.

'I have a group of friends now that I am regularly in contact with – four guys I went to secondary school with who are not involved in rugby at all. It's funny; all those friends have gone on to do academic things. All of them have a master's and some are doing PhDs and stuff! At school we certainly didn't achieve academically as we should have!

'In my early to mid-teens I got Osgood-Schlatter disease, a problem when kids grow too fast and the bones can't keep up. I got lumps below the knee. Lots of sporty kids go through it and I had to take two periods off, six months and nine months. I remember it was very tough when it was impinging on my performance. I'd come home in tears as I couldn't do what I wanted to do.

'Looking back it certainly gave me perspective that there's different things in life than sport and made me more rounded as a person. For me sport was a hobby that then became my profession, but I was lucky because it didn't encompass everything in my life. I believe this is something you have to be careful about, that rugby's not your hobby, your job, your social aspect, your friends etc. You need support and balance and not consume yourself in one clique. Looking back, I can see that problem allowed me to broaden my horizons.

'You can't value yourself solely as a rugby player.'

After he left school, Leinster became the focus of Shane's rugby but at that time Leinster was not a full-time province with a season-long fixture list so the Lansdowne club became the beneficiary of the big three-quarter's services with Leinster's demands being fitted in as required. This situation remained until the formation of the Celtic League and European Cup which generated a full schedule of games.

Unlike Scotland and Wales, Ireland's provincial structure was already established, with Ulster, Connaught, Munster and Leinster, and these provinces had the resources to survive in the new professional era.

As professional rugby was finding its feet Shane continued with his education by studying Law part-time at Portobello College in Dublin. 'The university were very good to me. The first year was almost full-time then I did it in dribs and drabs. I finished it a few years ago and I was very glad I did it. It wasn't too bad at all. It was different then because professionalism was still finding its feet, but with the demands of training etc. I think it would be more difficult to do what I did now.'

It was during this first year with Lansdowne and Leinster that Shane made his debut for Ireland Under 21s along with some of the now household names that have taken their place in the full national side over the last decade. 'We had a great team and won the Triple Crown – Ronan O'Gara, Dave Wallace, Leo Cullen, Frankie Sheehan, Bob Casey, Mick O'Driscoll. We probably could have won the Grand Slam but it was at the time when Ireland didn't win anything – you know, there was a real mental block. You didn't even think you could beat them. It really took the European Cup and familiarity with French sides to overcome that mental block.'

Progression within the national set-up continued very quickly as Shane was selected the next season for the Irish Provinces against the touring Springboks, which was a huge experience for the young lad from Bellewstown and he did not have to wait long for Ireland A honours. He scored on his debut against England but was on the losing side, a situation the team put right with a win against France in his second match.

That cherished first full cap came along when he took to the field against Scotland in 2000 at Lansdowne Road. A much changed team had been selected after a crushing defeat in the previous game against England. 'Ireland had just got badly beaten in England, by 40 points I think. Ronan O'Gara, Simon Easterby, Peter Stringer, John Hayes and I all came in together. Mick Galway was brought back from the wilderness and Dennis Hickey came back from injury.

'We won well that day and it gave us a bit of breathing room. The knives weren't out for us. We went on to have a couple of wins and this allowed us to develop as international players. There've been times when good guys have been picked but the team haven't done well on the day and they have not been given time to show what they can do.'

Shane's first full international cap, in which he scored a try, had been achieved when he was 21 years of age and by that time Leinster had become a full-time club. However, being professional is not just about being paid for playing and it took a while for a professional approach to be embraced in all club activities.

It was the Aussie coach Matt Williams – who came to Leinster as backs coach in 1999 and then assumed the mantle of head coach – who started to change attitudes and practice. 'I think the first real movement towards professionalism was when Matt Williams came in and he really moved Leinster towards being a more professional outfit, but looking back we were a long, long way from where we are now.

'Back then it was certainly more relaxed. I don't want to bring it all down to social aspects but I certainly remember playing European Cup games when there'd be a beer in the changing rooms after the match, before the shower. It was a different mentality. Matt just put in place the basic building blocks, but to us at the time it was a massive upheaval. After Matt, for a couple of years we didn't develop as a team and as an organisation. We had two coaches one after the other; each staying only a year and it's hard for things to progress, as it takes time to develop on and off the field.'

A word or phrase to describe you at 21 years of age?

Desperate not to make mistakes...

Leading up to my first cap I thought it's the most important thing and that's the top of the tree. As soon as you realise the dream of that first cap you become very greedy; you don't want to give up your spot.

It was like my caps for Ireland Youth – I was probably far to preoccupied with staying on the team, not making a mistake, rather than expressing myself and enjoying it. I'd enjoy the build-up, in the actual game with the fellas, the dinner afterwards and the craic. It wasn't until a couple of seasons in that I enjoyed being on the field and being in the game. I was just too worried, too stressed and it was very limiting. It took me a good number of caps to move on.

I was very lucky to be given those opportunities and the team was successful so I was given the chance to develop. Now I absolutely love actually being on the field and that is the most important thing to me, it's what I enjoy most rather than all the ancillaries.

That first cap was the highlight of the big Irishman's career at that point in time. However, that cap was a personal achievement and, as he has matured as a player, the importance of the team over the individual is the dominant mindset. 'Everything was about playing for Ireland. I'd had a good season the year before my first cap but I'd missed out on the tour to Australia. I was devastated. Everything is about getting capped so that's your pinnacle you strive for. Once you've got that cap in the bag you move on.

'As you get older it's about being successful with the team. You move away from personal achievements and realise how important winning is. The mentality in Ireland with old teams was that playing for Ireland was fantastic, but you realise that there is no enjoyment to be derived from playing and losing. It's the same with Leinster now. All the enjoyment and honour is based around winning.'

In the eight years since that first cap Shane has played at the top of the game and been a key figure in establishing Leinster as one of the foremost sides in European rugby and elevating Ireland to the status of feared opponents. Professionalism has been fully embraced, as Munster, Ulster and Leinster have pushed Irish rugby forward and raised expectations of supporters and players alike.

The provinces have been extremely successful and have dominated the Celtic League, subsequently the Magners League since its inception in the 2001–2002 season. Ulster were runners-up in 2004 and winners in 2006; Munster were runners-up in 2002 and 2005, winning the competition in 2003; whilst Leinster were runners-up in 2006 and have lifted the trophy twice in 2002 and then last season when they beat off the challenge of the Cardiff Blues. Munster are the current Heineken Cup Champions after an emphatic performance against Toulouse in Cardiff. They have also won the tournament in 2006 and been runners-up on two further occasions in 2000 and 2002. Ulster also won the competition in 1999.

These top-level performances have not happened by accident and the way Irish rugby embraced professionalism made the transition from the amateur era relatively easy. The game has continued to move forward and the way the game is now run is light years away from the early days of professionalism.

'Since Michael's [Cheika] come in, each year we've built to a higher standard and now I think we're at a really high level. I think what's also interesting is that there's a new generation of guys coming in that have come out of the academy system. They have been training from the age of 16 or 17 to a very, very high level of intensity. There are high demands on them and their level of professionalism is outstanding. The standard that these guys come in at physically is remarkable and far ahead of us at that time. These guys coming in have such a strong work ethic and it's demanded from them as an academy player. As a guy of 17, 18, 19, the commitment they give it's really remarkable.

'When we started we brought our bad habits. We also had guys in the organisation with bad habits and it took a while for us to get rid of them. It took us a while to really embrace this strict level of professionalism.

'The atmosphere around Leinster is really good; it certainly is at the moment. In truth, Leinster has underachieved really. I know we won the Magners League last year but from a European point of view the bar in Ireland's very, very high for Leinster as a result of Munster's recent success and also as a result of having good players.

'People recognise we have good players and that we haven't won a European Cup. If you said that to a team in England or maybe a supporter of 80 per cent of Premiership teams in England it won't even come on to the radar as it's so difficult to achieve. However, it's very prominent in Ireland and so it should be, as it's very important.

'In Leinster we have magnificent ticket sales and membership and with that there's a brilliant atmosphere. It demands a certain style of play and great results but does put a pressure on the team that can work both ways. It sets the bar high.'

It is no coincidence that the elevation of the profile of the national team has taken place at the same time. Ireland have the poorest record of all the nations involved in the Six Nations, formerly Five Nations, tournament but a smooth transition to professional rugby has led to three Triple Crowns in the four-year period from 2004 to 2007. The national team were benefiting from the experiences of the three major provinces as they competed on the European stage.

'We had a period of growth and before the 2007 Rugby World Cup we had really, really strong development. I think we brought a lot of strengths, knowledge and experiences from the provinces, good habits, a winning mentality, winning on French soil, exposure to higher levels of rugby and, I suppose, the willingness not just to lose. We brought those things to the Irish squad.

'There was a really, really exceptional buzz to the team and confidence. There was a recognition that we could beat any team and to a large extent over the years we almost beat everybody. New Zealand are the only team we didn't beat. Every time we beat South Africa, Australia and France, especially in France, these were milestones. We hadn't beaten such and such for 20 years and hadn't won at

Murrayfield for 20 years, hadn't beaten Wales in Cardiff, all these sorts of things. It was very exciting to be part of the team.

'That success came as a result of the development of the provinces.'

However, as performances and results reached new levels, expectations rose and the 2007 Rugby World Cup was going to be the world stage where Ireland would make its mark, but things don't always go to plan. Ireland never got going in the competition and were hugely criticised in the press. It was inevitable that there would be casualties. 'The World Cup was a bolt from the blue. There was a high expectation on us to go in and win and to not perform was shocking really, for us as individuals and for the general rugby public.

'The stagnation that was there was going to be very hard to shake off and the only way to do it was to do what we've done really – a new regime, new coaches and new backroom staff.

'I can't specifically pinpoint reasons for failure in the World Cup but largely what I drew from playing international rugby is that there are very fine margins. If you think about England, they looked down and out before the World Cup and there was a feeling they'd be embarrassed in France but they got to the World Cup final. England could have easily won that World Cup. It's a very thin margin between success and failure at international level. There is a fine tipping point between being super-confident and being able to express yourself the way you want, and then the confidence draining away and you questioning yourself.'

The lead into the World Cup was personally a difficult time for the Irish winger as he struggled with a knee injury, but the failure of the national team to perform on the biggest stage has certainly left its mark on the whole squad. However, dealing with personal and team disappointments is something that all professional sportsmen have to contend with.

Shane's injury problems in his early to mid-teens gave him a reflective perspective on these things and a previous coach's reliance on standard deviations to make his point have left a lasting impression. 'I remember a coach a long time ago talking to me about performance, and he drew a graph, standard deviation. I've thought about it a number of times since. The high points were high and low points were low, and I remember him saying you can continue on that way or you can raise the whole thing. Your high points are higher and your low points aren't that low. I try to use that mindset.

'I also glean a lot of my confidence on the rugby field by thinking it's never far away from something good happening. Even on the rugby field you can question yourself; you've dropped the ball or something else has gone wrong but something good will happen soon. It may not be something brilliant but it's a building block; the small things you get right, then the bigger things jump up.

'This is definitely something you can take from the rugby pitch to your career outside of rugby. It comes from the fact there's always another opportunity for good things to happen. People I know who've retired and gone on to the business world or whatever they've become involved in after rugby, they all have the mindset that tells them there's always another day.

'That's a good thing to take for your own mental health too, that we're always striving for something new. I've never wanted to see myself being judged for something I did in my twenties. A guy talking about something I did x amount of years ago when I was a young guy. That's innately depressing.

'I want to continue to set challenges for myself and they might not be as high-profile or as glamorous but they'll be important to me and ones that I'll be striving for. That's what rugby players do bring – when the game is over you take what you can from it . That's what we do – take the positives, leave the negatives behind and you move on.

'That's the same with challenges in life – question why did it happen, take what you need from it and leave the rest behind.'

As Leinster and Ireland have enjoyed a period of unprecedented success, there have been many special moments to be enjoyed and remembered. 'The England game at Croke Park was obviously an important moment and a lasting memory, but more for the historical and social implications than as a rugby match. I think beating Australia and South Africa was special; they were really big games for me. The fact that Ireland competed with Southern Hemisphere teams showed that we've moved on a lot. We were a different Irish team in that we weren't just competing for only 20 minutes; we could go the distance and grind out wins.

'I hope that we've left the standard of the World Cup behind us and can move back to that level where we are respected in the Southern Hemisphere. We played two tests down there in the summer and we lost to New Zealand and Australia, and there was a bit of "Didn't they do well". There was "They competed for long periods" and "They were very, very valiant in defeat", but I think that it's not acceptable to us that we were valiant in defeat; we want to move on from that. We have to win. We want to get back to the standard that we had reached. So the wins against the Southern Hemisphere teams stand out.'

The date 18 March 2006 is also a very special day in the life of the Irish winger as his last-minute try secured a 28–24 victory and the Triple Crown for Ireland at the home of English rugby, Twickenham. 'A very special moment for me was Ireland's Triple Crown win against England at Twickenham. Scoring the try in the last minute that gave us the Triple Crown, it does not get much better than that.'

A lot of players would put those magical moments in their sport as their standout, but, rather than a particular occasion, it is the same enjoyment of being a part of a team and the camaraderie that took Shane away from athletics and into Gaelic football and rugby that is most important to him. 'The major thing that stands out for me is that I've really been lucky; I've had some good laughs with the group of guys that I've played with. I've made some really, really strong friendships and I think without a shadow of a doubt that's what will stay with me. Of course I'll have memories of games, internationals and winning the Magners League and all of that but friendships that develop are much more durable because they'll be ongoing.

'At some stage I'll finish rugby and I won't be running out in front of the crowds and I won't be huddling up with the team, but I have friends I've made and had experiences with those guys that, if it weren't for rugby, I wouldn't have had. They'll continue on for the rest of my life.

'I think that's what I'll take out of rugby more than anything else. I haven't won a whole load of silverware. Touch wood this year or next year we'll be in good enough shape for the Heineken Cup, but again there's only so much value you can put on that.

'I was lucky to come into the side with a young group of lads.

There was a lot of change, rugby was changing at the time and we all came through it together. Now there's only Brian [O'Driscoll] and I left, but a lot of memories and friendships will endure.'

A word or phrase to describe you now?

Driven...

I'd say I'm more driven than at any other time in my life. That's something that's developed over a period of time. When you're younger you're more flippant about what you are doing but as you get a little older and move towards the end of your career, you don't want to waste any day, waste any game, waste any minute on the pitch.

I love being out on the rugby pitch and want to be out there every minute I can. You don't want any injuries, or to be rotated or dropped, you just want to be out there for every minute.

I'm certainly more driven now, probably more boring now as a rugby player and as a person than at any other time because the sport means so much to me. There is still so much to achieve.

I was always driven, you have to be. You're driving towards getting a cap and then you get to that maintenance period, there certainly was with me but then it's right I want success, success, success so you have to push on. That's where I am now.

The Leinster wing feels he still has much to achieve in the game and there is a very narrow and single focus to his, and Leinster's, ambition – lifting the Heineken Cup. Current champions Munster's fantastic record in the Heineken Cup has set the standards for Leinster to strive towards and success will be the perfect platform for anything else that might happen.

'I'm certainly ambitious to win the Heineken Cup with Leinster. My ambition is as focused and narrow as that and I don't make any apologies. I have two years left on my contract and hopefully I can do it within that time. That's certainly what drives me every day. I don't have personal goals. My goal is to win the European Cup with the team.

'Everything else that comes along in my rugby will be on the back of that. That's how I compartmentalise it. If I perform well enough to play for Leinster who are challenging for Europe, a by-product will be that I won't be a million miles away from Ireland and I won't be a million miles away from the British Lions. However, to say my goal now is to be on the Lions tour to South Africa is not really on my horizon because, if in some way my focus is taken away to the Lions or to Ireland, then I won't be taking care of my business in front of me for Leinster and I won't have anything. I need to focus on Leinster and the European Cup and be singular about it.'

There is not a lot of time away from the game that needs filling for Shane. Rugby has given him a certain lifestyle that is both challenging and rewarding at the same time and leaves him full of admiration for the guys who manage to cope with the pressures of the game and family. In World Cup year he was away from his own bed at least 35 weeks of the year at games, training camps and tours. 'I do have a girlfriend but I'm not married and don't have kids. It's different for guys like Cozza and I admire guys that have families because it's difficult when you're involved in rugby. There are long, long periods away from home and I have never really had to worry about that side of my life.

'I always put not having commitments down to rugby but it's funny that I am coming to the point where rugby will finish and I'll have to face up to the challenge!'

He has two years left on his contract and an obvious burning desire to bring Heineken Cup success to Leinster but the inevitable will happen. There will be a point at which he does not run out on to the turf of the Royal Dublin Society Showgrounds. His current focus is still very much on playing but life after playing will probably not keep him in the game. Unknown challenges beckon for which the skills utilised as an elite rugby player will serve him well in the corporate world.

'I don't think I want to stay in the game after I've finished playing. I've thought about it but I don't think I will. I'd like to look at different challenges and opportunities and that's what I'll push myself towards. I won't cut myself off from rugby 100 per cent but a couple of years away from it won't be a hardship. Although I have absolutely no regrets, it's taken a massive part of my life.

'What I've realised is that a lot of international rugby players are well equipped to go into business because of their work ethic. They're very driven and self-motivated; communicate very well with people and are good working with teams. These are qualities that people want in their organisations and I think the real issue is finding the right challenge, something that will really spark your imagination and initiative.'

Shane Horgan has been an important player in the establishment of professional rugby in Ireland. The playing record of the Leinster, Ireland and British and Irish Lion speaks for itself, but he is so much more than a big battering ram of a 1.93m, 104kg wing three-quarter. He is an extremely intelligent, articulate man who has a grasp of what he is and where he is. He is acutely aware of the need to be reflective and self-analyse but also of the importance of spontaneity and trusting your instincts in pushing the boundaries of personal performance.

'Particularly when you are younger you need external encouragement to reinforce your own beliefs to allow you to then develop the ability to self-analyse in an objective fashion. However, I believe a major thing that stifles rugby players and maybe people generally is when they think too much – just trust yourself, just do it. Go with your initial reaction, even if it's wrong; if you react to that initial thought and you do it 100 per cent you're going to be OK, something positive will come out of it. It's when you're caught between two stools, that's when you get problems.'

Whatever he decides to do with his life when he stops playing I am sure he will trust his instincts and give it 100 per cent because that's simply the only way he knows.

As I made my way back to Dublin Airport and a flight back to my beloved Newcastle I had two thoughts running through my head. The first was that I was pleased he did not come to Newcastle when we were chasing him in the summer of 1997 because it would have deprived me the experience of talking to a man who was so unashamedly

231

passionate and enthusiastic for his beloved Leinster. The second was that I hope it is not another 11 years until the next time we meet up for a chat. He is very good company and it's his turn to buy the coffee!

2008–2009 Season Update

A dream finally realised. Leinster lifted the Heineken Cup by beating Leicester Tigers at Murrayfield and for the big Irishman it just doesn't get much better than that.

Shane Horgan: Statistics	
Date of birth	18 July 1978
Birthplace	Bellewstown, Co. Meath, Ireland
Height	1.93m
Weight	104kg
Position	wing three-quarter; centre
School / university	St Mary's Diocesan School, Drogheda; Portobello College, Dublin
Present club	Leinster
Previous clubs	Lansdowne RFC; Boyne RFC
Nicknames	Shaggy
Favourite TV show	*The Sopranos*
Favourite film	*Withnail and I*
Favourite music	indie
Favourite book	Jack Kerouac, *On the Road*
Favourite food	anything good
Most like to meet...	John F. Kennedy
Least like to meet...	a plague victim
Best moment in rugby	England v Ireland Twickenham Triple Crown game 2006
Favourite place to visit	New York; Paris
I love...	family
I hate...	small-mindedness

GEORDAN MURPHY

Ireland; British and Irish Lions; Leicester Tigers

The 2008–2009 season will be a well-merited testimonial year for Geordan Murphy who has graced the Premiership stage with Leicester Tigers for ten seasons since his debut against Rotherham in November 1997. In the intervening years he has been an integral part of that great club's success in winning five Premiership titles, two Heineken cups and two EDF Energy Cups. He has appeared for the club in over two hundred games and is the top try scorer in the current squad with 74 scores to his name at the end of the 2007–2008 season.

Arguably one of the most naturally gifted players to play in the Premiership, he has earned 58 caps for Ireland and drawn plaudits from observers well respected in the game. The former Bath and England centre and now BBC Television pundit Jeremy Guscott compared Geordan to 'a grand chess master, always planning moves in advance', and Dean Richards the former Leicester coach, now in charge at Harlequins, has described him as 'the George Best of rugby'.

After his first season of senior rugby, the club coaches at his hometown club of Naas thought the 18-year-old had the talent to give the English Premiership a crack rather than being swallowed up into the Dublin club rugby scene. They wrote to a few clubs and it was Leicester Tigers who responded by offering Geordan and his big friend James Ferris a three-week trial. Those three weeks in August 1997 had the young Irishmen in awe of their surroundings. The whole experience was both intense and competitive but changed Geordan's life, as he grabbed the opportunity and the very special association with the Leicester Tigers club and their fans began. 'Leicester came back and said they'd be delighted to have James and myself for a trial. We came over and it was literally straight in at the deep end and a real eye-opener. I never thought I would be involved in professional rugby; I mean in May and June we had been watching the Lions tour in South Africa on the TV!

'We landed at Birmingham Airport and took a taxi to the club. They gave us our kit, we put on our boots and then out on to the field; there was no settling in period. Martin Johnson, Neil Back, Graham Rowntree and the like – we were with all of these players that we'd watched on TV so it was a complete wow-factor for me! I remember at the time thinking that this will be the best three weeks' training ever, working with these guys, and then I'll probably go back to Naas and do whatever.

'Leicester had about sixty guys who were made up from the First Team, Second Team and Academy squads and in that first week of training we were all together. It was very competitive. We trained and I was slotted in as part of probably the third-string back line. We moved around different groups and I basically ran at fly half. I remember asking one of my centres a lot of questions. Where did he want me to pass the ball? Where did he want me to run? Was the pass too wide for him? He talked to me and was really helpful. I did not know who it was; I didn't recognise him facially, but I knew I'd seen him play on TV. When he turned around and I saw "Joiner" on the back of his shirt, I was gobsmacked. I remember thinking, "Craig Joiner, I can't believe that!"'

A lot of youngsters freeze when put in 'make it or break it' situations but the young Murphy lived his dream and grabbed the chance to impress the Leicester management. Bob Dwyer was in charge of rugby at that time and he quickly recognised the natural ability of the young Irishman in both training and, more importantly, the Development Team trial game played on his first weekend at the club.

'The first weekend there was a trial game at the club so basically all of the Development Team were given a run-out. There were about 35 guys involved. That game was a dream come true for me. I remember Bob Dwyer was standing on the edge of the pitch watching and I scored three tries in about the first 20 minutes. Things just went really well for me. For one try I chipped the ball over the defensive line, caught it and scored under the posts; for another I remember taking a great line and scoring in the corner.

'Then Leicester had a winger called Mnamdi Ezulike who was in the Academy and went on to play for London Irish. We became very good friends but at that time I did not know him or the fact that he was lightning quick. In the game he made a break that I read; I kind of saw him coming and thought, "He's not really moving that fast," as he turned away from me. I corner-flagged him and managed to get him into touch just short of the line right where Bob Dwyer was standing. When I made the tackle Bob just said, "You can come off now," and I didn't know if that was good or bad.'

The World Cup-winning coach of Australia knew he had a special talent on his hands and Geordan was drafted into a very strong Tigers Second Team that were due to play Gloucester at Kingsholm the following week. 'After the trial game Bob said to me: "You're playing next week for the Second Team at Gloucester." We had a strong team with Dean Richards and John Wells in the back row as well as a lot of other big names, ex-England internationals and current England Under 21s. We drew the game and I was just amazed.'

In world rugby Martin Johnson can rightfully be described as a legend but in Leicester Martin's mother can be described in the same way. Geordan stayed at the Johnson household and this did nothing but heighten his feelings of wonderment at his surroundings. The shy young Irishman endeared himself to his temporary landlady. 'James and me were billeted in Martin Johnson's parents' house, and again it was an unbelievable thing. Living in Martin Johnson's bedroom, the room where he grew up!

'During the third week I was supposed to play for the Second Team again but for whatever reason the game was cancelled and I didn't know where I stood. It came towards the weekend and Mrs Johnson said, "What's the story with you two, when are you going back?" I told her that we were due to go back to Ireland the following Tuesday and she said, "Well, have they said anything to you because they've told me that they're very impressed with you." She told us she was going to come to the club with us and we were not going to argue.

'So she came in with James and me on the Monday to see Bob Dwyer. She was a legend; she literally stormed into the office and said, "What are you doing with them, are you keeping them or not?"

They had a chat for a bit and then Bob came out and said, "I'd love to keep you on a Development contract and find a university to keep your parents happy."

'So I went home, my parents were happy and my life had just changed. I guess Mrs Johnson was my first agent!'

George Edward Andrew Murphy entered the world in Dublin on 19 April 1978. He was named George after his father but his mother called him Geordan to avoid confusion. Naas in County Kildare, some 19 miles south-west of Dublin and whose Irish language name, Nás na R'ogh, literally means 'Meeting Place of the Kings', provided the surroundings within which Geordan grew up. His parents still live in Naas to this day.

The youngest of six children he refers to himself as his parents' 'little mistake' owing to the seven-year gap between him and the next youngest. His father was in the Irish army all of his working life and loved sport. He was involved in athletics when he was younger and played a lot of golf as the years passed by. His mother has always been at home and with six children to bring up has always had plenty to occupy her time, but in her youth she did play hockey. His siblings are all sporty, with his four brothers massively into rugby, and it was inevitable that sport would play a big part in his younger years. 'My mum said I always had a ball in my hand or on my lap. If I was eating dinner she would say, "No balls in the house," but it didn't really work. I was always playing or kicking about and, if it wasn't a football, it was rolled-up paper or a Kinder egg I remember at some stage!'

School started for Geordan when he was five and a pupil at the Christian Brothers' School where he was introduced not to rugby but Gaelic football; in that part of Ireland it is the number-one sport. A well-known Geordie Irishman, Jack Charlton, also had an impact on the sports followed and played by Irish youngsters at the time, because the profile of soccer was suddenly elevated.

'At that time rugby was really only played in the private schools. I attended the Christian Brothers' School, which was the school for the local kids, and we played Gaelic football, which was kind of my first love. I was at the school from about 1983 until I left in 1990 and during that time soccer became huge. Irish football came out of nowhere in 1986 and there was the 1988 European Championship and the World Cup in 1990.

'Everyone was playing and practising soccer but the opportunity to go and play for a team wasn't very big in Naas as it was all based around Dublin. It was more of a case of playing with your friends in the backyard. You'd have four-a-side games and stuff like that, but with Gaelic football you'd get a game at school and play in a team so that was the first sport that I got into.'

Rugby came into Geordan's life when he commenced his secondary education at Newbridge College, the private school that had provided the education for all of the Murphy children. 'My uncle had gone to the college years before and all of us were sent there. All of my brothers played rugby at the school and I played my first game when I was 13 years old. I absolutely loved school. I guess I'm lucky because I had some very good friends there and am still in contact with them. I loved the sporting side of things but generally had a great time. Looking back, I didn't work as hard as I should have done academically but I really enjoyed it.

'The Irish system is a bit different to England. We have the equivalent of O levels and we do about ten subjects and then we do our Leaving Certificate and study about six subjects. For my Leaving Certificate I did Irish Language and did OK. I still speak a bit and can get by, but I am not fluent. I did Irish, English and Maths, which I wasn't very good at but managed to scrape through my exams due to a very good teacher. I also did Biology, which was all right but I didn't do enough work. I was more into History and loved it. I am still a bit of a history geek and watch the Discovery Channel. I retain loads of useless information and can give you reams and reams of the stuff!'

Whilst Geordan admits to not working as hard as he might have at his studies, his sporting talents were being seen in both Gaelic football and rugby. He was playing Gaelic football for the town of Naas and rugby for Newbridge College until 16 years of age. However, at that time rugby was becoming more important as he got bitten by the rugby bug.

Gaelic football was not given up completely, with Geordan playing during the summer months outside of the rugby season. He had the opportunity to go for the Under 18 County trials and was selected to represent County Kildare, which he did on a couple of occasions. However, with an increasing desire to concentrate on his rugby and the need to focus on his Leaving Certificate exams, his attempts to keep everything going were causing his parents concerns and Gaelic football suffered the loss of a very talented sportsman.

The rugby bug had been planted by the coach Kevin West, a Kiwi who had come to Ireland to coach at the Naas club. 'We had a coach, Kevin West, who came to Naas Rugby Club when my brother Ross was captain. As well as coaching at the Junior 1 club, Kevin also helped out with coaching our senior cup team at the school. I was 16 years of age at the time and he said that some of us would benefit by going down to New Zealand.

'His wife's father had been the headmaster at Auckland Grammar School, the school that quite a lot of All Blacks had gone to, including the likes of Grant Fox and the Whetton brothers. It was a "mad into rugby" school, so in 1995 four of us from Newbridge College went there for five months. We lived with families and that's when I started to really enjoy my rugby. Before then I'd enjoyed playing rugby but when we got there we were totally immersed into it. Dougie Howlett was playing at the time we were there and he was a bit of a rock star at the school! It's a religion down there!

'We were training and playing for our school team pretty much every day and then on the weekends when we didn't have school games we signed up for the University Under 21 B team.

'I didn't actually play for the First Team in the school as it's weight-graded rugby down there so I played weight-graded-first-limit. For 16-year-olds it was physically a bit of a challenge but skills-wise we were up to it. We were just mad for getting as much rugby as we could. It was when I got back I realised I could play the game a little bit. I played fly half at that time and found that I was controlling games.'

On his return to Ireland Geordan continued his rugby with Newbridge College and, although the college was not one of the top rugby-playing schools in Ireland, the Schools Cup in his final year provided great memories for the young fly half. 'Our school in Newbridge wasn't a really big school and traditionally schools' rugby in Ireland is very strong and very competitive. There is a big Schools Cup competition in each province and it's massive. The whole school gets to come to the game and there's a big build-up.

'Our school hadn't been to a final since they won the cup in 1970, so we'd been through a long barren patch and been regularly beaten by some very strong Dublin schools like Blackrock, Castleknock, Clongowes, St Mary's and other big schools who had very good coaches. In my final year at the school in 1996 we got into the final. We got beaten in the game by Black Rock but played against a very strong team. They had seven or eight of the Irish Schoolboys team in there. It was very big for the school and it came after we had beaten our big local rivals, Clongowes, in the semi-finals. That match was huge and I played well but the best part was we managed to beat them. They had Gordon Darcy at fullback. I was about 18 and he was about 16, but he was still a tremendous player even then. The whole Schools Cup thing was great but the semi-final was a real standout moment for me.'

As Geordan's schooldays drew to an end, rugby was his driving passion. Ongoing education was an issue that needed to be considered but the choices taken were based upon not really knowing what he wanted to do and therefore keeping studies as general as possible. Waterford in Munster, about two hours south of Naas, provided the young student's home for the next year, although ties to Naas were not severed. Geordan studied a business and legal course at Waterford College, but rugby had to be fitted into the timetable and the emphasis and effort put into his rugby identifies clearly where his priorities were. 'I had only played schools rugby when I was at Newbridge College but when I got to 18 and left school a couple of clubs were interested in me to be a part of their Under 20 squads. Kevin West, the coach who sent me to New Zealand, asked me if I fancied playing for Naas.'

The Naas coach had seen something in the young fly half's game that suggested fullback may be the position that would enable him to fulfil his immense potential. Whilst Geordan's sights were on a higher level of rugby than Naas were playing, that very fact gave the opportunity to gain that fullback experience that set him on the road to the highest levels of the game. 'Naas played at Junior 1 standard, which is about five divisions down in Ireland. Kevin was telling me that he thought I would learn a lot by playing fullback. I wasn't sure, but he felt I was quick and had an eye for a break and running good lines. Eventually I decided to give it a go.

'The good thing for me was that Naas was a Junior 1 team and Water Park, the local team in Waterford where I was student, were a Senior Division Three team. Because one's a junior team and one a senior team I could do a "dual status" and sign for both teams.

'It was a bit difficult to fit it all in but I'd train down at Water Park on Monday and Wednesday and with Naas on Tuesday and Thursday. During a lot of the season I would play fly half on the Saturday for Water Park and fullback on the Sunday for Naas. Two senior games in a weekend when I was 18 was quite tough and pretty challenging. Water Park had a shocking year and we lost pretty much every game, but I really loved playing for Naas. We played pretty well and, although we didn't get the Towns Cup, we got promoted from the League.'

That first year of senior rugby was tough but international recognition came at the end of the season with inclusion in Ireland's Under 19 World Cup squad for the tournament held in Argentina. He warmed the bench for Ireland's first game of the tournament against Portugal, but in the second game Scotland were the opponents for Geordan's debut. The final game was against the hosts, Argentina, and, whilst representing Ireland for the very first time was a special moment, it was the weather conditions that are the most vivid memory of that time in 1997.

'It was so hot; it was boiling. I'd been on the bench for the first game and then played against Scotland in the second game. I remember being excited but so hot and thought, Jesus, I'm not going to get through this. I'm not the biggest of guys; I never was but I was very fit from all the rugby – but it was just unbelievably hot!

'Argentina beat us 42–32, but we were suffering from heat exhaustion. It was ridiculous. Looking back I suppose it was easier winning my first cap away from Ireland; there's not as much pressure so you can look forward to it and enjoy it. I felt so proud.'

It was on his return to Naas after the trip to South Africa that the opportunity to trial at Leicester came his way, and after the help of Martin Johnson's mother in securing his first contract he was very quickly promoted from the Development Team into the Second Team. The young Irishman was part of a team packed with former internationals, playing huge games against the likes of Bath in front of large crowds at Welford Road. In this environment he was learning a lot about the game very quickly and it was the autumn internationals in 1997 that created the opportunity for his First Team debut.

'There were another couple of fullbacks around at Leicester at that time but I was lucky enough. During the autumn internationals in 1997 Leicester had six or seven guys away with England so I got my chance in the First Team with my debut against Rotherham. I was playing in the team with Joel Stransky and other big names but not with the full-strength team. I scored a few tries and did all right.'

However, it is a match in January 1998 against Coventry that Geordan feels marked his acceptance into the Leicester family as he played in a full-strength side against Coventry in the Cheltenham and Gloucester Cup. 'Back at that time there used to be the Cheltenham and Gloucester Cup competition and I played in that. We were due to play away at Coventry, which was going to be a big game because Coventry were a serious team at the time and my friend James Ferris was picked to start at scrum half. The game got washed out, so was played the following week and they put me in because someone else was injured.

'I don't remember much about the game but I got a long-range drop goal that's taken on a legendary status due to Bob Dwyer's reaction. Coventry's fly half cleared the ball from his own 22; I was playing fullback and the ball kind of bounced in front of me on the halfway line about 15 metres to the left. I picked it up straightaway and instinctively thought drop goal and I went for it. I started to size it up and Bob Dwyer in a loud voice went, "Oh f***." He was sure I was going to miss it but before he finished the words got extended to "Oh f*** – he got it!" I hit it really well and it was still rising when it went over the post, which is surprising because I'm such a skinny man. In the changing room after the game Will Greenwood came over and said, "That was awesome, you've arrived."

'I felt really at home. People like that saying things like that makes you settle in quite quickly.'

By the end of the 1997–1998 season Geordan had played a lot of First Team games at fullback but Director of Rugby Bob Dwyer was replaced as a new structure was introduced at the Tigers with Dean Richards as rugby manager supported by John Wells. Under the new regime he slipped back to playing second team rugby but his versatility led to him regularly warming the First Team bench and coming on to the field at outside centre or wing. Versatility can be a double-edged sword as finding a position and getting the time in that position to develop is lost due to the ability to fill various holes. This issue was apparent again when in 1999 Joel Stransky the South African fly half became backs coach after playing at the Tigers for two years.

'For the 1999 season Joel Stransky was the backs coach and he wanted me to play at fly half but again I was chopping around different positions, starting at 10, then back to fullback in the second half and also sitting on the bench quite a lot.

'I wasn't first choice but if there was an injury I'd be there.'

A further change of backs coach brought more certainty over position as Wallaby centre Pat Howard saw in the young Irishman the same skills as Kevin West the Naas coach had seen, and Geordan played a lot of rugby at fullback in the Heineken Cup-winning season of 2000–2001 – the final where the Tigers beat Stade Français in their own backyard in Paris.

By the end of the 2000–2001 season, Geordan had just turned 21 years of age and, since his debut against Rotherham in the autumn of 1997, had been a part of a team that had won three consecutive Zurich Premiership titles and a Heineken Cup. Although playing at the highest levels of the club game at such a young age, international honours were somewhat elusive. 'The Irish RFU were getting a lot of heat from the press asking why I wasn't getting picked as I was probably playing to a higher standard than some of the lads who were picked. I didn't get picked for 1997–98 but I got into the Ireland Under 21s in the 1998–99 season and that was a big thing for me.

'My debut was against France and it was a big one because it was at home in Cork. I remember being on the bus on the way to the game and being very emotional about it all. Feeling very proud and feeling hyped up and literally about to burst into tears. I remember thinking about hearing the national anthem for the first time. I'm not usually like this before a game, I'm pretty relaxed. But I think particularly for a first international game in your home country I think everyone is nervous and shows it in different ways.

'For me personally once the whistle goes all nerves go. I think it's very easy to think about games and to get nervous about them, so I try to not think about it. I think about whatever else I can in the build-up to a game and cruise through, but then about an hour before kick-off, that's the time I switch on and run through what I have to do and what I want from it. I mentally imagine and focus on things I can see myself doing well and then probably get a bit nervous, excited, which is a good thing.'

Full international honours followed in 2000 when, after representing Ireland A, he made his senior debut against the United States, a game in which he scored two tries.

A word or phrase that describes you at 21 years of age?

Very shy...

At that age I was very quiet, very shy. I wasn't naive but I was very quiet back then. People who know me now would say I'm louder because I've been there and done a bit – though by no means everything that I want to do.

I'm probably a bit more confident in myself and that's not a bad thing, but I think when we were coming through we were a bit humble, which has maybe changed a bit these days. Young players get so much now.

When I broke through into the Leicester team I was in awe of the players and I didn't want them to think I'd let them down. I didn't want them to think I wasn't a good player. The older guys would keep the younger guys in check. I don't really see that happening so much now. Nowadays players are thrown in so young and given big plaudits. A lot of guys come out of the Under 21s and are flying around in their flash cars, with their white boots, dyed hair and Armani suits.

It's unbelievable how much it's changed in ten years.

Being a Heineken Cup winner, Premiership title winner and full Irish international by the age of 21 did indeed demonstrate that Geordan's emerging confidence came from having 'done a bit'. However, in a contact sport like rugby you never know if or, more likely, when your luck is going to run out in terms of injury. Bumps and bruises are the industrial injuries that are an integral part of the weekly existence of rugby players, but when more serious injuries come along they can be devastating in both a physical and mental sense.

In Ireland's last warm-up game before leaving for Australia and the challenges of the 2003 World Cup, the Irish fullback's world was turned upside down as his leg was shattered against Scotland at Murrayfield. 'We turned the ball over in our 22 and I passed it to Eric Miller, who ran the outside line. I moved in alongside him on a switch and, as I came back, Mike Blair was crouching in front of me. All my weight was on the left leg when he got in underneath me. He hit me low while the other fellow hit me high from behind. But I think Mike's knee crashing into my shin did it.

'I hit the ground and rolled and still managed to get the ball back on our side; that seems a worrying level of commitment now. I was lying on my right side and my left leg was dangling in the air. I had to somehow rest that leg on top of the other while this ruck was going on behind me. The pain wasn't unbearable, yet but I knew it was coming.

'I told the physio I'd broken my leg. He tried to be encouraging – "Maybe you haven't." I said it was definitely broken. He went quiet for about ten seconds and then called for the stretcher. I remember lying in the dressing room when the pain really kicked in and I knew they wanted me out of there before the team came in at half-time. They didn't want anyone to see me in that state.

'When I woke after surgery I thought the worst. I thought I was finished. The doctors came in and tried to be reassuring. They were brilliant but as soon as they were gone I was in bits. I was crying something terrible. A lot more bitter tears were cried the next few days. I was 25 years old and it felt like the end.

'Gary O'Driscoll, the Irish doctor, stayed with me those first few days and he kept saying that one of the best surgeons had operated on me and that [the former Celtic striker] Henrik Larsson had the same operation and he was playing top-class football again. So there was no reason I couldn't come back too. Eventually I started to believe him.'

At that time Geordan was arguably the most gifted player in the Premiership and was looking forward to playing on the biggest stage in international rugby, the World Cup, but it was not to be. Disappointments arise and need to be dealt with and the love of the sport drove him forward and gave him the incentive to get back to the top of the game.

The experience reinforces the need to be positive and forward-looking, not dwelling on the past. This mindset is important not just in coping with the trauma of serious injury but also in the day-to-day existence of professional sportsmen as they learn to draw a line under what has gone and focus on what is to come.

'At Leicester you're taught next game, next game. That's one of the good things about the Tigers, even when we were winning games and trophies when I started off the mindset was "Right, draw a line under that, fantastic we've won but...!" Even when we had played fantastic rugby it was "Right, next week we've got whoever. Even if that team was the bottom of the League they will want their points and if we let our guard down we will have problems."

'If we had setbacks we knew we had to draw a line under it and move on to the next job. This approach is really appropriate for players in terms of game management. Younger, inexperienced players can beat themselves up if they make a mistake; they can't stop thinking about that last mistake and the next time they get the ball this negativity can lead to another mistake.

'Players need to say: "Bang, that's done, I've made a mistake and I'll make up for it. Where's the next ball, I'll make something happen." It's tough to do because no one wants to make mistakes or feel like they've let the team down but that's what you have to do.'

Geordan's return to the top of the game was rewarded by a place on Sir Clive Woodward's difficult Lions tour to New Zealand in 2005. A tour that was both enjoyable and disappointing. The change from being an Irishmen to being a Lion in New Zealand brought an interesting reaction from the rugby fans down under. 'Being selected for the Lions tour was a huge honour and it was tough. Older guys said to me that it would be tough-going down there playing for the Lions but I just thought, well, you know, playing for the Lions with these guys, we'll win the series. I just wanted to get in the team and had such admiration for other players who were selected.

'I'd obviously been there with Ireland but it's a huge difference going there with the Lions. I mean Ireland had never beaten New Zealand, so immediately we're the brave, plucky Irish and they all love the Irish. They give you great support walking down the street, but to go there with the Lions was very, very different.

'England had beaten New Zealand in a massive test match before the 2003 World Cup, which was the last time Clive Woodward had been there. He came back with the Lions and a massive backroom squad including the likes of Alastair Campbell and they automatically took a dislike to us. It was built up so much over there. They were really looking forward to getting stuck into the aloof British Lions. It was a completely different kettle of fish.

'That tour is something I'll remember for the rest of my life. I met guys I'd never had a chance to speak to before and you're in each other's pockets. You get to know them really well. Though it was disappointing tour rugby-wise, I did enjoy it.'

A word or phrase that describes you now?

More confident...

I don't think I'm cocky or arrogant but I think I'm more confident, some would say mental!

From all that I know about the man 'cocky' and 'arrogant' are certainly not adjectives that you could use in relation to the softly spoken Irishman but 'relaxed' and 'confident' are. There is also that sparkle in his eye that maybe underpins the 'mental' tag!

Whilst he has possibly never reached the heights set by his Ireland colleague Donncha O'Callaghan for being 'mental', Murphy's ability not to get the blame rankles with the big Munster second row. O'Callaghan is infamous for various incidents including pulling down Alastair Campbell's trousers on the 2005 Lions tour; running on to the field and contesting a line-out in red silk underpants; enticing a family of ducks with a trail of cornflakes into a Munster team meeting and hiding them behind the curtains; and buying a lobster whilst on holiday, putting it on a leash and walking it down the promenade. 'That's Geordan Murphy putting that around, the pet lobster thing. Because it's me, if any story gets bandied around everybody tells everyone and everyone believes it. Now if someone like Geordan does something a bit strange, which believe me he does, often, it all stays quiet.'

The Murphy glint in the eye maybe does betray the mischievous streak that turns Shane Horgan into a nervous wreck. 'I roomed on and off with Shaggy over the years. Our relationship is based on me trying to frighten the life out of him. It started on an away trip when I saw him walking down the corridor talking on his phone. I hid in a doorway and grabbed him as he passed. He screamed this unbelievably high-pitched scream, just like a girl. We've all grown up a little since then but it's still fun to scare him occasionally.'

Outside of rugby it is no surprise that socialising with friends is high on the list of things he enjoys doing and the relaxation toy of choice for rugby players, the guitar, plays its part. 'I love golf and try to play when I can. It's difficult to fit it in during pre-season training but I played a lot in the summer when I was off. I see myself playing a lot when I've finished my rugby. I really enjoy it.

'I'm really sociable and I just really enjoy hanging out with my friends. A lot of the guys are into playing the guitar and I enjoy just relaxing with them and their families after games. Some of the lads say I'm too chilled out really! When you're younger it's hectic because you're hanging around with girls trying to catch one, but when you're older you just want to relax with your mates.

'Music's a big thing for me too.'

Music does have a special place in Geordan's life as his fiancée is the charming and beautiful singer-songwriter Lucie Silvas.

His long list of rugby achievements span his whole career from his first season as a Tiger in 1997–98, and when he identifies standout moments a list of memories is reeled off. His Tigers debut against Rotherham, his drop goal against Coventry, winning Premiership titles, the unbelievable experience of winning the 2001 Heineken Cup, his international debut and the 2005 Lions tour are all special memories.

However, I think it is an insight into the nature of the man that, when reflecting on his career, he constantly makes reference to other players and friends. An example is his recollection of the game which secured the Premiership title for Leicester when they won 30–23, away at Bristol in May 2000. Whilst winning the game was obviously important, it was his friendship with other players that was at the forefront of his mind. 'At the time we won the League down in Bristol in 2000 I was very friendly with Lewis Moody and Leon Lloyd, and all three of us scored tries in the match. The try I scored I really enjoyed. I was playing on the wing and Pat Howard was playing centre. I had the ball but Pat was falling behind and the fullback was coming at me. I chipped it over him but didn't gather it; I kicked it on and it was kind of going towards the corner flag. I thought it was going to go out of play but chased it anyway. It bounced right back to me and I managed to score under the posts. Tries like that when you win the League are very special.'

The 2008–2009 season will be the sociable Irishman's testimonial year and he has two years left on his contract at Leicester, two years he very much wants to use to add to his already impressive list of achievements. 'I'd like to play a lot more for Ireland and hopefully I'll finish on my terms. I think good players have a lot of self-confidence and self-belief they will know when they are not good enough. When I know I'm not good enough then that's it, I'll retire from international rugby.

'I'd love to try play for the Lions next summer. Everyone knows that if you're not in the national team that year, you're going to struggle to get into the Lions squad. All of the international players want to give a good account of themselves with the hope that they might get selected. I played for the Barbarians in 1999 and absolutely loved that. I love the spirit of the Barbarians, throwing the ball around and the social side of the whole thing. It would be great to that again.

'Sometimes I think I'd like to experience a different rugby culture, perhaps abroad in France, Italy or Japan. Guys I speak to say the lifestyle is fantastic; they train and play hard but have time to relax and have coffee with friends, socialise. It would be good to experience a different lifestyle. I haven't kids to tie me down, so it may be something for the future.

'Leicester has been very good for me and I want to win more

things with them. The way I see it is that they took me in and looked after me as a youngster and gave me a chance; but not only the club but the fans and senior players. They kept me in check, taught me valuable lessons about hard work, keeping your head down, being humble and all of that. It was what they did.

'Nowadays it's "Can you show them this or that?", but back then the senior players didn't have to be told. As a youngster if you came in a bit flash with dyed hair or something, then they'd give you a load of abuse and it wouldn't be long before you changed it back! The club taught me a lot and over the years the fans have been good to me. I've met great guys like Cozza [Martin Corry] and Johnno [Martin Johnson], guys you want to go out and play for. It's a family-orientated club and it's very special.'

When the time comes to hang the boots on the changing-room peg and take the ceremonial retirement photograph a new chapter will open but what that chapter will hold is not certain at this point in time. 'I think it's going to be quite difficult for a lot of us when we finish playing as we have flexibility of hours, so a nine-to-five existence is going to be hard! I only did one year of a Property and Business degree at De Montford University but I am not sure if I will ever go back and finish the course.

'At the moment I enjoy my rugby and would like to stay involved on some level, possibly coaching though not sure what, perhaps Under 8s or Under 10s. I really enjoy it. I've got ideas and aspirations, nothing definite, but some ideas of what I want to do.'

Geordan Murphy has played the game at the highest level since arriving at Leicester in 1997. His closeness to the Leicester club and fans is something that is very special to him and his desire to bring more silverware to the East Midlands in the 2008–2009 season has seen him add to his try tally with only two games played.

When chatting to Geordan at his beautiful Leicestershire home he asked his fiancée what word or phrase describes him now. Lucie's response may be inspired by the philosophy of Forest Gump: 'You're like a box of chocolates, darling. We don't know what we are going to get next.' But as Geordan plays his part for Leicester Tigers and Ireland it may be opposition defences that will not know what they are going to get next.

2008–2009 Season Update

Geordan's testimonial season must have been one of mixed emotions.

On the international scene he mostly got on to the field from the bench, but he did play his part in the Grand Slam triumph of the Irish.

Martin Corry's injury problems and ultimate retirement led to him assuming the role of captain of Leicester Tigers. He put in a man-of-the-match performance as the Tigers took the Premiership crown at Twickenham, defeating London Irish 10–9. However, disappointment followed the next week. At Murrayfield he left the field injured as his friend and sometimes international room-mate, Shane Horgan, realised his dream when the Leinster team lifted the Heineken Cup after defeating the Tigers 19–16.

Geordan Murphy: Statistics	
Date of birth	19 April 1978
Birthplace	Naas, Co. Kildare, Ireland
Height	1.86m
Weight	86kg
Position	fullback; wing
School / university	Newbridge College; De Montford University, Leicester
Present club	Leicester Tigers
Previous clubs	Naas; Waterpark
Nicknames	Chicken Legs; Skinny; Godfather
Favourite TV show	*Prison Break*; *CSI*
Favourite film	*The Quiet Man*; *The Sound of Music*
Favourite music	rock; anything with guitars
Favourite book	Paulo Coelho, *The Alchemist*,
Favourite food	Mum's chocolate roulade with raspberries
Most like to meet...	Hitler; Jesus – I'd need a time machine but I'd love to know what is not written in books about these people.
Least like to meet...	nobody
Best moment in rugby	2001 Heineken Cup final win; first cap in Ireland v Scotland
Favourite place to visit	Melbourne, Australia
I love...	winning
I hate...	losing